Christmas '96.
for Ruth
from Phil x.

Border Wares

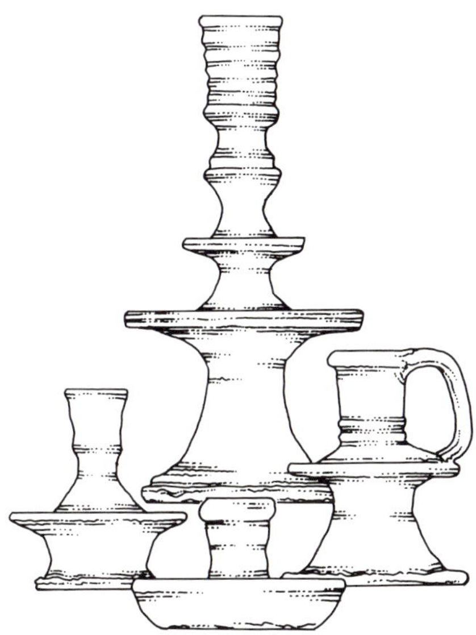

MUSEUM OF LONDON

POST-MEDIEVAL POTTERY IN LONDON, 1500–1700

VOLUME 1

Border Wares

Jacqueline Pearce
with contributions by J E C Edwards and D Lakin

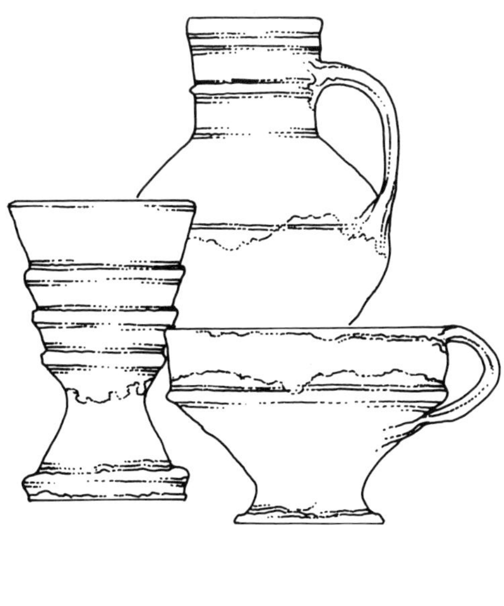

LONDON: HMSO

First published 1992

ISBN 0 11 290494 7

British Library Cataloguing in Publication Data
A CIP catalogue record of this book is available
from the British Library

Front cover:
Border ware vessels from London. From left to right (clockwise): Type 1 mug, flanged dish, tall ornamental candlestick, globular drinking jug and porringer.

Back cover:
Border ware costrels from London.

HMSO publications are available from:

HMSO Publications Centre
(Mail, fax and telephone orders only)
PO Box 276, London, SW8 5DT
Telephone orders 071–873 9090
General enquiries 071–873 0011
(queuing system in operation for both numbers)
Fax orders 071–873 8200

HMSO Bookshops
49 High Holborn, London, WC1V 6HB
071–873 0011 Fax 071–831 1326 (counter service only)
258 Broad Street, Birmingham, B1 2HE
021–643 3740 Fax 021–643 37140
Southey House, 33 Wine Street, Bristol, BS1 2BQ
0272 264306 Fax 0272 294515
9–21 Princess Street, Manchester, M60 8AS
061–834 7201 Fax 061–833 0634
16 Arthur Street, Belfast, BT1 4GD
0232 238451 Fax 0232 235401
71 Lothian Road, Edinburgh, EH3 9AZ
031–228 4181 Fax 031–229 2734

HMSO's Accredited Agents
(see Yellow Pages)

and through good booksellers

Printed in the United Kingdom for HMSO Dd 295269 12/92 C13

Contents

Illustration References

Fig, No(s), Plate relate to items in this work and are given with an initial capital letter. Figs 19–46 are further subdivided into 460 individually numbered items, e.g., Fig 20 (No 32).

References to illustrations in this book are shown first when appearing in conjunction with references to other publications; references to illustrations in the latter use lower-case initials for fig, no, pl.

List of Illustrations

Figures

Plates

Acknowledgements

The free and constant availability for study of the Museum of London's Tudor and Stuart pottery has been of inestimable value in the preparation of this volume. I am indebted to Rosemary Weinstein and Hazel Forsythe for making this accessible and for all their help.

I am extremely grateful to Felix Holling, whose name has long been associated with Border ware, for the considerable amount of time and effort he contributed in response to queries about the original excavations. The help of those museums holding the pottery excavated from the various kiln sites is also fully acknowledged, and I would like to express my thanks to Sue Roggero at Castle Arch Museum, Guildford and to David Allen and Kay Ainsworth of the Hampshire County Museum Service. David Gaimster, of the Department of Medieval and Later Antiquities, British Museum, kindly commented on imported whitewares from Embroiderers' Hall.

Throughout the preparation of this volume, invaluable advice and support have been given by Roberta Tomber and Angela Wardle in the preparation of statistics, retrieval of material and data, and editorial comment. Clive Orton and Tony Dyson read the completed script and made many helpful comments and suggestions. Wendy Garrett spent much time patiently typing and emending untidy typescripts. Thanks are also due to the editorial, design and production teams at HMSO.

The preparation of Appendix 1 The Excavations was undertaken by David Lakin, with additional material contributed by Julie Edwards. Excavations prior to 1983, and all the analysis and research for this study, were funded by HBMC (England) and its predecessor within the Department of the Environment.

I am also thankful for the help and advice of colleagues past and present in the Finds Research section of the Department of Urban Archaeology (DUA; now the Museum of London Archaeology Service – MOLAS) at the Museum of London: Alex Bayliss, Lucy Bown, Francis Grew, Anne Jenner, Beverley Nenk and James Robinson. All illustrations are the work of the author. The photographs were taken by Edwin Baker.

Finally, my husband Michael helped type much of the original manuscript and was an invaluable source of support. Any errors, inconsistencies and inadequacies are naturally mine alone.

Introduction

This study initiates a series which will examine, by source, fabric and form, the pottery from the major industries supplying the capital during the 16th and 17th centuries.

The early post-medieval period in England was a time of economic growth and expansion. During the 16th and 17th centuries, the period dominated by the Tudor and Stuart dynasties, the country's ceramic industries underwent a great transformation, characterised by technological advance and the adoption of new methods of manufacture. Improved communications accelerated the exchange of ideas and influences between the major potteries, both in this country and on the Continent. The latest fashions were quickly assimilated, new forms proliferated, and new patterns of marketing emerged to meet the growing demand for pottery from all sections of society. Many small-scale or non-specialist centres were unable to compete in the march towards industrialisation, and disappeared. Other industries correspondingly expanded. The importance of London cannot be overestimated as a consumer centre and as a market for pottery of all kinds, the mundane and the esoteric, both from local centres of production and from a diversity of sources extending to the Far East.

The Museum of London houses a considerable collection of pottery from the Tudor and Stuart periods, built up over the last 150 to 200 years, and numbering several hundred individual pots in a state of total or near completeness. One of the main drawbacks of this collection, for the archaeologist, is the very fact that it is a 'collection'. The principles of modern scientific excavation and stratigraphical association played little or no part in the discovery of the bulk of the pottery acquired by the Museum. The survival of any one vessel was largely dictated by the care and observation of workmen or excavators, the commercial appeal to antique dealers who were generally less interested in the mundane accessories of everyday life than in the aesthetically appealing, and the personal whim and taste of the collector. Repeatedly, lack of information on context or circumstances of discovery reduces the archaeological value of a pot that has found its way into the Museum. Nevertheless, the sheer size of this collection, and its state of preservation, make it an invaluable tool for studying the ceramic history of the capital.

Since 1973, controlled excavations carried out in the city of London by the Department of Urban Archaeology (DUA) at the Museum of London have yielded vast amounts of pottery which can, in the archaeological sense, be related to context, and which can be scientifically dated on the basis of stratigraphy and associated finds. A number of well dated, closed groups have been selected as the basis of the present series (site summaries are given in Appendix 1). Since the occurrence of complete pots is much less frequent than in the days before earth-moving machines, the largely fragmentary nature of the excavated pottery means that some forms are known imperfectly and that technological evidence may accordingly be lost through the difficulty of reconstructing complete profiles. The information derived from this source is, therefore, both supplemented and complemented by the more complete pottery in the Museum's Reserve Collection.

This series was initially conceived as a limited project covering a group of well dated post-medieval pit groups. However, it soon became apparent that the quantity and quality of the material warranted a much more extensive study which could best be treated as a series of fascicules, with each volume devoted to a particular ware. This first volume covers Border wares; subsequent volumes Tin-glazed wares and Redwares.

The aim of the series is to present corpora for the major post-medieval pottery industries in a format similar to that adopted for publication of the medieval pottery from London (eg Pearce *et al.* 1985; Pearce and Vince 1988).

The nature and quantity of materials make it impossible to cover the entire post-medieval period and therefore the 18th century is excluded from the series, although many of the major industries supplying London in the 16th and 17th centuries, such as Post-medieval redwares and Tin-glazed wares, continued into the 18th century.

However, the rise of the Staffordshire ware industries and their subsequent dominance of the market in the 18th century, make the end of the 17th century an appropriate point at which to conclude the series.

The subject of this first study is the pottery made in the early post-medieval period at a number of centres situated along the borders of Surrey and Hampshire, and known collectively as 'Border ware'. The known kilns produced a wide range of domestic pottery, principally whitewares, but also redwares. They used common clay sources and were linked by shared forms and manufacturing techniques. The industry continued a long-standing medieval tradition of potting in the area. London was a major consumer of Border ware, which constitutes a high proportion of pottery from excavations in the City. (For discussion of Border ware terminology, sites, clay sources, fabrics and technology see Chapters 1 and 6.)

A comprehensive type-series forms the nucleus of this volume, illustrating, as fully as possible, the variety and range of Border ware forms found in London. Fabric analysis is given for both whiteware and redware, and the late-medieval fineware commonly known as 'Tudor Green'. Aspects of technology and function are also examined. Quantified data are presented from the excavated contexts used to provide the chronological framework for the type-series. Border ware is also considered in its relationship to the other pottery sources supplying London during the 16th and 17th centuries, largely in terms of influences and affinities.

In so fluid a discipline as archaeology, this study cannot claim to be exhaustive or definitive. New finds are constantly adding to, expanding or altering our understanding of any ceramic industry. It is not the intention to present a complete history of the Border ware industry, the extent and chronology of which are only imperfectly known, since much of the excavated kiln material still awaits full analysis and publication. Consequently, questions of the wider distribution of Border wares and their significance in the country as a whole, or even in the south-east, cannot be addressed. What is presented is a picture of Border ware as it relates to the city of London over a 200-year period. The evidence from London may be selective, but it is hoped that as a major consumer centre yielding large domestic assemblages, it will complement and expand the current state of knowledge derived from production sites.

· 1 ·
Background to the Border Ware Industry

Terminology

'Border ware' is the term, first used by Orton, to denote the various products of the extensive pottery industry which flourished in the border area of north-east Hampshire and west Surrey during the 16th and 17th centuries (Orton and Pearce 1984, 35–6). The term includes both fine, sandy whitewares with an off-white to buff fabric and with yellow, green, olive or brown glaze; and fine redwares, with clear, green to olive or brown glaze. 'Border ware' is here used to describe the products of the industry as a whole, and specifically the whitewares. The redwares are called 'Red Border ware' (ibid.).

The main kiln deposits are dated to the late 16th century, the second quarter of the 17th and the late 17th century (see Production Sites below).

The manufacture of whitewares probably ceased during the early 18th century, and this is taken as the chronological limit of Border ware as such, although redwares continued to be made in the area into the 19th century. Common characteristics of fabrics, glazes and forms allow the 16th- and 17th-century pottery to be recognised as the products of a single industry. Within this industry, certain chronological distinctions can be identified, as well as minor differences of form and specialisations related to individual sites. Holling (1971, 70–2) recognised the problems resulting from the lack of evidence for production from the early 16th century, as well as the period covering roughly the last quarter of the 16th century and the first quarter of the 17th century. Firm dating for the late 17th century is also lacking. Unfortunately these gaps in our knowledge remain, and the considerable quantities of pottery from the known production sites (see below) now held by Castle Arch Museum, Guildford, and the Hampshire County Museum Service have yet to be fully analysed and quantified. A small collection of pottery from 137 High Street, Guildford, dated by association to the early 16th century, includes some whitewares, but no evidence for production (Holling 1984).

Border ware developed from a flourishing and long-standing medieval tradition of potting, known by the term 'Surrey whitewares' (Pearce and Vince 1988). Kingston-type ware is found in London as early as *c.* 1250. Later whitewares belong to two main groups: Cheam whiteware, known from kilns at Cheam in Surrey, and Coarse Border ware from the area of the Surrey–Hampshire borders. The prefix 'coarse' is used to differentiate the medieval products of this area from those of the post-medieval industry. Coarse Border ware probably ceased to be used in London by the early 16th century (ibid., 18), although the final stages of the medieval industry cannot be clearly established archaeologically. Cheam whiteware may still have been in production in the early 16th century (ibid., 88–9). However, the evidence from London becomes less clear during the second half of the 15th century, and the history of the late medieval Surrey whiteware industries is consequently more difficult to chart in this crucial period in the development of the post-medieval Border ware industry.

The place of 'Tudor Green' in the growth of the post-medieval industry is equally problematic. Rackham (1952) was the first to discuss the fine, untempered, thin-walled, green-glazed pottery made in white-firing clay, which has come to be associated with the term 'Tudor Green'. He also connected the green-glazed whiteware drinking jugs, now known in large numbers from the Inns of Court (Matthews and Green 1969) with a likely source in the Farnham area, an association which was made by Hobson almost 70 years earlier

(Hobson 1903). The origins, dating and distribution of 'Tudor Green' have since been examined in some depth (e.g. Holling 1977; Moorhouse 1979). Holling considered 'Tudor Green' a myth, and suggested that the term be dropped since it referred to a natural development of the Surrey whiteware industries into the post-medieval period. This view was based on the clear association of 'Tudor Green' wasters with Coarse Border ware cisterns and other forms typical of the medieval industry at the late 15th-century kiln at Farnborough Hill. Moorhouse (1979), however, recognised 'Tudor Green' as part of the development of the Surrey industry, but not a 'natural' one. He saw it rather as a new element introduced into an existing tradition in the late Middle Ages, and believed that it was better defined as a separate class which gave the impetus for the expansion of the industry and the development of new forms within the general tradition. For the purpose of this volume, the name 'Tudor Green' ware is retained, but in quotation marks. It refers to the green-glazed finewares made principally in the late 15th-century phases of the various Surrey whiteware industries, but with a broader overall date range of *c.* 1380–1550 (Orton 1988, 297; Pearce and Vince 1988, 17, 88). 'Tudor Green' has been found in many early 16th-century assemblages from various parts of the country, for example Overton, Hampshire (Moorhouse 1971a) and Farnham Castle, Surrey (Moorhouse 1971b); and since it plays a critical part in the development of the Border ware industry, it comes within the scope of the present study. It is both distinct from Border ware and, at the same time, a part of the same tradition, produced at the same kilns. Its relationship with fully developed Border ware is discussed further in Chapter 7.

Orton allowed that Red Border ware, although principally denoting fabrics made alongside whitewares in the industry centred on the Surrey–Hampshire borders, may include material from outside this area (Orton and Pearce, 1984, 35–6). At least two possible sources in Buckinghamshire, at Brill (Farley 1979) and Potter Row, Great Missenden, were noted. Although more study is necessary to clarify their relationship, the use of the term here remains unaffected, since it includes only those sandy, glazed redwares comparable in form with the white Border wares from the kiln sites, and in fabric with the redwares made at those sites. Further study is also needed to define the area of distribution of Border wares. The thorough survey required lies beyond the scope of the present volume, which can only present the evidence as it relates to the city of London.

Production Sites

The pottery industry of the Surrey–Hampshire borders was first described as such by Felix Holling, who identified 11 sites, concentrated in the area north-east of Farnham, which could be associated with pottery production by documentary sources, finds or excavation (Fig 1; Holling 1971, 60–2). Three sites in particular yielded pottery which formed the basis of a preliminary type-series, widely used as the standard reference for this pottery to date. These sites are:

1 Farnborough Hill Convent, Hampshire (SU 875566): waste pottery associated with at least three different kilns, dated to the late 16th century (Holling's phase 1). One kiln was subsequently given an archaeomagnetic date of *c.* 1560–75, and the overall range for the three kilns was estimated to be between 1550 and 1580 (Holling 197, 64). A fourth kiln was also excavated, and dated to the late 15th century (ibid.).

2 'Ye Olde Malthouse', Chapel Lane, Hawley, Hampshire (SU 861581): large quantities of pottery associated with part of a kiln, dated to the second quarter of the 17th century (Holling's phase 2).

3 'The Lime', Ash, Surrey (SU 895505): late medieval pottery, and waste and kiln furniture dated to the mid- to late 17th century (Holling's phase 3; see also Holling 1969).

All three sites produced both whitewares and redwares, although whitewares predominated at each.

A fourth major collection of Border ware was found at Cove, in east Hampshire. Dumps of pottery, both whitewares and redwares, were found in excavations by the M3 motorway at Sandy Lane, Minley Road (SU 846569), although no kiln was located (Haslam 1975). The pottery was dated by the excavator to the second quarter of the 17th century. A second large collection of waste pottery from Cove was found at Yeoman's Potteries, Cove Road (SU 861555), and is housed by the Hampshire County Museum Service. However, it has not yet been fully studied or published, apart from a brief note (Millett 1981). A cursory

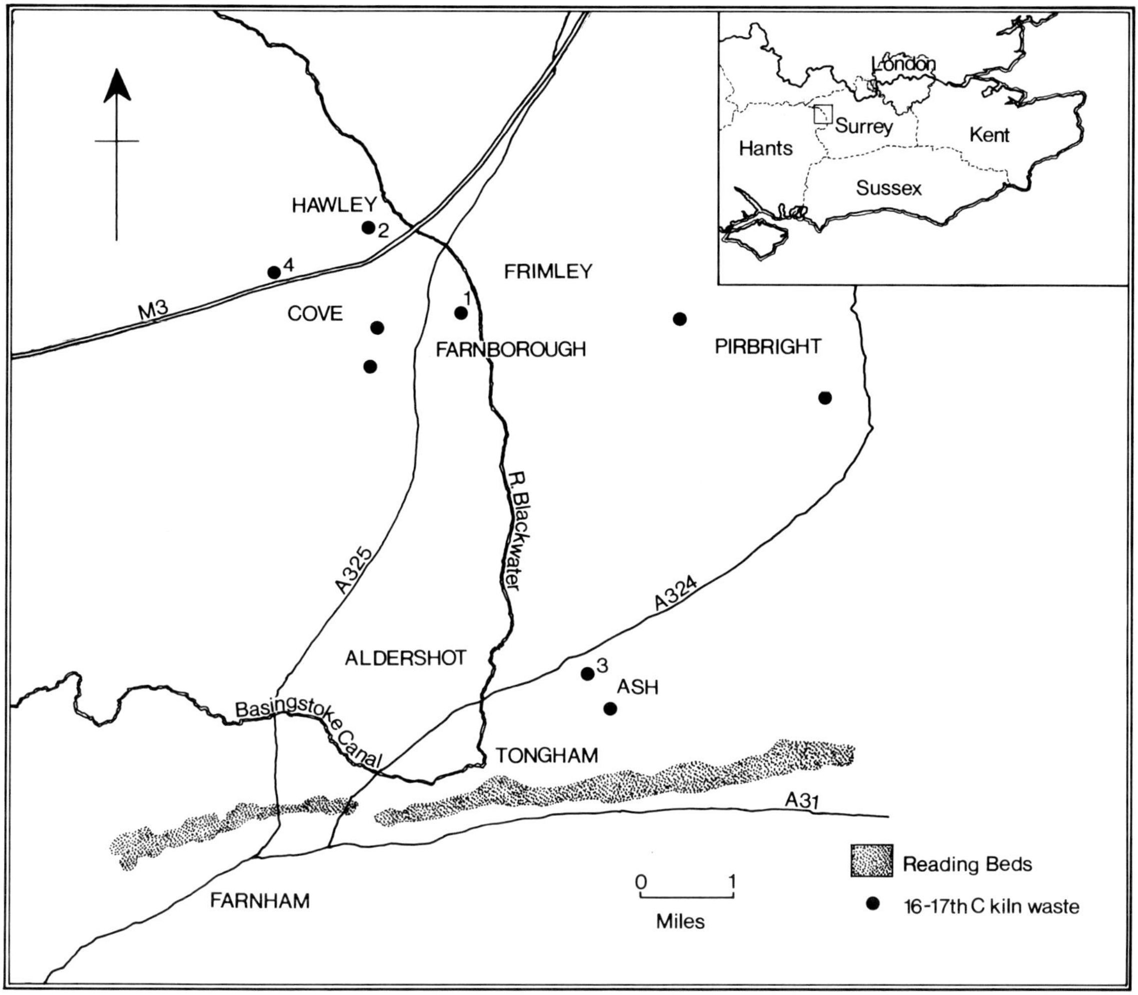

Fig 1 *The location of the known Border ware kiln sites and finds of kiln waste in the Surrey–Hampshire border area. The main sites mentioned in the text (p 2) are numbered. (After Holling 1971 and Haslam 1975)*

examination revealed a wide range of 17th-century types, including material unknown elsewhere in the Border ware industry, notably stove-tiles (Gaimster 1988a).

To date, the Minley Road site, and the sites at Farnborough Hill, Hawley and Ash constitute the main published evidence for the production of Border ware during the 16th and 17th centuries, although there are significant published collections from consumer sites. One of the largest comes from Basing House, Hampshire, dated between c. 1540 and 1645, from the initial occupation of the house until its destruction (Moorhouse 1970).

Clay Sources

All the known Border ware production sites lie within six miles to the north of extant sources of white-firing clay at various places in the outcrop of the Reading Beds which runs through Farnham and Tongham. Farnham Old Park was highlighted by Rackham (1952) as a source of white clay used to make the green-glazed, white-bodied drinking vessels purchased by the Inns of Court. His publication of a letter, dated 1594, written by Sir Julius Caesar, Treasurer of the Inner Temple, concerning the continued digging of white clay from the Park to make 'greene pottes' has contributed to the association of this area with the production of 'Tudor Green' and Border ware. The name 'Farnham ware' is still inscribed on some of the Border ware drinking jugs in the Museum of London. Experimental firings further demonstrated the similarity of the clay from a site in Claypit Wood, Farnham Old Park, to that of whiteware drinking vessels from the late 16th-century kilns at Farnborough Hill (Holling 1971, 62–3). An entry of 1603 in the Pipe Rolls of the Bishop of Winchester also mentions the carting of white clay from Farnham Park (Holling 1969, 19). Tongham, near Ash, is indicated as another possible source of clay by a reference of 1574 to the 'digging of potters' clay', and by 19th-century references to the area as an established source of clay for local potteries (ibid.).

The presence of good white-firing clay in the Farnham area was undoubtedly influential in the location and growth of the medieval and later pottery industries. A second advantage was the proximity of fine red-firing clays which could be used to produce Red Border ware. Outcrops of London clay lie adjacent to the Reading Beds both in Farnham Old Park and Tongham, and provided the raw material for local potteries well into the 19th century. Gault clay, which produces redware in the same firing conditions as for whiteware, was used, at least until recently, at the Wrecclesham pottery in Surrey (Holling 1971, 63). In the light of petrological analysis of Red Border wares (see below), it is interesting to note that white-firing clay was mixed with Gault clay at Wrecclesham. Both sources of red-firing clay would have been available to all the known Border ware potteries.

Not all the medieval Surrey whiteware industries which relied on the Reading Beds were as ideally situated as the Border ware potteries of the 16th and 17th centuries. Distance from the Reading Beds may have been one of the factors which led to the decline of the Kingston-type ware industry during the late 14th century (Pearce and Vince 1988, 11). The coarse Border ware potteries were situated closer to the desirable white clay, and this would have contributed to the continuation of a flourishing pottery industry in the area into the early post-medieval period. Raw clay would have had to be carried only relatively short distances to any of the known kiln sites, generally no more than six miles, either by cart or along the River Blackwater. No doubt many other factors were involved in the decline of the Kingston-type and Cheam whiteware industries, but the greater distances involved in carrying finished pots from the Farnham area to the capital appear not to have hindered the development of the medieval or later Border ware industry.

Fabrics

Border ware fabrics, both from the city of London and from the kiln-waste found at Farnborough Hill, Cove (Minley Road and Yeoman's Potteries), Hawley, and Ash have been examined by binocular microscope (x 20 magnification) and thin-section analysis. The main fabric characteristics are given for whitewares, redwares and 'Tudor Green'. Type-sherds are housed in the DUA Ceramic Reference Collection. Glaze and fabric colours are coded according to the Munsell colour chart (Munsell 1969). Minor fabric variations are expressed by different fabric numbers which are combined under group codes. The assignment of different codes to different glaze colours does not necessarily signify variations in fabric; it is simply a means of characterising type-sherds as a whole and this includes additives or colourants in the glaze. The various Border ware fabric codes, the common name codes used in the Museum of London computerised record and their expansions, are given below and in Appendix 3. Methods of fabric characterisation are explained fully in Tyers 1984, which may be obtained on application to the Museum of London.

Full name	Computer code	Fabric code no
Green-glazed whiteware	BORDG	Sgw 2335
Yellow-glazed whiteware	BORDY	Skw 2344
Brown-glazed whiteware	BORDB	Skw 2367
Olive-glazed whiteware	BORDO	Skw 2396
Unglazed whiteware	BORD	Sw 1703
Red Border ware	RBOR	Skw 1688 1701
'Tudor Green' ware	TUDG	Sgw 1475

A list of thin-sectioned Border ware sherds in the DUA Ceramic Reference Collection is given in Appendix 4. Results from that analysis are here considered in conjunction with those from examination under binocular microscope. Border wares, both whitewares and redwares, from excavations in the city of London and from the various kiln sites, share the same basic characteristics and fall within the ranges expressed below. The clay matrix is densely packed, with fine, silt-size quartz grains. Slight textural variations were noted between some samples, generally in the density of inclusions. Little chronological or geographical significance could be attached to these variations, and it was not possible to relate them to individual 16th- and 17th-century kiln groups as specific forms. The small number of more densely packed samples may simply represent the limits of the range. This is not unexpected, since the sites are all within easy reach of the same clay sources. The range, frequency and size of inclusions visible under binocular microscope are given first, followed by the additional inclusions noted in thin section. The same general results were obtained by both methods.

Whiteware fabrics

Texture and colour: fabrics are hard with a smooth or fairly smooth feel and a fine texture. Surface, core and margins are generally, but not invariably, uniform in colour. The range of colour is quite wide and includes pale grey (Munsell colour code 2.5Y 9/0); yellow- to pinkish-buff (2.5Y 7/2; 5YR 7/6, 8/4; 7.5YR 7/2, 8/6, 9/3); and very pale brown (10YR 7/6, 8/2–8/4, 9/2–9/4). Some kiln sherds from Minley Road, Cove (e.g. TS 1502) have pale salmon-pink streaks or patches within a buff fabric, particularly where the clay is thick, as at a rim, base or handle. This may be caused by leaching of iron-rich compounds, or the poor mixing of clays. This last possibility will be discussed more fully below, in relation to Red Border ware fabrics.

Inclusions: moderate to abundant, ill-sorted, sub-rounded, angular and sub-angular quartz up to 0.25 mm in size, colourless, milky and greyish. Moderate rounded quartz, iron-stained to varying degrees to give a reddish or rose colour, up to 0.25 mm in size, with occasional grains up to 0.5 mm. Sparse rounded red and black iron-rich compound up to 0.25 mm, and sparse flecks of mica up to 0.1 mm which, because they are generally much smaller, are not a notable characteristic under the binocular microscope. In thin section, the matrix is seen to be very micaceous (mostly muscovite, with rare biotite mica). Sparse to rare inclusions of quartzite, although not in every sample; flint or microcrystaline silica, some heavily iron-stained; and felspar could also be identified. The clay matrix is usually optically anisotropic.

Glaze: crazed, and finish varies from thick and glossy to thin and sparse, sometimes pitted. Within each of the main glaze colours used the range of hues is wide. Clear, lead sulphide (galena) glaze appears yellow on a whiteware body and ranges from a lemon colour, through amber to a dull, sandy shade, depending on the colour of the fabric and the thickness of the glaze (2.5Y 8/6–8/10; 7/8). The distinction between glaze which appears yellow and olive glaze may be far from clear. In many cases, a clear lead glaze appears olive because it has been applied over a pale grey body. However, true olive glazes (7.5Y 8/4; 6/6) are also found on lighter, pale buff fabrics, and the distinction is retained here. Yellow-green glazes, with only a small amount of added copper, come close to giving an olive colour. The presence of an iron-rich compound may cause brown streaks or spots in or under the glaze and these are sometimes quite profuse over the glazed surface. Individual spots can be up to 1.0 mm in size or even greater, or they may simply be visible as tiny pin-pricks, prominent enough to be tactile. The addition of varying amounts of copper produces different shades of green, ranging from a dark cucumber colour to a pale apple-green (2.5GY 6/8–4/4; 5GY 5/6–4/4; 10Y 6/8–5/4). Green glazes, of whatever hue, may be even or mottled. Brown glazes result from the addition of manganese or iron to the basic lead solution. The colour varies from dark, heavy brown to a pale golden or honey colour, generally with darker mottling or streaks (5YR 4/2–6,3/2; 7–5YR 6/8–5/6).

The fabric of the late-medieval fineware or 'Tudor Green' has been described by Pearce and Vince (1988, 10–11). The range of inclusions is comparable with other medieval Surrey whitewares and with Border wares, but is not visible to the naked eye. The significance of this fabric in relation to the present study lies in its presence in early 16th-century contexts from London and elsewhere, in the transitional period for which there is no kiln evidence. The only thin-sectioned early 16th-century sherd from London (TS 1514, Bridewell Place) was noticeably more densely packed with very fine quartz than sherds from later contexts and from the kiln sites, with only rare inclusions larger than 0.05 mm. The sample is closer in appearance to Border ware proper than to 'Tudor Green' and may be representative of the transition to a more robust fabric. However, a much larger sample is needed before any conclusions can be reached.

Redware fabrics

Texture and colour: the fabric has a smooth to slightly rough feel, and smooth to subconchoidal fracture. There is wide variation in colour within the fabric of individual vessels and between vessels. The most characteristic colour is pale brick-red to reddish-yellow (2.5–7.5YR 7–8/6–8, 7/10). Dark brick-red fabrics are also found. Lighter buff, pale brown or yellowish margins are common, particularly the external margin where the body is thick (10YR–2.5Y 8–9/4). The surface may be darker red (7.5YR 7/6).

Inclusions: moderate to abundant, ill-sorted, sub-rounded, sub-angular and angular, greyish and colourless quartz up to 0.25 mm, with sparse to moderate iron-stained (reddish and brownish) quartz up to 0.5 mm. Sparse to moderate, well-sorted, rounded black and/or red iron-rich compound in the same size range as the quartz. Sparse mica up to 0.1 mm (see whitewares above), and sparse, ill-sorted red clay pellets, quartzite and ?flint. The fabrics are far more variable than the whitewares. A coarse, dark red storage jar from Minley Road, Cove (TS 1500) was distinctly different in thin section from any of the whitewares sampled. However, the clay matrices of the coarsest whitewares and the finest redwares appear similar in all respects other than the frequency and grain size of the iron-rich compound, which in the latter is both more common and larger. In view of the fact that redwares and whitewares were fired together (Chapter 6), it appears that increased iron content rather than firing conditions is responsible for the distinctive colour of Red Border ware.

There are differences in the degree of siltiness of the matrix, and many Red Border ware fabrics have noticeable buff or off-white streaks throughout. On this basis, it is suggested that it was made by mixing red-firing clays (London clay) with white-firing clays (from the Reading Beds) to varying degrees. The presence of clay pellets probably indicates poor or inadequate mixing.

Glaze: finish is variable, from thick and glossy to thin and sparse. As with whitewares, more than one colour of glaze is used. Clear, lead glaze may appear reddish-brown to orange (2.5YR 5/6–; 5YR 5/8, 6/12), depending on the colour of the underlying fabric. Green glaze, coloured by the addition of copper, gives a dark green to khaki colour (2.5Y 5/4–6; 5Y 5–4/4). Dark brown, manganese-stained and speckled glazes are also used on certain forms.

Description and Type-Series

Border wares from London are here described by class, such as 'dish' or 'bowl', and within this by form. Where necessary, forms are further subdivided into types, which differ from each other in minor details (Pearce and Vince 1988, 19). Whitewares and redwares are discussed together for all classes and forms, but in all cases whitewares predominate. No forms are known in Red Border ware alone. Each form is described in terms of shape, rim, base and handle form, decoration (if any) and finish. Questions of function are also considered. The capacities of certain forms, such as drinking jugs, were measured to the nearest 10 ml using dry rice.

Within each class and form, the minimum number of individual vessels recorded in the DUA corpus is given. This sample, which is drawn from the Reserve Collection and from excavated assemblages, consists both of illustrated 'type-vessels' which were given a 'corpus number', and unillustrated parallels which are sufficiently similar to be assigned the same number as an illustrated example. Type-vessels are selected on the basis of significant variations in shape or details of construction (but not of glaze colour); for example, pots which have the same shape but different rim forms are given different corpus numbers. Excavated vessels which are too incomplete to be compared with the corpus are not given any reference number, but are recorded in the quantified data for individual contexts, and are noted in the text where relevant. Proportions given throughout the type-series are based on the number of vessels in the corpus and do not reflect trends in the real assemblages, nor consequently, trends in actual use. The relative proportions of forms from excavated assemblages are given in Appendix 3. It is these which are used in Chapter 7 rather than figures derived from the corpus, since certain forms such as candlesticks and costrels are no doubt over-represented in the Reserve Collection as a result of collector bias.

Figs 19–46 illustrate Border ware vessels by class and form. In addition to a number, each vessel illustrated has a letter code to denote its glaze or fabric type. The codes are:

T 'Tudor Green'

B brown-glazed whiteware

G green-glazed whiteware

O olive-glazed whiteware

U unglazed whiteware

Y yellow-glazed whiteware

R Red Border ware

· 2 ·
Dishes and Bowls

Dishes

Throughout the type-series, the term 'dish' has been used in preference to 'plate' or 'platter' for open or flatware forms whose height is approximately 1/3 to 1/7 of the rim diameter (Bloice and Dawson 1971, 121–3; Orton 1980, 34). These parameters, which are derived from the classification of Tin-glazed ware forms and Roman pottery studies (Webster 1976, 17–18; Millett 1979, 37) are inevitably arbitrary. Nevertheless, they provide a convenient across-the-board classification which has proved to work with Border wares, and which carries only the most general of functional implications. All corpus vessels were systematically measured, and their height and rim diameter recorded. On the basis of their rim: height ratio, they were recorded as either 'dish' or 'bowl'. The terms 'plate' and 'platter' have not been used for Border ware forms from London and are restricted to vessels which are much closer in profile and 'flatness' to modern plates, as in late 17th-century Tin-glazed wares. By comparison, Border ware vessels are deeper and are therefore classified as 'dishes'. They are subdivided into 'flanged dishes' and 'deep dishes'.

Flanged dishes

Figs 2–4; Figs 19–20, Nos 1–32; Fig 21, Nos 33–42

This form, which is a shallow dish with a broad flange, corresponds to Holling's Class A1–3 'plates, platters and dishes' (Holling 1971, 72–4, fig 2) and Haslam's 'plates and platters' (Haslam 1975, 168–9, fig 3). There are 90 flanged dishes in the corpus and of these only 13 come from the Reserve Collection. There are no reliably dated dishes from the early 16th century in London. All the available excavated material dates from the late 16th and 17th centuries.

Flanged dish rim diameters range from 210–440 mm, although the majority of vessels fall within a more restricted range of 230–330 mm. Base diameters range from 80–220 mm, but most commonly from 100–140 mm. Height ranges from 36–80 mm, with an average of 40–60 mm.

Rim flanges can be up to 52 mm across. The change of angle in the dish profile at the flange is sometimes quite sharp, especially inside (e.g. Nos 18, 20), in which case a tool would have been used to emphasise the shape. More gently sloping profiles were also made (Nos 25, 32) and flanges may be relatively flat (e.g. Nos 15–16, 19) or, more commonly, angled to varying degrees from the horizontal.

A variety of rim forms were made. Although certain broad chronological distinctions can be recognised, these may not allow individual sherds to be dated, since there is considerable overlap. Simple bevelled and slightly thickened rims (No 12) which can be compared with Holling's Class A1 at Farnborough Hill, are found in late 16th-century contexts from London and continue into the second half of the 17th century. The great majority of rim forms from late 16th- to early 17th-century contexts are thickened, usually underneath the flange, and may be bevelled inwards, or rounded at the outer edge (e.g. Nos 9–11, 13–14, 18). These forms again continued to be used into the late 17th century, together with a wide range of folded and beaded rim forms. In groups dating from the mid-17th century and in Great Fire deposits, the rims are most commonly thickened both above and below the flange, with a rounded outer edge, or above the flange only, leaving the underneath flat (Nos 19–27). The thickening or beading was generally produced by folding the edge of the rim downwards and inwards to meet the flange, and in many cases this may clearly be seen in sherd profiles (e.g. Nos 35, 38, 39). The amount of thickening above and below the flange may be increased to give a hammerhead effect (No 40), a feature which seems largely to be found in groups dating from the late 17th century. Single grooves on the outer edge of the rim, or defining the upper or lower thickening, would have been made with a pointed tool. These generally occur on rims dating from the mid- to late 17th century, although they are also known on dishes from earlier contexts (e.g. Nos 12, 29). Folded and beaded thickened rims from mid- to late 17th-century contexts in London can be broadly paralleled by the range of rims found at Cove, dating from the second quarter of the 17th century (Haslam 1975, fig 3, nos 1–13), and at Ash from the mid- to late 17th century (Holling 1969, fig 5, B3–B8). There seems to be little difference between dishes from these two kiln groups.

Flanged dishes are thrown with a flat or slightly indented base. The sides may be straight, like those of an inverted, truncated cone (e.g. No 8), or, more commonly gently curved, giving a slightly convex profile (e.g. Nos 24, 28). All vessels whose bases have survived were knife-trimmed to some extent, and they are the only form to have been regularly treated in this way. The trimmed area can extend from the base-angle to the flange, obscuring throwing-marks. However, it was generally restricted to a shallower zone between 1/4 and 1/2 the height from the base. Trimming was executed with a knife, rib or similar tool in a series of horizontal strokes around the body of the dish, sometimes giving the base-angle a distinctly rounded profile (No 33). Fine drag-marks are common, where inclusions were pulled along by the trimming-tool, although some dishes are very smoothly trimmed, with an almost polished appearance.

Of the vessels examined, excluding small flanged dishes, 25% showed some sign of blackening or sooting from cooking or keeping food warm (for example, on a chafing dish). Heating usually blackened the surface just under the base, especially around the circumference, suggesting that the dishes had been left standing on a heated, flat surface. Some, however, are quite heavily burnt and sooted outside right up to the rim, and must have undergone a more robust form of heating. The remaining unblackened flanged dishes, that is, the majority, were probably used solely for serving food.

Only 12% of all flanged dishes carried any sort of decoration, the most basic form consisting of two or three incised concentric grooves inside the base (No 10). This is a feature which Holling ascribed to the mid- to late 17th century, from the material at Ash (Holling 1971, fig 2, A3), but which in London occurs on dishes dating from the late 16th and early 17th centuries. In one instance, three bands were made with a four-pronged comb (No 16). Wavy lines in a single or double interwoven band around the flange and in patterns inside the dish were made using a pointed tool (Fig 2; No 18) or a comb with four to eight prongs (Fig 3; Nos 27, 29). This form of decor-

Fig 2 *Detail of flanged dish rim with incised decoration*

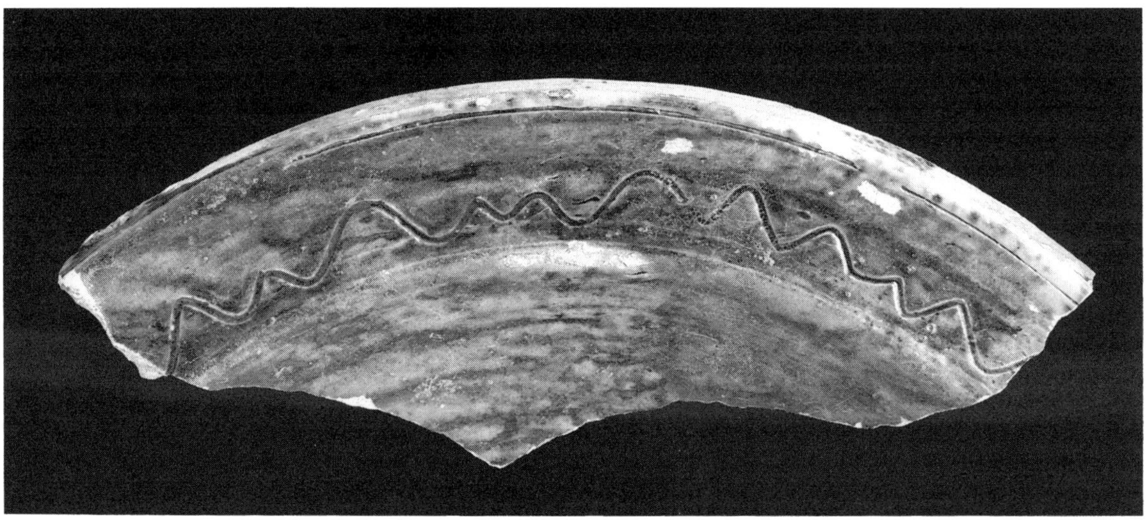

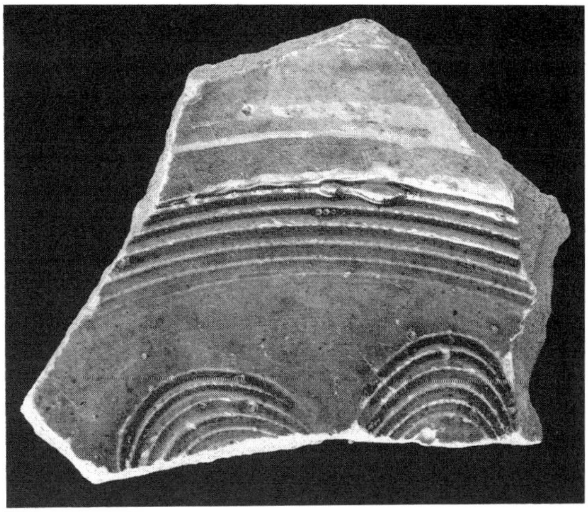

Fig 3 *Detail of flanged dish with combed decoration*

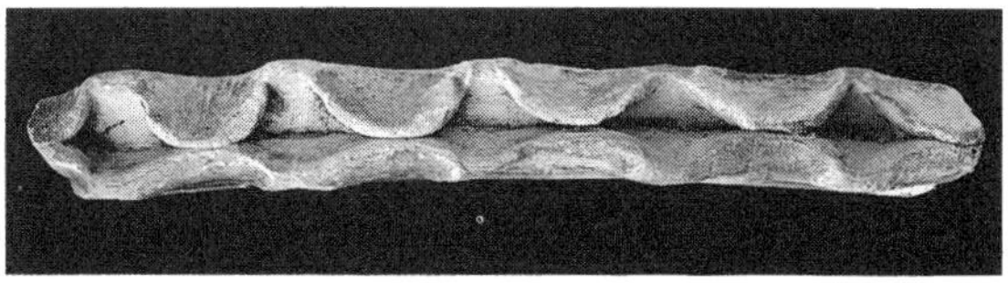

Fig 4 *Detail of flanged dish rim with piecrust decoration*

ation is found in London on dishes dated to the late 16th century and throughout the 17th century. Piecrust decoration, made by pinching the rim at regular intervals around both the upper and lower edges (Fig 4; Nos 17, 31), is found on vessels made in the late 16th and 17th centuries. Incised decoration was found at Cove (Haslam 1975, fig 3, nos 9–13) and at Farnborough Hill, Hawley and Ash (Holling 1971, fig 2, A1–A3); and piecrust decoration at Hawley and Ash.

Flanged dishes were glazed inside only, up to the edge of the rim and just over. Occasional patches, dribbles and spots outside, not always of the same glaze colour, often resulted from contact with other vessels during firing. Green and yellow glazes are found on vessels from the late 16th century and throughout the 17th century, without any apparent chronological implications. The commonest colour is yellow (52% of corpus vessels). Fewer dishes were green-glazed (35%) and olive glaze is very rare. Brown glaze is found only on dishes dating to the mid- to late 17th century (constituting only 6%). Red Border ware flanged dishes also date from this period but were never common in London (6% of the corpus).

A distinct range of small flanged dishes was recognised (12% of all flanged dishes (Nos 1–7)). They are comparable in size to modern saucers or teaplates, although deeper. Rim diameters range from 116–168 mm, base diameters from 55–80 mm and the height from 16–40 mm. Two particularly flat dishes (Nos 1, 4) should properly be defined as plates, but since that term is not otherwise used here they have been included with the small flanged dishes, which they closely resemble in form and probably function. Holling (1971, 72–4, fig 2, A1) suggested that dishes of this size were generally earlier in date than the more common larger forms. Those with a simple bevelled rim were dated to the late 16th-century phase at Farnborough Hill. The small flanged dishes from London correspond closely with this form, and rims are usually either bevelled inwards or outwards, or simply rounded. Thickened, rolled rims are also known (Nos 2–3). Examples of this type of dish are found in London in contexts dating from the late 16th century, but also throughout the 17th century, and at Cove dating from the second quarter of the 17th century (Haslam 1975, fig 3, no 8). Moreover, larger flanged dishes were also found in London in late 16th-century contexts, so size may not be as good an indicator of date as is suggested by Holling's type-series. Only one of the small flanged dishes from London shows any sign of having been heated. It is also the only example in Red Border ware. Whiteware forms are glazed green or yellow in almost equal numbers. In all other details of form and finish, small flanged dishes conform to the larger flanged dishes with which they have been classified.

Deep dishes

Fig 21, Nos 43–9; Fig 22, No 50

A group of unflanged dishes (11 vessels) are classified as 'deep' to distinguish them from the flanged form. Their height in relation to rim diameter tends to be greater, with a ratio of 3–4:1 as opposed to 5–6:1 for flanged dishes. A range of small dishes can be distinguished (Nos 43–4), with rim diameters from 128–155 mm, base diameters from 60–110 mm and height from 39–44 mm. The larger or 'standard' deep dishes range in rim diameter from 230–360 mm, in base diameter from 170–280 mm and in height from 64–80 mm.

In all other respects, the two ranges of deep dish share the same distinctive characteristics. Since they have no rim flange, their base diameter is greater in relation to that of the rim than flanged dishes.

Rims are mostly folded and either simply hooked (Nos 43–4) or folded right back to meet the wall of the dish (Nos 45–6, 49). Exceptions are a rim with a very shallow ledge, similar to a flange (No 50) and simple upright, unthickened, rounded rims (Nos 47–8).

Bases, as with flanged dishes, are either slightly indented or kicked, or flat, and most vessels show some degree of knife-trimming. This is generally much less noticeable than on flanged dishes, being restricted to a shallow zone just above the base-angle, occasionally as much as 1/3 to 1/2 the height. Only one vessel showed any evidence of heating. One dish (No 46) has closely spaced, horizontal ribs and grooves running around the body from the rim to just above the base. Incised or pinched decoration seems to have been restricted entirely to flanged dishes which were probably intended for the table.

Deep dishes were glazed inside only, and 64% have yellow or clear glaze. The glaze colour of the remaining dishes is equally divided between green, olive and brown. Only one small Red Border ware deep dish was found.

No chronological distinctions within the form were recognised, and deep dishes were found in contexts dating from the late 16th to the late 17th centuries.

Bowls

Bowls are defined here as open forms whose rim diameter is greater than that of the base, and whose height is 1/3 or more of the rim diameter (Bloice and Dawson 1971, 123; Orton 1980, 34). A great variety of shapes and sizes of bowl was made, including several forms adapted for specific uses, some of which are unknown. Such forms, including colanders and the putative 'stool pans', have been included with bowls because they conform to the criteria used to define this class. Three main forms of bowl are recognised in London – wide, deep, and handled.

Wide bowls

Fig 22, Nos 51–64; Fig 23, Nos 65–73

This form resembles the deep dish in shape (see above), although the height: rim ratio is greater, thus classifying them as bowls. There are 44 wide bowls in the corpus, including 15 from the Reserve collection (54% of all bowls). Of these, 59% have a flanged rim. As with flanged dishes, the breadth and angle of the flange vary, and a number of bowls have a distinct internal ledge, akin to a lid-seating (Nos 52–7). Rim forms are quite varied. Flanged bowls may have a simple everted rim, slightly thickened and bevelled or rounded (Nos 51, 58–9, 62), sometimes with an incised groove made with a pointed tool around the outer edge and/or the upper surface. This form can be paralleled at Farnborough Hill in the late 16th century (Holling 1971, fig 5, O1), and is found in London in contexts of the same date, but also in 17th-century deposits. The edge of the flange is more commonly folded or thickened to produce the internal ledge described above, which may be emphasised by the use of a pointed or blunt-ended tool. The outer edge of the rim is left rounded (Nos 52–5), or may be shaped with a tool so that the edge is folded right back underneath the flange (Nos 56–7, 65). Bowls without a flange tend to have simpler rim forms. These may be hooked, that is bent downwards, but not back on themselves (Nos 70–1, 73); slightly thickened (No 67) or folded, with or without a central groove (Nos 66, 68, 72).

Wide bowls are more consistent in size than dishes. Rim diameters generally range from 172–320 mm, but the great majority fall between 200–260 mm. Base diameters range from 80–160 mm, with an average of 100–140 mm, and height from 60–123 mm, with an average of 64–90 mm. The majority of the corpus vessels (72%) were made with more or less straight sides, resembling an inverted, truncated cone. The remainder have curved sides, giving a slightly convex profile. Bases are flat or slightly indented or kicked, as with dishes, but knife-trimming is not common. Only 9% of the bowls in question had definitely been trimmed, and then in a shallow zone just above the base-angle (e.g. No 60). A small proportion may have been lightly shaved or turned to tidy up the lower sides, and a number of bowls have smooth outer walls which show little sign of the more prominent turning-marks often apparent inside. In this respect, wide bowls contrast with the more noticeably trimmed flanged dishes. Signs of heating or burning were found on 25% generally restricted to the lower part of the body and base. Heavy sooting or blackening resulting from protracted or intense subjection to heat is rare. Two bowls have a shallow band of ribbing just below the rim (Nos 62–3), and one has a single cordon in a similar position (not illustrated). None are decorated.

Glaze was applied to the inside only, with splashed patches and spots on the outside. Yellow glaze was used on 54% of the vessels, and 32% were green-glazed. Red Border ware is uncommon (9%) and brown and olive glaze are extremely rare.

Wide bowls show little recognisable chronological development. Holling's type-series illustrates bowls in phase 1 only (Holling 1971, O1), although they are also recorded at Hawley in the early 17th century. In London, this form continues throughout the 17th century. The other rim variations and shapes of wide bowl illustrated here also span the late 16th and 17th centuries, and no useful typological criteria emerge to enable individual forms to be dated. However, the great majority of wide bowls from London date to the mid- to late 17th century, and only 9% of corpus examples come from late 16th- or early 17th-century contexts. Most of the variations of wide bowls from London were found at Cove, where they were termed 'wide bowls and pans' (Haslam 1975, fig 5, nos 34–9) and at Ash (Holling 1969, 27, fig 6, E1–E5).

Deep bowls

Fig 23, Nos 74–81; Fig 24, Nos 82–93

This form includes bowls in a variety of shapes, whose height is greater than half the rim diameter. They are noticeably deeper than wide bowls and 28 examples are recorded (12 from the Reserve Collection). Three main types of deep bowl are found in London.

Type 1 (Nos 76–9) is more or less straight-sided or has only a slight curvature and an upright, slightly thickened rim, rounded or bevelled internally. Shallow ribs and grooves run around the body, made while the bowl was on the wheel. This type can be paralleled at Ash (Holling 1969, fig 6, E11–E13).

Type 2 (Nos 74–5, 80–1) is a carinated bowl which resembles a large porringer without handles. The rim is beaded or folded and the upper part of the body is almost straight-sided, with regularly spaced, horizontal ribs and grooves. These were made either with a tool or by squeezing the clay between the thumb and forefinger while the bowl was on the wheel. The base-angle is thickened and probably turned. The bowl illustrated by No 79 is something of a hybrid between Types 1 and 2. Type 2 bowls were made at Farnborough Hill in the late 16th century (Holling 1971, 81, not illustrated) and at Hawley and Cove (unpublished material in Castle Arch Museum, Guildford).

Type 3 (Nos 87–93) are generally deeper than the previous types and their height may be greater than their rim diameter. They have straight sides or a slightly convex profile, with or without ribbing. One vessel from London has a pronounced cordon just below the rim (No 93). Rims are folded and thickened (Nos 88, 92–3); hooked (No 87) or everted (Nos 89–91). Bowls of this form are recorded at Cove as 'tall bowls' (Haslam 1975, fig 5, nos 40–2), at Hawley (unpublished) and at Ash (Holling 1969, fig 6, E10). The late 17th-century bowl illustrated by No 91 has a very broad flange and conical profile, and may be compared with a similar green-glazed Border ware vessel found in a late 18th-century group from Crosswall in London (Vince 1981, 162, fig 163, no 10). This has been interpreted as a stool pan, and conforms with Amis' (1968, 11) definition. A small Red Border ware bowl of similar shape (No 90) was found in a late 17th-century context and is paralleled by five more vessels in the Reserve collection (not illustrated). All are in redware and are remarkably uniform in shape and size. However, there are few other examples from London or elsewhere, and none published from the kiln groups. They are rather small for stool pans, but resemble some of the larger whiteware examples (e.g. No 89) so closely that they are included with them. Their function must remain conjectural.

Light knife-trimming is generally restricted to the area just above the base-angle, but is not as common as on dishes – only 21% of all deep bowls are trimmed. Type 3 shows no sign of heating, but blackening and indications of burning occur on about half of all others.

Decoration is uncommon and, apart from ribbing, is found only on two incomplete Type 2 bowls of similar shape (Nos 74–5) dated to the mid- to late 17th century. Otherwise unparalleled in London, both have at least two rows of rouletted, nicked decoration running around the maximum girth. The larger bowl has an additional band of rouletting around the edge of the rim.

There is no apparent correlation between glaze colour and bowl type. In all cases, clear or yellow glaze is predominant (43%), with 14% green-glazed. Only one olive-glazed example (No 88) is recorded. The number of Red Border ware vessels is particularly high (39%). All bowls are glazed inside only.

One deep bowl from London (Fig 5; No 86) is unique in having a maker's mark scratched underneath the base in the form of four intersecting straight lines. Such marks are known, albeit rarely, on medieval pottery from the London area, for example, on London-type ware (Pearce *et al.* 1985, fig 38) and Surrey whitewares (Pearce and Vince 1988, fig 106, no 416; fig 68, no 93), and may record specific orders or batches.

All the deep bowls from London come from 17th-century contexts. None have been found in the late 16th-century London assemblages considered here.

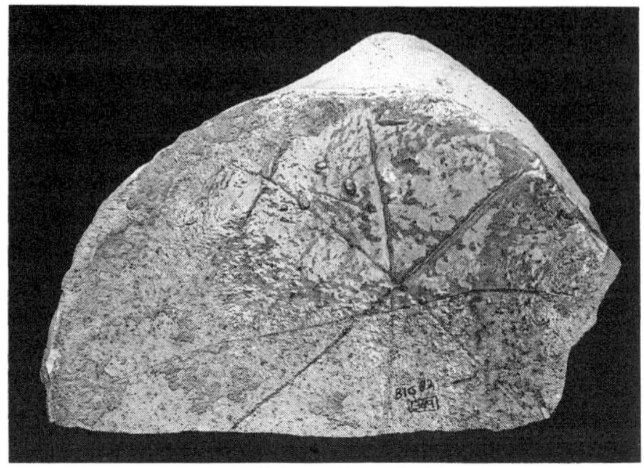

Fig 5 *Detail of deep bowl base with incised maker's mark*

Handled bowls

Fig 24, No 94; Fig 25, Nos 95–101

The third main form of bowl includes large, deep, substantial vessels, thickly potted and provided with one or two loop handles. Rim diameters range from 130–230 mm, bases from 110–170 mm and height from 85–137 mm. Rims are either folded and rounded or bevelled (Nos 94–5), or upright with a broad external lid-seating (Nos 96–8). No lids have definitely been associated with these forms, although large lids which could have fitted them are known in Border ware (e.g. Fig 45, No 439).

Bases are either flat or slightly indented and may be lightly knife-trimmed just above the base-angle. Handles are mostly applied as horizontal loops of rod or squashed oval section. Two diametrically opposed handles are more common than one. This is appropriate for such large and heavy vessels, which could hardly be carried when full by one handle alone. They were applied in the same way as porringer handles (see p 16), and one of the most substantial examples (No 96) has a single deep thumb impression at each end, securing it to the body. One unusual and particularly deep bowl (No 98) has two opposed vertical loop handles, sub-rectangular in section. Handled bowl bodies may be plain, or have a band of incised grooves, or a cordon running level with the handles (Nos 95, 97), which could have acted as a guide for their positioning.

In form, handled bowls resemble modern casseroles. A similar function, for stewing and simmering food, is suggested by blackening and sooting at least around the base and lower sides of most vessels, including all two-handled bowls. All are glazed inside only, with yellow the predominant colour (85% of corpus vessels). The remaining bowls are all green-glazed.

Parallels for the handled bowls illustrated by Nos 94–8 are sparse, limited to one published example from Cove (Haslam 1975, fig 5, no 43) and unpublished vessels from Hawley, all dated to the second quarter of the 17th century. The only dated vessels from London come from late 17th-century deposits.

Three vessels closer in form to wide bowls have a single vertical loop handle (Nos 99–101). All have externally thickened, bevelled rims. One (No 99) has a groove around the top of the rim, and is thinly potted with a convex profile. The largest vessel (No 100) has straight sides and all have handles of sub-rectangular section attached in the same way as chamber pot handles (Fig 54). They are glazed inside only, the largest bowl with yellow and the others with green glaze. The large bowl (No 100) in particular resembles late 16th-century forms termed 'stool pans' by Holling (1971, 81, fig 5, M1). This common type at Farnborough Hill was also found at Cove, where examples are referred to as 'flanged bowls [?stool pans]' (Haslam 1975, fig 4, nos 22–7). They appear to be a well defined type here, all thinly potted and perhaps made by the same potter. Holling (1971, 81) suggests that the form may have served as a rather lightweight type of sanitary vessel, supplanted during the early 17th century by the more substantial and widespread chamber pot. This seems feasible, if the bowl did have a sanitary function, which is suggested by late medieval illustrations of handled bowls used for this purpose in the chamber rather than in a close stool (Amis 1968, figs 8, 14). The form of the 16th- and 17th-century stool pan described by Amis (ibid., 11) is much closer to the Type 3 deep bowls illustrated by Nos 90–1. The London vessels are probably best referred to as 'handled bowls'. They may have had a sanitary function, but not, strictly speaking, as stool pans. They come from early to mid-17th-century contexts.

Colanders

Fig 25, Nos 102–6

Border ware colanders are wide bowls perforated liberally with holes in the body and base to allow the straining of foodstuffs. There are five examples in the corpus with a convex or straight-sided profile. Rim forms reflect those of wide bowls, and are mostly folded. Holes are punched through the walls from outside, in a random pattern and are generally closely spaced. In all but one example, the holes are round. The exception (No 106) has holes made with a tool of pentagonal section. The excess clay left behind on the outside when the tool was removed from each hole was shaved off as the colander was trimmed, probably on a turntable. This cleaning process tended to leave the exterior of the vessel quite smooth, with slight impressions and cracks around the edge of each hole. As expected, none of the London colanders was burnt. Two vessels have yellow glaze, one brown glaze, and two are in Red Border ware. All come from mid- to late 17th-century contexts. No parallels have been published from the kiln groups, although fragments were found at Farnborough Hill (unpublished material in Castle Arch Museum, Guildford).

Porringers

Figs 6–7; Fig 26, Nos 107–30; Fig 27, Nos 131–3; Fig 53

The term 'porringer' is used to describe a vessel shaped like a small bowl or large cup, with a horizontal rather than vertical handle. The form, which was common in the early post-medieval period both in England and on the Continent, was intended to hold a variety of foods, such as broth or porridge (Coleman-Smith and Pearson 1988, 162). Large numbers of vessels defined as porringers were found at Cove in a variety of shapes, with or without handles (Haslam 1975, 170, fig 4, nos 14–21, 28). Holling prefers the term 'cup' for vessels of this form (Holling 1971, 74, fig 2, B1b–B3). They may have been used as cups, or, as the evidence from London suggests, as bowls for food, or the functions may have been interchangeable. The term is used here to distinguish the form from generally smaller open drinking vessels with a vertical handle made in the so-called 'Tudor Green' fabric (Fig 31, Nos 194–7).

A total of 70 vessels was examined, including 20 from the Reserve Collection. Only three were found which correspond to Holling's form B1b, from Farnborough Hill, all too fragmentary to illustrate. One comes from a late 16th-century context, which agrees with Holling's dating; the other two were from mid-17th-century deposits. The great majority of porringers from London fall into Holling's form B2b–B3, typified by material from Hawley and Ash, dated to the early and late 17th century respectively, and from Cove (see above). Form B2b porringers are also found at Farnborough Hill (Holling pers comm), and this dating is reflected by the London material, where forms corresponding to Holling's B2b are found in late 16th-century contexts and throughout the 17th century.

Porringers are invariably carinated at or just below the mid-point of the profile. The majority are also ribbed around the upper part of the body, above the carination. There are generally three or four ribs and grooves, which may be quite pronounced, particularly when made with a tool. Shallower ribbing was made with the fingertips alone, as the pot turned on the wheel. A number of porringers (13%) have no ribbing at all, or only very slight ribs and grooves (Nos 127–33). These

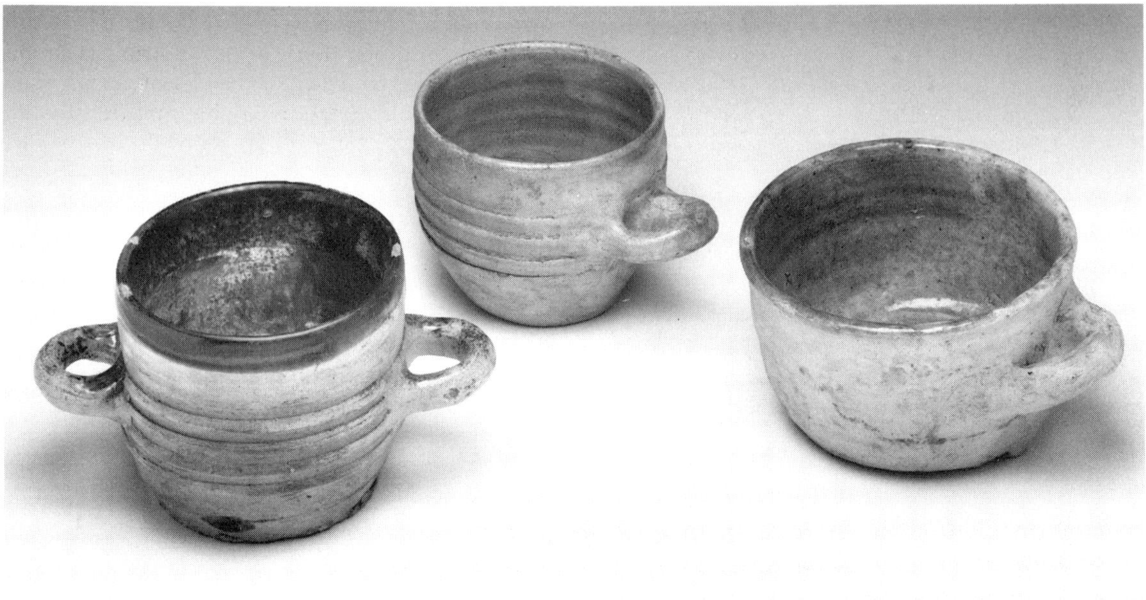

Fig 6 *Porringers. From left to right: 17th century, brown-glazed (height 80 mm); yellow-glazed (height 77 mm); late 17th century, green-glazed*

vessels form a distinct group which appears to be late in date, and is not paralleled in the published kiln groups. In London they are found in contexts dated to the late 17th century as well as in 18th-century groups, and half the corpus vessels were made in Red Border ware. They have a sharp carination, lower on the body than in Holling's form B2b, and a greater base diameter in relation to the rim.

Rim diameters range from 100–160 mm, with most between 120–140 mm. Base diameters have an average range of 70–90 mm with outer limits of 55–112 mm. Height varies from 56–80 mm, with the majority from 60–70 mm. The capacities of 10 vessels were measured at 450–740 ml, but this sample is not large enough to determine whether specific size ranges were made.

The commonest rim form is simply rounded and unthickened (51% of the corpus; Nos 108–16) and is found on ribbed porringers from the late 16th and throughout the 17th century. A smaller number (*c.* 20%) have a slightly everted rim, occasionally with a narrow incised groove just below (Nos 117–19). These are found in mid- to late 17th-century deposits but not earlier. Only one inturned porringer rim is known from London (No 107). Other rim forms are externally thickened with an internal bevel (Nos 121–2); internally thickened (No 124); and rolled or beaded (Nos 123, 125–6), all found in deposits dated to the mid- to late 17th century.

One porringer has two diametrically opposed, horizontal loop handles (Fig 6: No 114), unique both in London and the kiln groups. Another vessel of porringer form (not illustrated) has one very short, stubby, horizontal handle, complete and hardly suitable for holding the vessel. This is again unique, and the form may originally have had two such handles. Only one vessel definitely has no handle, although 37% are incomplete and may or may not have had one. The remaining porringers have one horizontal loop handle, attached over the ribbing, either at the carination or just above. Few handles are truly horizontal (e.g. Nos 114–15), but are generally tipped upwards, sometimes to quite a degree, so that they almost reach the body of the vessel. Porringer handles are of rod, oval, square or sub-rectangular section, and a small number have a shallow groove on their outer surface. In all cases, the length of handle to be attached was luted on to the body at the desired point (here the ribbing may have helped secure the attachment) and smoothed into the body all round. It was then bent round to form a loop, and the other end was simply pressed on to the wall, but not wiped or smoothed into the body in the same way (Figs 7, 53). Single thumb or

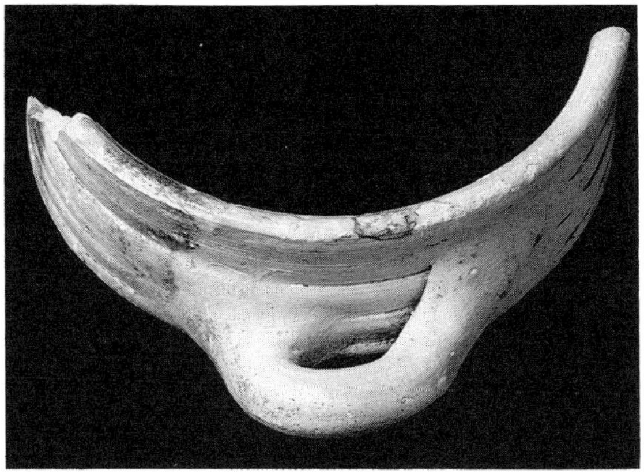

Fig 7 *Detail of porringer handle showing method of attachment*

finger impressions at this join are common. Many porringer handles are either so small, or attached at such an acute angle to the body, that it would have been difficult, if not impossible, to hold the vessel by the handle alone, especially for drinking. They are more likely to have been used to hang the vessel from a hook.

Porringer bases are slightly indented or kicked, or almost flat. There is little evidence for knife-trimming. Marks left by the process of removal from the wheel-head often remain unobscured by finishing. Excess clay, which may have spread at the base-angle, was lightly shaved away, often leaving a slight, smooth ridge just above the base, part or all of the way around the vessel.

A large proportion of the porringers from London (40%) are blackened and sooted from use. The commonest pattern of burning is around the lower part of the body, more or less below the carination, but not around the handle. Some vessels are very heavily sooted up to and around the rim, and others show signs of slight blackening just around the circumference of the base. Porringers were certainly used for heating food, such as broth or porridge, or for keeping individual portions warm. Since 60% were not burned in any way, the form may have been used to hold liquids as well, but the number of rims unsuitable for drinking and the awkward handles suggest that it was made for food. Although certain forms used for drinking, such as goblets, have thickened rims, it seems likely that the function of drinking vessels was generally fulfilled by cups, drinking jugs and mugs and that porringers were made for semi-solid food.

No Border ware porringers are decorated. They ar glazed inside and just over the edge of the rim. Many also have a thin covering of glaze outside, giving a slightly glossy sheen. The majority have clear, yellow glaze (54%); 27% were green-glazed; 9% have brown glaze, while olive glaze is rare. Red Border ware vessels account for 9% of the sample. At all periods, from the late 16th century to the late 17th century, there were twice as many yellow-glazed porringers as green-glazed. Brown-glazed and Red Border ware porringers are found only from the mid-17th century onwards.

· 3 · Cooking Vessels

Tripod Pipkins

Fig 8; Fig 27, Nos 134–46; Fig 28, Nos 147–54; Fig 29, Nos 155–68

The term 'tripod pipkin' is used to describe jar-shaped cooking vessels with three feet and at least one handle. The reference to feet is included in the form name to distinguish it from the simple 'pipkin' without feet made in medieval Surrey whitewares (Pearce and Vince 1988, fig 95, nos 311–17). Although the latter term is used in the published kiln groups (Holling 1969, 24, fig 5, A1–A10; Holling 1971, 76–7, fig 3, E1a–E3; Haslam 1975, 179, fig 8, nos 90–5), the same form as defined here is being described. A total of 59 corpus vessels from London was examined, including 26 from the Reserve Collection. Holling (1971, 76) concluded that the form displayed 'reliable chronological features' for the Border ware industry as a whole, the most significant of these being the presence, or absence, of ribbing on the body, and the position on the profile of the maximum girth. On this basis, London vessels fall into two main groups: those with a ribbed body (56%) and those without (44%). Both groups include vessels with internal and external lid seating, a feature which Holling recognised as just beginning in the late 16th century at Farnborough Hill, and becoming more common later (ibid.). Otherwise, rim forms do not have any chronological significance. Everted rims (Nos 134–48, 155–64) are the commoner form in London (75% of the sample, both ribbed and plain). Of these, 44% have a definite internal step or ledge to accommodate a lid (e.g. Nos 156, 158–62), although this does not preclude the use of lids for the remainder. It may be significant that the stepped rim is more prevalent on plain-bodied pipkins from mid- to late 17th-century contexts in London (76% of the examples, as opposed to 30% of ribbed vessels). The rim may simply be bent outwards, with a rounded or flattened outer edge (Nos 135, 140, 147), and a few rims are folded back on themselves (No 143). Those with a definite internal ledge or step tend to be bevelled externally to give an upright outer edge, sometimes with a light central groove (Nos 136–7, 161–2). External lid-seating was provided by a simple flange positioned 16–20 mm below the rim (Nos 149–54, 165–8). This could be rounded in profile, like a cordon, or curved upwards, and in most examples the rim simply has a rounded, unthickened top, slightly inverted.

Holling noted that late 16th-century vessels from Farnborough Hill had light grooves separated by ribs on the upper half of the body. Those from the early 17th-century group at Hawley had more pronounced corrugations, covering more or less the whole body. Ribbing appears to end *c.* 1640, and was not found on any late 17th-century tripod pipkins from Ash. At about the same time, slight changes in shape can be seen, the maximum girth being positioned lower on the body to give it a more pear-shaped appearance (Holling 1971, fig 3, E2b-E3).

In London, tripod pipkins with ribbed bodies are found in contexts dating from the late 16th and throughout the 17th century. The extent of ribbing does not seem to be chronologically significant and can, of course, only be determined where the profile is substantially complete. Those with light ribs and grooves (e.g. Nos 135–41) covering the upper half of the body are found in mid- to late 17th-century contexts and vessels with close-set grooves, or 'corrugations', covering at least 3/4 of the body (e.g. Nos 143–6) are found in late 16th- to late 17th-century groups. In all but a few instances (e.g. Nos 152, 154, undated) vessels with ribbed bodies have an even convex profile with the maximum girth at approximately the mid-point. Light ribbing could well have been made using the fingertips only, although it is more pronounced than normal throwing-marks. Deeper corrugations were probably made with a tool while

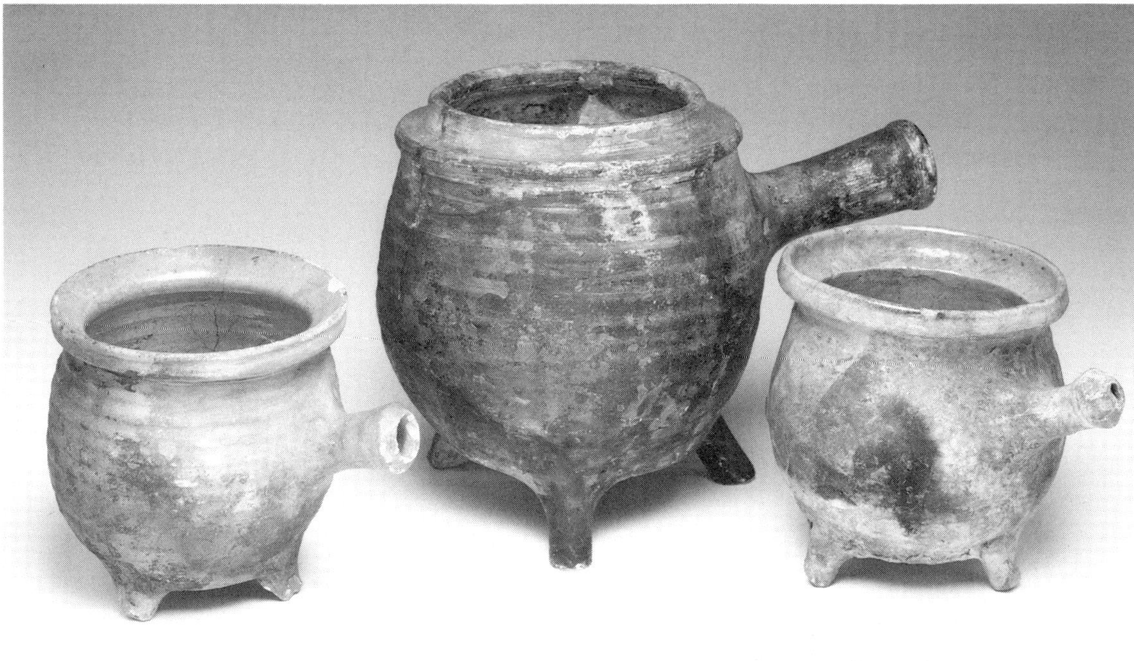

Fig 8 *Tripod pipkins. From left to right: early 17th century, with yellow glaze (height 130 mm); mid- to late 17th century, with olive glaze (height 189 mm); late 17th century, with yellow glaze (height 130 mm)*

the vessel was turned on the wheel. Tripod pipkins with plain, unribbed bodies (Nos 155–68) are found in mid- to late 17th-century contexts. They are absent from late 16th- or early 17th-century deposits from London. External lid-seating, with or without ribbing, is found in London from the mid-17th century onwards.

Examination of the excavated kiln groups suggested that tripod pipkins were made in graduated sizes, although the dimensions were not standardised (Holling 1971, 76–7). Too few London examples are sufficiently complete to allow measurement of the capacity. Those which could be measured ranged from 340–2510 ml. Rim diameters range from 76–212 mm, peaking at 80–100 mm; base diameters range from 50–188 mm, peaking at 60–85 mm, 100–120 mm and 140–155 mm; and heights range from 76–243 mm, peaking at 85–105 mm, 115–140 mm and 185–195 mm. Different size ranges were found in both ribbed and plain vessels, although the majority of tripod pipkins with external lid-seating come at the larger end of the range.

Handles are tubular in all but one instance, a solid handle attached in the same position as the normal form (No 158). All handles were thrown, however small, and were secured at or just above the mid-point of the body, at an angle of about 25–45° from the horizontal. They were luted on to the body and smoothed radially into the clay, obscuring ribbing when present. A number of vessels have thumb- and finger-impressions around the handle/body join, making the attachment more secure (e.g. Nos 141, 144, 150–4). Most, but not all, of the larger tripod pipkins are treated in this way. The number of impressions varies from one beneath the handle (No 135) to four equally spaced around it (No 141). Three impressions, one each side and one below, are most common (No 151). Handle length varies from 32 to 88 mm; the larger the vessel, the more substantial the handle required to support it, although one example (No 143) has an unusually large handle for its size. The terminal of the handle may be slightly flared and then tapered (Nos 135, 137), thickened with beading (Nos 159–60) or, rarely, flared and cut straight across (No 145). Moorhouse commented on the linking of the first type with late 16th-century material from Farnborough Hill, and the second with Hawley and Ash (Moorhouse 1970, 43–5), suggesting that these terminals could be the trademarks of particular potters. In London, both main types are found on ribbed and plain tripod pipkins alike and it would be unwise to use this criterion as a dating feature. Most surviving bases are slightly indented or kicked, although some are almost flat (Nos 136, 141) and a few are markedly indented (e.g. Nos 144–50). One unusual vessel has a pronounced convex or sagging base (No 154) – a form which is otherwise virtually unknown in Border ware, and is associated rather with medieval Surrey whitewares.

Knife-trimming was not easy to detect on tripod pipkins. If present, it was obscured by burning and the application of feet. However, as far as could be seen, a fairly small number of vessels whose bases survived were lightly trimmed in a shallow zone just above the base-angle, and sometimes underneath (22%). One vessel (No 157) had been vigorously trimmed around the sides, giving it an almost carinated profile.

Feet were applied at more or less regular intervals on the circumference of the base and smoothed into the base and lower sides of the vessel (Fig 49). In most cases, this process was carried out carelessly, leaving cracks around the join. The feet were splayed outwards at a slight angle and were generally oval, triangular or sub-rectangular in section. The larger the vessel, the more substantial the feet required; one particularly large example (No 153) has three shallow vertical grooves in the outer surface of each foot, running across the join with the body, presumably to make it more secure.

Tripod pipkins were made for heating food, and 75% of the London vessels are burnt to some extent. Evidence of heating may simply take the form of slight blackening under the base, on the ends of the feet, and around the lower sides, especially opposite the handle. A sizeable proportion (41%) are burnt heavily, with encrustations of soot remaining, and heavy blackening as far as the rim and around most of the body, showing lengthy or frequent use on an open fire. A small number (10%) shows no signs of burning or heating at all.

Glaze was applied to the interior only, although streaks and patches are found on the outside. The predominant glaze colour is yellow (68%), while 12% have an intermediate yellow-green or olive glaze. True green glaze is uncommon (6%) and Holling found that it was not used at Ash in the latest phase of the industry, after c. 1640 (Holling 1969, 24; 1971, 83). In London, green glaze is found on a very small number of ribbed and plain pipkins from the mid- to late 17th centuries. There are no brown-glazed tripod pipkins in the corpus. The number of Red Border ware vessels is comparatively small (10%), although this fabric was used for both ribbed and unribbed forms.

Skillets

Fig 9; Fig 30, Nos 169–84

The vessels described here as 'skillets' are small bowls or dishes with one handle and a pouring lip, used for cooking. They may or may not have three feet. As found in London, the form includes Haslam's 'skillets or ladles' from Cove (Haslam 1975, 71, fig 4, nos 29–33) and Holling's 'saucepans or skillets' of the same date (Holling 1971, 77, fig 4, F2). There are no skillets of Holling's form F1 from Farnborough Hill in London. However, the range of skillets recorded in the corpus is wider than illustrated in the published type-series from the kiln sites. They come from contexts dating to the late 16th century and throughout the 17th century, with no apparent chronologically distinctive features.

Skillets vary in profile and in detail, although two main shapes can be recognised in London: one with a more or less straight-sided profile (Nos 179–84) and the other with a carinated or convex profile, resembling a porringer in form (Nos 169–72, 174–8). Rims are commonly everted, with a rounded or bevelled edge (Nos 176–7, 180), and four have an internal ledge or step to provide a lid-seating (e.g. Nos 179, 183). The other main rim form is folded or beaded and thickened externally (Nos 169–72, 178). There are two unusual forms: a simple upright, unthickened rim (No 175) and an unthickened, everted rim above a constricted neck (No 173). All reasonably complete skillets have a pinched and pulled pouring lip positioned at 90° from the handle. None is definitely without a lip. Rim diameters range from 110–152 mm (with the majority 115–125 mm), bases from 60–92 mm, and height from 38–88 mm. No capacities were measured, but the vessels were obviously not made to hold a single large meal for a number of people. They were

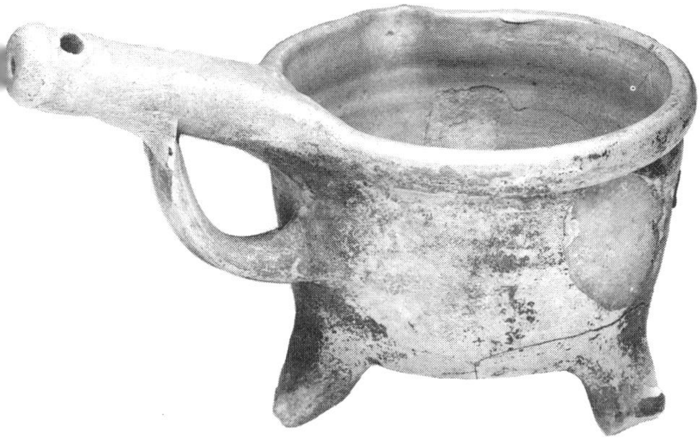

Fig 9 *Mid-17th-century skillet with yellow glaze (height 88 mm)*

probably used to heat certain ingredients or parts of a meal, or individual portions.

The majority of skillets (c.77%) have a solid, more or less horizontal handle attached either over the rim or at the maximum girth. Some handles are very short and stubby and hardly practical (e.g. Nos 171, 178) and sections vary from rod to sub-rectangular. Two unusual vessels have vertical loop handles (Nos 169–70), and two skillets have tubular handles, also attached over the rim (Nos 177, 184). The handle of No 184 (see also Fig 9) is particularly long (84 mm) and has a curved, supporting strut of sub-rectangular section springing from the mid-point underneath to the wall of the vessel just above the foot. The strut is very poorly bonded and a circular hole runs diagonally through the end of the handle, perhaps for hanging the vessel from a hook.

Bases are slightly indented or kicked, or almost flat, and may have a slight, untrimmed thickening around the circumference (e.g. Nos 171–2). Two vessels were definitely trimmed around the lower sides (e.g. No 184), although the application of feet, when present, may have obscured evidence for this process. Feet are short and stubby, with a squared or oval section and flattened or slightly pointed ends. All but two skillets show signs of heating, and seven were heavily burnt and sooted. The remainder were only slightly blackened around the feet.

All skillets are glazed internally. Most of the corpus vessels (55%) have yellow glaze, 33% have green glaze and, apart from one mid- 17th-century Red Border ware example (Fig 30, No 183), the rest are olive-glazed.

Saucepan

Fig 30, No 185

One cooking vessel found in London, in a context dated c. 1650–1700, resembles a skillet in form, but has a much larger capacity. Its shape is that of a deep bowl, with a pulled and pinched lip positioned at 90° from a handle of sub-rectangular section, attached over the rim. The handle was originally supported by a strut, which is now missing. The rim is folded and thickened externally, with a slight undercut, but no lid-seating. A horizontal band of incised grooves runs around the body just below the rim. The base is missing, so it is uncertain whether the vessel had feet. It is very heavily burnt, blackened and sooted externally, up to the rim. A mottled green glaze covers the interior. No parallels are recorded from the kiln groups.

Chafing Dishes

Plate 1; Fig 30, Nos 186–7; Fig 31, Nos 188–93

Chafing dishes are bowls set on a deep pedestal base, used to hold charcoal or embers for cooking or keeping food warm in a dish placed over the lugs or knobs around the rim (Coleman-Smith and Pearson 1988, 217). Eight chafing dishes from London are recorded in the corpus; only four (from the Reserve Collection) have a complete profile and, although the sample is small, there is some variety in both shape and detail.

Four vessels are very heavy and substantially built, with the thick walls necessary to support a large or heavy dish of food (Nos 186–7, 191, 193). Rim diameters range from 132–212 mm, bases from 90–140 mm and the height (including lugs or knobs) from 89–123 mm. Only one example (No 186) has squared lugs. The remaining vessels whose rim supports have survived, have thick knobs with rounded terminals, crudely made and clumsily applied. One vessel (No 192) is extremely unusual and without parallel in any of the kiln groups. Instead of having lugs or knobs, the sides of the bowl are cut into a continuous series of V-shapes all round, giving a 'crenellated' effect, and making the bowl itself very shallow.

Rims are generally externally thickened and

folded, and rounded or squared externally (Nos 188–9, 191) or bevelled internally (Nos 186–7). The sides of the bowl are more or less straight and vertical, and half the corpus examples are ribbed above the carination, one of them with close set, deep ribs and grooves (No 190). The sides of the bowl are pierced with circular airholes in five examples. Additional apertures of different shapes, such as square (No 189), may also be included. The most elaborate chafing dish from London (No 191) has an irregular row of circular holes, interspersed with double triangles, with smaller holes above and below. Three vessels have no airholes at all (Nos 186–7, 192).

Handle forms are varied. Three chafing dishes have two diametrically opposed vertical loop handles (Nos 187, 189, 193) attached, at the top, over the rim, and, at the bottom, over the carination of the bowl. One vessel (No 186) definitely has only one such handle and the handles of two excavated examples are now missing. The remaining chafing dishes have two opposed horizontal loop handles, attached over the carination (Nos 191–2). The handle section may be round, subrectangular or roughly oval.

Whenever the base of the bowl has survived it is both pierced and applied separately to what would have been thrown as a form resembling a large cup (e.g. Nos 195–7). As on the walls, various patterns and numbers of holes were made with different types of tool. The most common are circular (Nos 186, 190), but patterns made with a knife-tip are also known (Plate 1; No 187), and No 191 has an unusual arrangement of circular holes and irregular, roughly curved slits.

All the more complete chafing dishes have a closed pedestal base, slightly kicked underneath. Half the recorded examples have regularly spaced horizontal grooves running around the outside of the pedestal (Nos 186–7, 191, 193). Two vessels have large triangular apertures cut clumsily in the side of the pedestal just above the base (Plate 1; Nos 186–7). There is one example with a single rectangular opening (No 192) and one very unusual vessel with four large, regularly spaced, rectangular apertures around the pedestal (No 193). This is a particularly large vessel, whose upper part is missing. It is included here because of its general resemblance to chafing dishes, although its precise identification remains uncertain. Another chafing dish has an entirely closed pedestal, with no apertures of any sort, although the base of its bowl is pierced (No 191). The pattern of pierced bases and pedestal apertures suggests that the chafing dishes found in London were made to hold embers or charcoal, rather than hot water or spirits (Moorhouse 1970, 66). None could have held fluid, apart from No 191, which could only have contained it in the pedestal. However, none of the London examples shows any sign of the burning or blackening which would have resulted from their holding embers, so their actual usage remains enigmatic.

No Red Border ware chafing dishes have been found in London. This is unexpected, since they are more common than whiteware examples at Farnborough Hill in the late 16th century (Holling 1971, 79). The majority of chafing dishes from London are glazed inside the bowl only, including the knobs or lugs. Small patches of glaze frequently seeped through the airholes to the exterior surface. Two vessels are glazed externally as well: No 191 (which is the only chafing dish with brown glaze), and No 193, whose pedestal base is unglazed inside, apart from spreads of glaze around the apertures. Half the London vessels are green-glazed, and, apart from the single brown-glazed example described above, the rest have yellow glaze.

Holling recognised two types of Border ware chafing dish from phases 1 and 2 of his type-series (Holling 1971, 79, fig 4, J1 and J2). Of the London examples, only one (No 186) corresponds with form J1, with its squared lugs and heavy body. However, this vessel closely resembles No 187 in all respects other than rim supports – the latter has the rounded knobs considered by Holling (ibid.) to be typical of phase 2 at Hawley, and found also at Cove (Haslam 1975, 182, fig 9, nos 103–10). A simple squared lug was also found at Cove (ibid., fig 9, no 110), so this feature in itself is not necessarily diagnostic of date. Only three of the London chafing dishes can be dated, all to the mid-17th century.

· 4 ·
Drinking Vessels

A great variety of Border ware drinking vessels are found in London. The comparative wealth of types in use from the 15th century onwards contrasts sharply with the range of medieval ceramic vessels made for drinking. The term 'drinking vessels' should be taken in the broadest sense, without placing restrictions on the uses to which the forms may have been put. The forms considered here – cups, goblets, drinking jugs and mugs – were made over a long period of time, developing and evolving out of forms which came into use in the 15th century and earlier.

Cups

Fig 31, Nos 194–7

There are four reasonably complete cups in the Reserve collection whose forms and fabrics are derived from the 15th-century fineware element of the late medieval Surrey whiteware industry, or 'Tudor Green'. Both forms illustrated here are represented by sherds from early 16th-century London contexts.

There is no evidence that the tall, waisted cup form (No 194) was made in the late 16th-century kiln at Farnborough Hill, although it was found in the late 15th-century kiln material (Holling 1977, fig 1, no 4), where it had two handles. The London vessels and the excavated kiln parallels are all thin-walled, very fine and light. The elegant profile has a flared neck above a pronounced waist from which the body curves to the base. The rim is rounded and not thickened, and the base is slightly kicked. The strap handle has a slightly concave upper surface and is attached over the rim, and below the waist. The lower end is wiped to each side in the same way as drinking jug handles (see below). The cup has green glaze inside, and outside as far as the waist, with numerous splashes and spots below this. Although there is no evidence that cups of this form were made in the 16th century, they are quite often found in early 16th-century contexts outside London (Moorhouse 1970, 62, fig 14, no 133; Moorhouse 1979, 57). The presence of cups in early 16th-century contexts from London may be accounted for by curation of intrinsically desirable fine pottery. However, in the light of other finds from around the country, and the lack of any early 16th-century kiln material to elucidate the industry at this period, it may be suggested that the form was still being made after 1500 (Holling 1977, 65–6).

The other form of early fine cup included here was also made at Farnborough Hill in the late 15th century (Holling 1977, fig 1, no 7) but not at the later kilns. All three illustrated cups (Nos 195–7) have the thin walls and fine fabric associated with 'Tudor Green'. The body is straight-sided above a carination at the mid-point of the profile with a narrow, pedestal foot. Rims are unthickened and rounded and the foot slightly splayed and thickened around the base-angle. They are green-glazed inside, and outside over the upper half of the body. Handles are attached in the same position and in the same manner as on the tall cup described above, and have a similar section. One cup (No 196) and sherds from at least two different vessels of the same form come from early 16th-century contexts in London.

Goblets

Fig 31, Nos 198–203; Fig 32, Nos 204–6

Goblets are tall drinking vessels without handles. There are nine in the corpus, only one of them from an excavated context. They have an approximately straight-sided body with a constricted pedestal base. Rim diameters range from 80–110 mm, bases from 65–85 mm and height from 110–142 mm. Measured capacities fall between 250 and 340 ml. Rims are either externally thickened and squared or bevelled (Nos 198, 200–1) or simply unthickened and rounded (Nos 202–4, 206). The body has two to three regularly spaced horizontal cordons or ribs, which can give a distinctly stepped appearance to the profile (e.g. Nos 201, 205). The cordons were formed either by using a tool to give a sharp, angular profile (Nos 198–9) or by hand during throwing, giving a more undulating profile (Nos 204, 206). The base is thickened and trimmed to give an upright bevel, and one (No 204), in addition, is pinched or thumbed all the way round. Diagonal twisting marks are visible inside the pedestal where the clay was squeezed during throwing. Goblets are glazed externally from the rim to the top of the pedestal and just inside the rim. Only two have yellow glaze; the rest are green-glazed. Two also have blackened and sooted bases (Nos 198, 206).

Goblets were found in the late 15th-century and late 16th-century kiln material from Farnborough Hill, where they were classified as form B1b (Holling 1971, 74, fig 2; 1977, fig 1, nos 6a–b). They were not found at any of the later kiln sites. Small sherds which probably came from goblets were found in early 16th-century material from London.

Drinking Jugs

These are among the best represented Border ware forms in the Reserve Collection. The corpus totals 93 examples, including only six from excavations. Many more fragments are found in excavated material than is suggested by this, but because they are fine and generally thin-walled, they break easily into small sherds. Even the more distinctive of these could well belong to a number of type-vessels, but are too incomplete to be assigned a corpus number. The Inns of Court have produced the largest published collection of drinking jugs to date (Matthews and Green 1969). The term 'drinking jug' is used here in preference to 'jug' because the great majority are of a size suitable for drinking, rather than serving, and because of the documentary evidence for this usage from the Inns of Court (see below). Although the largest vessels may have been used for serving, they are few in number and are best included here on account of their obvious similarity to the standard range. Drinking jugs in the corpus correspond broadly with the types recognised by Green at the Inns of Court. Two main types are represented.

Rounded drinking jugs

Fig 32, Nos 207–17; Fig 33, Nos 218–33; Fig 34, Nos 234–5

This type consists of drinking jugs listed by Green as 'wares in the Surrey tradition' (Matthews and Green 1969, 7–8) and includes both the 'tall jugs' of the 'early tradition', dated to the 16th century, and the 'squatter' jugs of the 'late tradition', dated to the second half of the 17th century. The term 'rounded drinking jug' is here preferred for the form as a whole, on the basis of profile. The body curves gently down to the base, which has no thickening or waist. The neck is distinct from the body and is either straight-sided or slightly flared. There are variations of profile and proportions within this, but not enough to merit separate terminology.

There is a total of 60 rounded drinking jugs in the DUA corpus (64% of all drinking jugs). They can be graded roughly according to size, on which basis 12 (Nos 207–15; 20% of this type) could be seen as belonging to Green's 'early tradition' (ibid., fig 1, nos 5–12). These are the tallest of the drinking jugs and share certain distinctive features which suggest a chronological grouping. It is difficult, however, to make hard and fast rules, and there are a number of intermediate types between the 'early' and 'late' traditions (e.g. Nos 216–17). The rim diameters of the taller group range from 58–85 mm (the majority are 60–70 mm), base diameters from 70–80 mm, and height from 185–215 mm. Capacities are between 740–990 ml. There are 48 rounded drinking jugs (Nos 217–35) which, on the basis of size, could be classed as the squatter, 'late tradition' (ibid., fig 2, nos 13–21), including intermediate examples. Their rim diameters range from 55–90 mm (with the majority 60–70 mm) and height from 115–174 mm. The overall capacity range is quite wide, from 260 to 670 ml, although most fall between 440 and 590 ml. It is notable that the shorter the vessel, the wider its rim diameter and the taller its neck in relation to the overall height. Those less than 130 mm tall tend to have a 'waisted' appearance, with the neck taking up almost half the height, and a correspondingly less rounded body. Moreover, for the majority, there is little more than 10 mm difference between base and rim diameters.

Rims are most commonly unthickened and simply rounded (Nos 213–15); steeply bevelled internally (No 216); or slightly thickened with an internal bevel (Nos 211, 217–18) or flattened top (Nos 207, 209). One (No 210) is unusual in having an internal ledge or step. All rounded drinking jugs with reasonably complete rims have a pouring lip diametrically opposite the handle, or almost so (e.g. No 217). The taller jugs of the 'early tradition' and intermediate forms, have a deep lip, pulled and pinched, and often extending the whole length of the neck (e.g. Nos 213–14). The shorter, squatter jugs of the so-called 'late tradition' have a smaller V-shaped lip, pinched rather than pulled (e.g. No 223). Matthews and Green (1969, 7–8) draw attention to contemporaneous continental paintings depicting lipped jugs with their contents being poured directly into the mouth rather than into a mug or cup.

Handles are always luted on to the body, without any of the disruption associated with many medieval forms (Pearce 1984). At the top, they are attached to the neck below the rim, commonly as far down as the shoulder (e.g. Nos 208, 213). The lower end is pressed on to the body at or just above the maximum girth and simply wiped to each side across the join. Rarely, there is a single thumb or finger impression over the lower join (Nos 211, 231). Strap handles are associated particularly with the tall 'early' group, and generally have a slightly concave upper surface. The remaining drinking jug handles are thicker with a sub-rectangular, oval or rod section.

The bases of all rounded drinking jugs are either flat or slightly indented or kicked. None are thickened, and at least 28% show clear signs of having been lightly shaved while being turned on the wheel to remove surplus clay just above the base-angle. A large number also have diagonal twisting marks visible in the clay, especially inside the neck. This results from the squeezing of the clay during throwing to produce the neck constriction. A few vessels (12%) have one or more lightly incised grooves running around the neck or shoulder (e.g. Nos 211, 228, 233).

Glaze was applied to the outside of the drinking jug, over roughly the top half of the body, and just inside the rim. There are plenty of splashes and patches of glaze on the lower half, and runs of liquid glaze show that most drinking jugs stood upright in the kiln. Only one rounded drinking jug from London has yellow glaze (No 223). The rest have green glaze of varying hues from pale to dark. Occasional accidental patches of yellow or brown glaze, and in one instance a kiln scar of red clay (No 225), show that the form was fired with other vessels, both whitewares and redwares, and not necessarily on its own as a specialised item made for specific orders. An interesting feature of the London vessels is that 38% had been heated in use, and are blackened and sooted around the base, especially the circumference, and partly up the side opposite the handle.

Border ware drinking jugs continue the tradition established by the medieval Surrey whiteware potteries. Small biconical jugs or drinking jugs, and small rounded jugs were made in Kingston-type ware and Cheam whiteware (Pearce and Vince 1988, figs 79–82; fig 122, nos 543-51). London was supplied with drinking jugs by the Border ware potteries throughout the 16th and 17th centuries. Institutions such as the Inns of Court obviously bought in bulk and had long-standing orders or contracts with particular potters and potteries specialising in these forms (Rackham 1952, 50–1). Lincoln's Inn is recorded as using green-glazed pots as early as 1482/3 (Matthews and Green 1969, 6). By the mid-16th century, they had probably taken over from wooden cups altogether. The main types of drinking jug found at the Inns of Court and included in this corpus were made at Farnborough Hill in the late 16th century and fragments, not reconstructed, were found at Hawley and probably at Ash (Holling 1971, 76, fig 3, D1), as well as at Cove (unpublished material in Castle Arch Museum, Guildford). Rounded drinking jugs were also found in the early 16th-century material from Guildford High Street (Holling 1984, fig 1, no 2), and in the 15th-century kiln dump at Farnborough Hill (Holling 1977, 2, fig 1, no 1).

Sherds of drinking jugs found in well dated contexts in London confirm the dating at the Inns of Court. Fragments of at least seven different vessels of the so-called 'early tradition' come from a single late 16th-century context in London. A reasonably complete drinking jug (not illustrated) comes from a Great Fire deposit and belongs to the 'late tradition', dating to the second half of the 17th century. Small sherds from rounded drinking jugs which cannot be given a corpus number are found in contexts from the 16th and 17th centuries.

Conical drinking jugs

Fig 34, Nos 236–9

Conical drinking jugs are a minor variant of the above type. Only four examples are recorded, two complete. They are particularly tall, their height being two to three times the maximum girth. The rim and base diameters fall within the average range for rounded drinking jugs; the heights of the two complete vessels are 205 and 236 mm, their capacities 660 and 600 ml. They are not all strictly conical, but neither are they rounded. The sides may curve only very gently, or be almost straight, and the maximum girth is hardly greater than the base or rim diameters, if at all. The two complete vessels have a flared neck with pulled and pinched lip. The handles are of strap form. One has a lightly incised spiral groove running twice around its body (No 239). The extent of glaze is similar to that of rounded vessels, with the exception of No 237 which has only a 'bib' of glaze under the lip. All are green-glazed and two are in 'Tudor Green'. The form is illustrated in published material from the Inns of Court, where it is dated to the late 16th century (Matthews and Green 1969, 8, fig 2, no 22).

Globular drinking jugs

Plate 2; Fig 10; Fig 34, Nos 240-51; Fig 35, Nos 252–62

This is the second main type of drinking jug found in London, represented by 28 examples in the corpus. It has a full, bulbous body with a more or less straight-sided neck, and a slight constriction or 'waist' above a thickened base. Rim diameters range from 43-70 mm, with the majority between 50–60 mm, base diameters from 50–80 mm, and height from 103–146 mm. Capacities are between 180–630 ml.

All but two globular drinking jugs (Nos 246, 252) have a simple, rounded and unthickened rim with a raised cordon 12–28 mm below, forming a collar which may be quite prominent. The top end of the handle is almost invariably attached over the cordon. Handles are typically sub-rectangular in section and are attached at the lower end in the same way as on rounded drinking jugs. Only four examples have a thumb- or finger-impression at the lower join (e.g. No 245). In addition to a collar or neck cordon, globular drinking jugs may have from one to three incised grooves around the shoulder and/or at the maximum girth, where they probably acted as a guide for the positioning of the handle. Bases are nearly always indented or kicked, and were probably turned, to shape or bevel the thickened base angle. In section, a few clearly show that the splayed foot was folded back and upwards, rather than trimmed away (e.g. Nos 247, 252). Some were also quite heavily trimmed around the lower part of the body (No 259). Three are unusual in having thumbed bases (e.g. Plate 2; Nos 260–1), one of these also having a closely ribbed neck. A distinctive feature of this type is the absence of a pouring lip of any kind. Only three show signs of having been heated. These two features, taken together, may be related to the type of drink for which they were used.

Globular drinking jugs are glazed in a similar pattern to the rounded type. Only one (No 260) is glazed completely outside from rim to base. The majority are green-glazed (71%), one is in Red Border ware (Fig 10; No 249) and 25% are yellow-glazed. As a type, globular drinking jugs are recognised by Matthews and Green (1969, 8, fig 3, nos 28–35) as 'jugs imitating German stoneware' and are dated at the Inns of Court to the late 16th century. They were found in both the late 15th- and late 16th-century kiln material at Farnborough Hill (Holling 1971, 76, fig 3, D1; 1977, fig 1, no 2). The two almost complete drinking jugs with thumbed bases (Plate 2; Nos 260–1) are probably copies of the common Raeren form exported to Britain in the first half of the 16th century (Hurst *et al.* 1986, fig 94). A thumbed drinking jug base sherd of this type was found in a late 16th-century context in London. None of the other illustrated London examples come from datable groups, although sherds have been found in excavated contexts dating from the early 16th century to the early 17th century. The one Red Border ware drinking jug (No 249) is an undated find, but the redware fabric is not found in London before the early 17th century.

The neck of an incomplete drinking jug, with yellow glaze (No 262), probably comes from a type made in imitation of the baluster-shaped Siegburg *Trichterhalskrug*, current in the 15th and early 16th centuries. The neck is tall and flared above a very

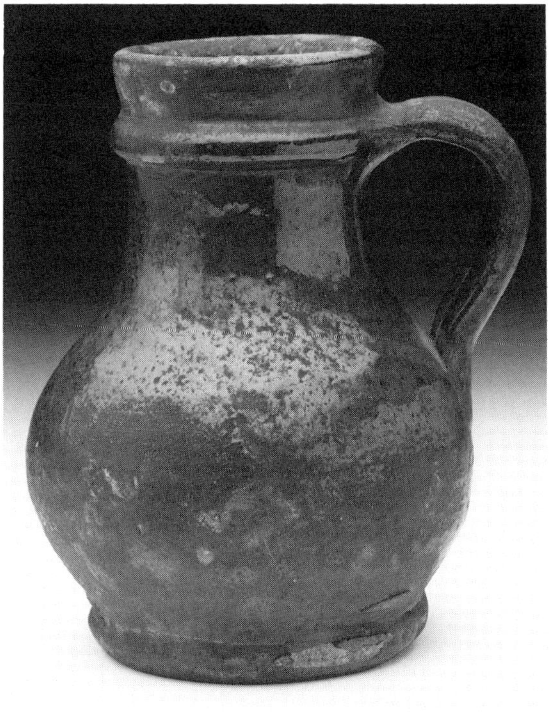

Fig 10 *17th century Red Border ware globular drinking jug (height 127 mm)*

narrow constriction at the shoulder, from which the upper end of the handle springs. Drinking jugs of similar type, copying Siegburg stoneware, were also found at the Inns of Court (Matthews and Green 1969, fig 2, nos 25-7), and one of them was dated to the early 16th century.

Mugs

A mug is defined here as a drinking vessel with vertical loop handle(s), whose rim and base diameters are similar and whose height is greater than either. Thirty-one mugs are recorded, 18 from the Reserve Collection. All are finely made and well-finished, and include some of the most highly decorated products in the Border ware repertoire. Cove, in particular, specialised in the production of high quality mugs, and something of the considerable variety made there is represented in London. Since Cove yielded the widest range of mugs found at any of the published kiln groups, Haslam's typology is used here (Haslam 1975, 173–9, fig 6, nos 53–8; fig 7; fig 8, nos 77–82)

Most of the London finds fit comfortably into Haslam's Types 1–3 with one possible exception, described separately below. No mugs of Haslam's Types 4 and 5, which were rare at Cove, have yet been found in London.

Haslam Type 1

Plate 3; Fig 11; Fig 35, Nos 263–70; Fig 36, Nos 271–4

These are described as 'globular or barrel-shaped vessels' (Haslam 1975, 173, fig 6, nos 53–63), a type also found at Hawley and Ash (Holling 1971, 74–6, fig 3, C2). There are 12 vessels in the corpus (38% of all mugs). The size range is fairly limited, with rim diameters from 80-100 mm, base diameters from 65-85 mm, and height ranging from 100-140 mm. The capacities of two vessels (Nos 272, 274) were measured at 700 and 880 ml respectively. Those with a 'globular' or 'bulbous' profile (Nos 268–73) have no neck, or only a slight change of angle between the neck and the body, and a constriction or 'waist' just above the thickened base (e.g. No 272). 'Barrel-shaped' profiles have an even, convex curve from rim to base (No 274). Rims, as in all Border ware mugs, are simple, rounded and unthickened, the ideal form for a drinking vessel. All Type 1 mugs have from one to four raised cordons 16–32 mm below the rim and may have, in addition, up to four cordons above the base at the waist. In most examples the base is slightly indented or kicked and the thickened base-angle may be folded and rounded or bevelled externally. The handle is attached at the top over the neck cordon(s), but at the lower end, approximately at the maximum girth, above any cordons near the base. The upper cordons would probably act both as a guide for the position of the handle and help to provide a more secure attachment. The lower end of the handle was simply pressed on to the body and wiped to each side, as on drinking jugs and chamber pots (Fig 54). Only one mug has a faint finger- or thumb-impression at the lower handle attachment (No 271). Handles may have a sub-rectangular, square, oval or rod section. Type 1 and all other Border ware mugs have a good cover of glaze inside and out, and partly underneath the base. The majority of this type (66%) have a brown glaze, manganese-speckled and streaked, and one (No

273) has brown glaze outside and green inside. There are no completely green or yellow mugs of this type, and three vessels are made in Red Border ware with dark brown glaze (e.g. No 271). All datable Type 1 mugs from London come from mid to late 17th-century contexts.

A group of eight mugs (Nos 263–7) is related in shape to Haslam's Type 1, but is not paralleled at Cove or in any of the published kiln material. They have a squat, globular, profile, with a slightly kicked and unthickened base. Handles are attached in a similar position to those of Type 1 and are oval or sub-rectangular in section. As a rule, cordons or decoration are absent, with one exception (No 263), which is in Red Border ware and is the only example with a slightly pinched and pulled pouring lip. This feature is typical of drinking jugs, although in shape the vessel more closely resembles mugs and is therefore included with them. This vessel is also unusual in having, under its lip, opposite the handle, a faint, round stamp of a winged horse, probably Pegasus, the mark of the Inner Temple (Fig 11). The form and the stamp can be paralleled by material from the Inns of Court (Matthews and Green 1969, 8, fig 2, nos 23–4). The badge is also found on a candlestick in the Victoria and Albert Museum (Rackham 1952, pl V). Two other undecorated mugs of this form are in Red Border ware. One has green glaze (No 267) and the rest have a light brown manganese-speckled and streaked glaze inside and out. The only dated example comes from a mid-17th-century group (No 266).

Haslam Type 2

Plate 3; Fig 36, Nos 275–80

There are six mugs of this type in the corpus (19% of all mugs). In form, they resemble Type 1, but have 'encrusted' decoration (Haslam 1975, 176, fig 7, nos 64–6). Similar fragments were also found at Hawley (Castle Arch Museum, Guildford, unpublished). Rim diameters range from 65–96 mm, bases from 60–100 mm and heights from 114–176 mm. Type 2 mug profiles are globular with a constriction or waist above the foot (Nos 278–80), or barrel-shaped (No 275). Both shapes have up to three cordons at the neck and above the foot. Handles, of oval, rod or square section, are attached in a similar position and manner to those of Type 1. The main difference between the two

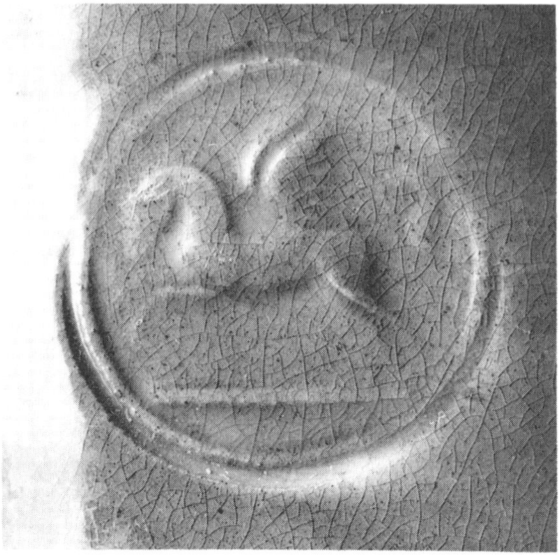

Fig 11 *Winged horse stamp on Red Border ware mug*

types lies in the decoration. 'Encrustation' refers to the application of densely packed, angular flint chippings around the body. Most commonly, a broad band of chippings, on a 'cladding' of clay, was wrapped around the body of the mug between the neck and base cordons, stopping short of the handle (Nos 275, 277, 279). The 'cladding' is a separate layer of clay, up to 4–5 mm thick, rolled out and 'encrusted' with chippings while still wet. Two rather more elaborately decorated mugs use flint chippings in simple patterns. One (No 278) has eight regularly spaced, broad vertical stripes placed around the body. A more unusual pattern is made on the second mug (No 280) by three arrangements of four triangular panels, forming a 'Maltese cross'. The use of flint chippings adds considerably to the weight of a mug and makes holding it uncomfortable, even when empty. All Type 2 mugs are glazed inside and out, although glaze is much thinner over the chippings. Two of the London mugs (Nos 277, 279) have green glaze, although it is unusual for any mugs to be covered entirely with this colour. The remaining four have brown glaze, undoubtedly the preferred colour for mugs. One of the green-glazed encrusted mugs from London (No 277) was found with its lid (No 276), also green-glazed. The lid can be paralleled at Cove (Haslam 1975, fig 7, nos 64–5). Its encrustation stops short of the missing knop, which shows nail-marks around the base. The only datable Type 2 mug from London (not illustrated) comes from a mid-17th century context.

Haslam Type 3

Fig 36, Nos 281–2

This is the least well represented type from London, with only four examples in the corpus (13%). It was made at both Cove (Haslam 1975, 176–9, fig 7, nos 67–76; fig 8, nos 77–82, 84), and Hawley (Holling 1971, fig 3, C2). In form, the mug has straight or slightly flared sides. The London finds differed considerably in size, but were too few in number for a realistic range of dimensions to be given. All have cordons around the body: from one to four at the neck, and from two to six above the base. One incomplete, green-glazed example, which came from a mid-17th-century context, is decorated with regularly spaced incised vertical grooves, made with a three-pronged comb (No 281). The other mugs were made in Red Border ware (not illustrated) and were undecorated. One (No 282) is unique in London in having two handles, a feature which can be paralleled at Cove (Haslam 1975, fig 7, nos 67–8, 72).

A significant proportion (27%) of Border ware mugs of all three Haslam types show signs of having been heated, with blackening and soot around the base and lower sides. This bears comparison with the relatively high proportion of rounded drinking jugs which had been heated.

· 5 · Other Forms

Costrels

Two forms of costrel, or portable flask, were recognised in the Border ware kiln material (Holling 1971, 79, fig 4, K1–2). Both are found in London.

Mammiform costrels

Fig 12; Fig 36, Nos 283–4; Fig 37, Nos 285–7; Fig 48

This form (Holling's K1) was thrown with a domed, enclosed body, resembling a large, squat money-box in shape. A short, narrow, thrown neck was applied over a hole cut or pushed through the side of the vessel at approximately the maximum girth (Fig 48). Two ear-shaped lugs, one each side of the neck, were pierced with circular holes for suspension, probably from a leather thong. The side diametrically opposite the neck was flattened slightly to allow the costrel to stand upright. The corpus includes seven mammiform costrels, only two of them from excavations. All are similar in shape and details of manufacture, although there is some variation in size. Rims are consistently small (25–30 mm), but bases, as thrown, range from 48–105 mm, with the majority 48–70 mm. Height, when standing, ranges from 124–187 mm (with most between 124–150 mm). The capacities of two vessels (Nos 284–5) were measured, both at 550ml. All the London costrels had a patchy covering of mottled green glaze over more or less the top half of the vessel, particularly on the domed 'front' side rather than on the flat 'back'.

Mammiform costrels were succeeded by the bottle-shaped form in the late 16th-century kiln material at Farnborough Hill and were not found in any of the later kiln waste from Hawley, Cove or Ash (Holling 1971, 79). The form was, however, represented in the early 16th-century group from Guildford High Street (Holling 1984, 299, fig 2, no 25). It continues the medieval Surrey whiteware tradition of 'Tudor Green' (Pearce and Vince 1988, fig 126, nos 587–8) and was made in redware at Kingston in the late 15th to early 16th centuries (Nelson 1981). The neck and one lug from a 'Tudor Green' mammiform costrel (not illustrated) were found in an early 16th-century context from London. Other excavated examples in Border ware proper can be dated to the late 16th and the late 17th century. The latter (No 283) is probably residual.

Bottle-shaped costrels

Fig 12; Fig 37, Nos 289–300; Fig 38, Nos 301–10

A total of 23 bottle-shaped costrels (Holling form K2) is recorded, all from the Reserve Collection, and all complete or nearly so. As the name implies, the form is that of a bottle or flask, but with pierced lugs for suspension. The body is generally evenly rounded and globular, with the maximum girth more or less at the mid-point of the profile. The neck is generally straight-sided, and between 1/4 and 1/3 of the total height.

Rim diameters are consistently narrow (25–40 mm); base diameters show greater variety, ranging from 35–105 mm, with the majority between 60–85 mm; height ranges from 85–198 mm with most between 115–150 mm. The capacities of 19 costrels were measured, and appeared to fall within three ranges: small (100–230 ml, Nos 289–91); medium (340–640 ml, with 38% of all examples between 410–470 ml, Nos 292–307); and large (1190–1730 ml, Nos 308–10).

Rim forms display a surprising variety. They include externally thickened rims with an internal bevel (Nos 289, 294), triangular (Nos 291, 306, 309) or beaded rims (Nos 297/–8), simple upright

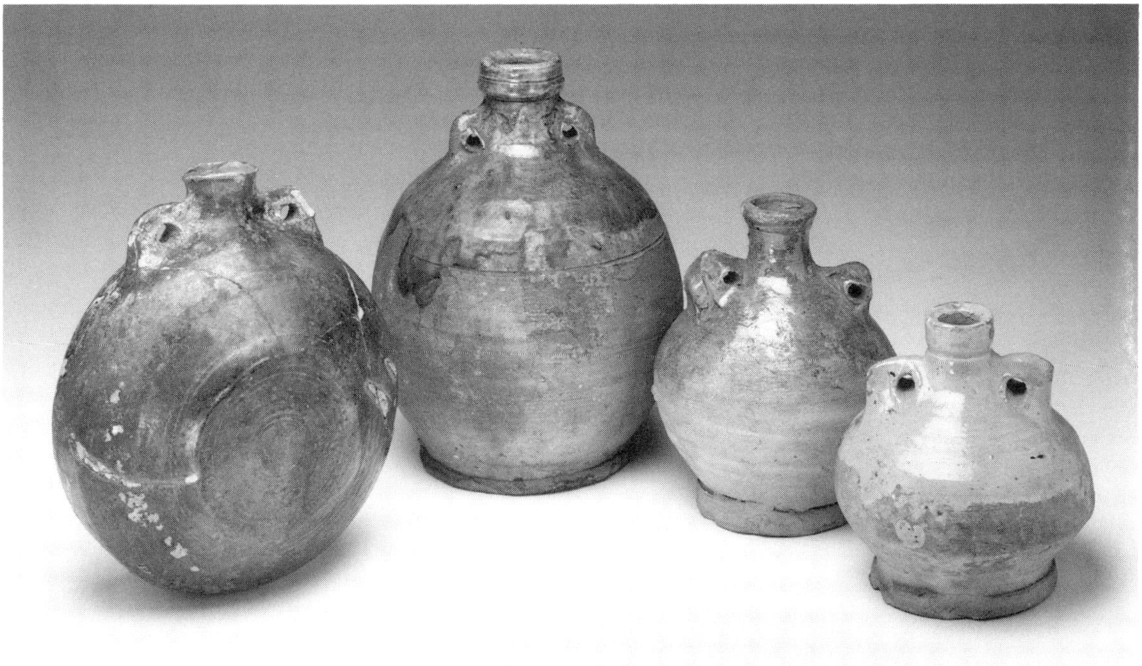

Fig 12 *Costrels. From left to right: late 16th century, mammiform, with green glaze (height 165 mm); 17th century, bottle-shaped, green-glazed (height 182 mm); bottle-shaped, green-glazed (height 134 mm); bottle-shaped, yellow-glazed (height 115 mm)*

rims (No 310) and upright rims with a collar (Nos 295–6).

All bottle-shaped costrels have two lugs, one each side of the neck, generally attached over the junction between the neck and the body, or just below, on the shoulder. The lugs may be gently rounded in shape, semi-circular or more angular. Some are very small in relation to the body, hardly strong enough to support the weight of the vessel when empty, let alone full (e.g. No 309, the largest London example). All lugs have a single circular hole pushed through the centre, leaving an untidy ring of clay on one side, which was seldom trimmed away. The majority of costrels have clumsy, poorly finished lugs, which may be domed, triangular or square in section.

Almost all but the two smallest costrels (Nos 289–90) have a kicked base, below a slight constriction of 'waist'. Only four examples from London have no such constriction (e.g. No 301). The base-angle is generally thickened, and may be bevelled, using either the fingertips or a trimming tool while the vessel was 'turned'. A large number of vessels (48%) were also lightly shaved just above the base. The clay at the base of one costrel (No 295) was clearly folded upwards and back to meet the body.

Six vessels have one or two incised horizontal grooves around or just above the maximum girth (e.g. Nos 294–5, 303, 308); two also have light grooves around the neck (e.g. No 310). All bottle-shaped costrels have external glaze only, extending from the rim and covering between 1/3 and 2/3 of the body, or, rarely, almost to the base. The main area of glaze cover is generally very uneven, with plenty of spots and patches over the rest of the body. The majority are green-glazed (78%), and the rest are yellow, bearing out the suggestion that green was the traditionally preferred colour for this form (Holling 1977, 63). There are no olive- or brown-glazed costrels and none in Red Border ware.

Bottle-shaped costrels, which have been compared with Bellarmines in form (Holling 1971, 79), were found at Farnborough Hill (Holling 1977, fig 1, no 16) and at Hawley and Ash, but not at Cove. They appear to have replaced the mammi-form costrel by the start of the 17th century. No complete, or even nearly complete, bottle-shaped costrels have been recorded in the excavated groups under consideration. However, base sherds, which are typically unglazed internally, were found in contexts dating from the mid- to late 17th century. It was not possible to assign any of these fragments a corpus number.

Miniature costrel

Fig 37, No 288

One very small costrel from London could hardly have been intended for practical use and may well have been a toy. It is a perfect replica of the bottle-shaped form, no more than 48 mm in height, with collar rim, splayed foot and pierced lugs. It has brown glaze, unknown in the standard form.

Chamber Pots

Holling noted that the form of the chamber pot, like that of the tripod pipkin, underwent great changes during the period covered by the available kiln groups (Holling 1971, 79–81, fig 5, L1–L2c). Certain distinctive and variable features were associated with the waste material from Farnborough Hill and Hawley, the chief of these being rim form and shape. A wide range of chamber pots has been found in London, showing greater variety than the published pottery from the kilns, but on the basis of shape and rim form they can largely be correlated with Holling's type-series. A total of 39 is recorded in the corpus, 20 from the Reserve Collection.

Type 1

Fig 13; Fig 38, Nos 311–13; Fig 39, Nos 314–22; Fig 40, Nos 323–30; Fig 54

The first, and most numerous, type of chamber pot (28 examples or 72%) can be compared with Holling's L2a–b (ibid.), although a greater variety of rim forms is found. Rims are most commonly everted and externally thickened, with a rounded or upright, bevelled outer edge (Nos 311–18). Everted rims may also have an internal ledge or stepped profile, giving an internal lid-seating (21% of this form; Nos 319–23). Other rim forms included here may be externally thickened and folded back on themselves, with a slight undercut (Nos 325–6, 328), or squared externally with a flat or bevelled top (Nos 327, 329–30). Chamber pots with any of these rim forms tend to be consistent in shape and size. The body profile is evenly rounded, with the maximum girth near the mid-point. Rim diameters range from 150–180 mm, bases from 95–115 mm and height from 130–167 mm. The measured capacities of five vessels fell between 2000 and 2350 ml. There are three chamber pots whose rim forms cannot be paralleled by any of the published kiln material, although similar forms are found in the unpublished field collection from Yeoman's Potteries, Cove (held by Hampshire County Museum Service). They appear to be intermediate between Holling's L2b and L2c (Nos 327, 329–30) and are noticeably wider than the others included with this type; their rims measured from 190–205 mm, and bases from 125–130 mm, although heights are 140–150 mm.

Handles are attached over the rim and are quite thick, with a sub-rectangular, oval or strap section. Many have a slightly concave upper surface (e.g. Nos 314, 316, 319), and the broader examples have shallow vertical grooves made with the finger-tips running down their length (e.g. Nos 326, 329). At the lower attachment, the end of the handle was either wiped to either side and smoothed into the body in the same way as drinking jug handles (Fig 54), or pressed into the wall of the vessel, leaving a single thumb- or finger-impression (e.g. No 313).

All London Type 1 chamber pots have a kicked base with a thickened base-angle. This may be turned and bevelled (Nos 314, 316–17), or left untouched (No 322). There is no evidence for knife-trimming. Glaze covers the interior only, coming just over the top of the rim, and yellow is the predominant colour (54% of this type). Olive glaze is found on 18% of the vessels examined, and green glaze on 14%. A further 14% are made in Red Border ware.

Type 2

Fig 13; Fig 40, No 331; Fig 41, Nos 332–6

The other main type of chamber pot found in London (11 corpus examples) can be identified with Holling's form L2c, or a development from it. The rim is broad and more or less flat-topped.

Some examples have a lightly incised groove running around the outer edge of the top of the rim (e.g. Nos 333–4). In shape, Type 2 chamber pots are squatter than Type 1 which they appear to succeed typologically. The maximum girth is much lower, and the average rim and base diameters wider (the measured ranges are 180–210 mm and 130–155 mm respectively). The height is noticeably less in relation to the rim and base, ranging from 109–126 mm. Handles are attached as described above, and are all of strap form. Only one chamber pot of this form has a thickened base (No 332); all the others have a simple unthickened base angle and 54% have a flat rather than kicked base. There is some evidence for knife-trimming, generally in a zone up to 20 mm from the base, and probably removing any thickening at this point. All Type 2 chamber pots from London are glazed inside and out, down to the base, and sometimes partly underneath. Green is the principal glaze colour (82% of this type), and only two yellow-glazed vessels are recorded (e.g. No 332). This confirms the unusual trend from predominantly yellow to green glaze noted at Farnborough Hill and Hawley (Holling 1971, 81). Very unusually, one chamber pot (not illustrated) from a mid-17th-century context has a thick, mottled brown glaze.

An invariable feature of all chamber pots is the presence of at least one cordon, or two to five incised horizontal grooves, positioned between the neck and the lower handle attachment. Of all the vessels from London, 51% have only one cordon, produced by squeezing the clay between the thumb and forefinger as the pot turned on the wheel. In many cases the thumbnail has dug into the clay on top of the cordon. Sharper, more pronounced, cordons were made with the aid of a tool. No squat Type 2 chamber pots have incised grooves. The presence of cordons has been explained as an imitation of silver prototypes (Amis 1968, 13).

Amis (ibid., 5) notes that the use to which chamber pots were put 'is not always the one generally suspected' and that the form could even be used for 'kitchen purposes'. In this respect, an interesting feature of the London material is that 31% of all vessels show signs of having been heated, as if used for cooking. Patterns of blackening and sooting around the base and in patches on the body, especially opposite the handle, bear a strong resemblance to the blackening of tripod pipkins. Chamber pots with an internal lid-seating may or may not be burned, suggesting that lids were considered desirable for either cooking or sanitary functions. None of the Type 2 pots are burned, and all are glazed externally, a feature which is not normally associated with vessels intended for heating food. The majority of chamber pots, whether heated or not, have a dull, buff,

Fig 13 *Chamber pots. Left: early to mid-17th century, with yellow glaze (height 147 mm). Right: late 17th century, with green glaze (height 115 mm)*

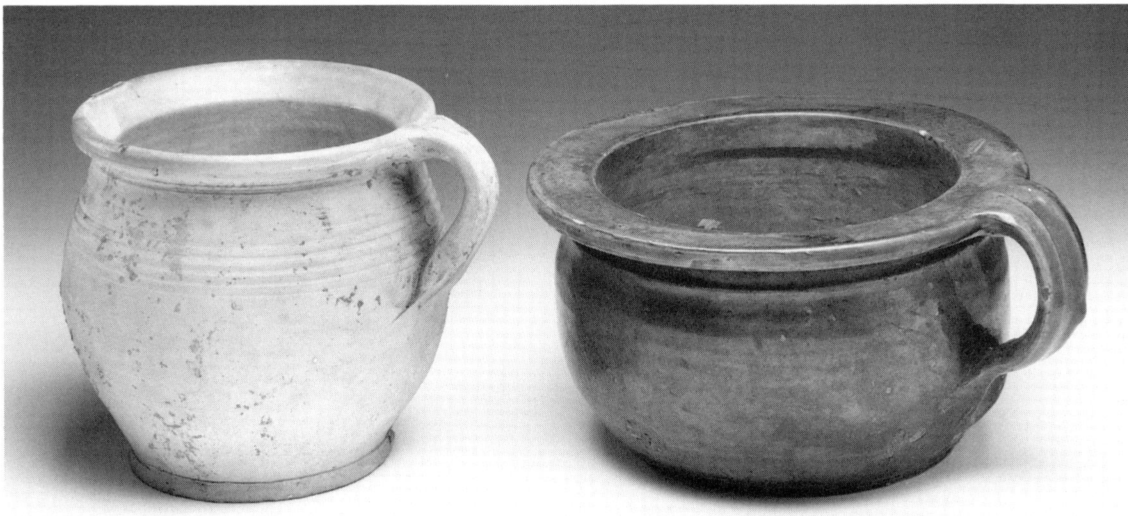

flaky deposit covering the interior, which seems to be associated more with the sanitary function than with food preparation.

Holling's forms L2a–c are all dated to the first half of the 17th century at Hawley, L2c coming stratigraphically later than the other forms, and suggesting that the flat-topped rim evolved from the everted types. Flat-topped and intermediate rim forms were found at Yeoman's Potteries, Cove (see above under Type 1). Chamber pots which conform to Holling's L2a–b were found in large numbers at Minley Road, Cove (Haslam 1975, fig 9, no 96) dated to the second quarter of the 17th century. No chamber pots of Holling's L1 have been identified in London and only one reasonably complete vessel has been found in a late 16th-century context (No 311). All other corpus examples, Types 1 and 2, were found in contexts dated to the mid- to late 17th century.

Five unusual vessels (Fig 41, Nos 337–9), from both excavated contexts and the Reserve Collection, resemble chamber pots in form but have an external lid-seating more akin to tripod pipkins (Fig 28, Nos 149–54). They are included here, rather than with the cooking vessels, because of their closer analogy to chamber pots and because of the ambiguity of their function. Rim diameters range from 108–160 mm; bases from *c.* 90–120 mm and height from 92–150 mm. All have a simple, slightly inverted upright rim and a substantial external lid-seating. They have a kicked base, no feet and little sign of any knife-trimming. A single vertical loop handle of strap or subrectangular section paralleled by chamber pot forms, springs from the lid-seating rather than the top of the rim. The lower end of the handle is wiped on to the body on each side. Two vessels (Nos 337–8) are burnt and sooted around the base and sides in patches, especially opposite the handle. However, one (No 337) also has a thick, flaky, buff deposit covering the entire interior in common with the majority of chamber pots. Four vessels have yellow glaze inside only, and just over the rim as far as the lid-seating. The fifth has no glaze at all. Dated examples come from mid- to late 17th-century contexts.

Candlesticks

There are 40 candlesticks in the corpus, only eight from recent excavations, although more are found as small sherds. They display some variety, but fall essentially into two forms – upright and saucer – each with its own variations. Both forms were made in all three phases of the Border ware industry outlined by Holling (1971, 81, fig 5, N1–N3), and at Cove (Haslam 1975, 183, fig 10, nos 114–17).

Upright candlesticks

Plate 4; Fig 14; Fig 41, Nos 340–5; Fig 42, Nos 346–57

This form, also referred to as 'table candlesticks' (Moorhouse 1970, 45), seems to have been the most common at the excavated kiln sites, and continues with little change from Phase 1 to Phase 2 in Holling's type-series. Ascription of the London finds to any of Holling's forms is made difficult by the fragmentary nature of the kiln material. No sockets were found at Hawley, and the reconstruction of the forms made there is therefore incomplete.

A total of 22 upright candlesticks was recorded, including variations on the basic form (55% of all candlesticks). All come from the Reserve Collection, and 17 (Nos 340–52) are simple upright forms, with a socket or candle-holder above a drip- or grease-tray on a pedestal base. The size range is fairly standard. Socket rim diameters vary between 30 and 40 mm, the base of the pedestal between 55 and 90 mm, and overall height between 108 and 131 mm. They were throw in one piece, with a separate ball of clay plugging the base of the socket, to keep the candle in place. The plug was smoothed into the socket at the top, but was left rough and untouched underneath. All but two of the simple upright candlesticks are plugged in this way. The exceptions (No 350; the other not illustrated) are constricted below the socket to keep the candle from dropping. A number of plugged candlesticks also have such a constriction. When present, the length of the socket from rim to plug is between 36 and 50 mm. Rim forms may simply be unthickened and rounded (Nos 345, 348). More commonly, they are thickened externally and folded or beaded (Nos 346, 349) or collared (Nos 344, 347). The majority of sockets are also lightly ribbed or rilled, and/or have one or two raised cordons at their base above the drip-tray. Closely ribbed sockets are a feature of Holling's

N1 candlesticks from Farnborough Hill, and four of the London examples can be paralleled to this form (e.g. Nos 340–1).

The single drip- or grease-tray is positioned approximately at the mid-point of the candlestick, or just below. They have either a slightly upturned rim (Nos 342–4), or a thickened rim with an internal groove running around the edge (Nos 341, 347–8), to help contain the molten wax. One rim (No 346) has an almost hammer-head appearance, with thickening above and below.

All upright candlesticks have a heavy, flared, pedestal base, thick-walled in comparison with the socket. They are thickened at the bottom, to give them a firm footing, and may be turned or shaved lightly to give an upright external bevel. Inside the pedestal, the clay always shows signs of twisting, at least up to the drip-tray, as a result of having been squeezed during throwing. All but two upright candlesticks are open at the bottom, and were quite crudely pared or trimmed by hand inside the base, often as far as the drip-tray. The exceptions (No 350 and one not illustrated) are closed at the bottom and are the only vessels in London which may correspond to Holling's type N3 from Ash (Holling 1971, fig 5). On the basis of incomplete material from Hawley (ibid.) and Cove (Haslam 1975, 183, fig 10, nos 115–16), the remaining upright candlesticks, apart from the putative N1 examples (see above), may belong to Holling's type N2b. It is not possible to be more definite than this. Only pedestal bases survive in the excavations considered here and they come from contexts dated to the mid- to late 17th century. In form, Border ware upright candlesticks can be compared closely with a metalwork type with incurved base, current from the mid-16th to at least the mid-17th century (Caspall 1987, 82–6, figs 146–54).

Two unusual, upright candlesticks, which cannot be paralleled by any of the published kiln material, have a vertical loop handle, sub-rectangular in section. Both handles are attached at the top to the socket rim. At the lower end, one (No 351) is luted over the edge of the rim of the drip-tray; the other (No 352) is folded across the top of the tray to join the base of the socket. In all other respects, these candlesticks resemble the form described above.

All upright candlesticks are glazed inside the socket, and outside as far as the drip-tray and just over its rim, leaving the pedestal unglazed. Yellow glaze is used on 59% of the simple upright form; 18% have green glaze, 18% are in Red Border ware, and one has olive glaze. Most of the candlesticks, of whatever form, have signs of blackening and traces of soot around the top of the socket.

Five ornamental upright candlesticks have been recorded (Nos 353–7). Their rim diameters and socket lengths are comparable with the simple upright candlesticks, but they are at least twice as tall and have up to twice the base diameter. One (No 355) has a broad drip-tray with vertical notch decoration around its upright, bevelled rim, around the edge of the pedestal base, and around four prominent raised cordons spaced at regular intervals up the stem as far as the rim. The socket is plugged in the usual way. Two other candlesticks with notched decoration must have been similar in appearance (Nos· 356–7). The other complete ornamental candlestick (No 354) can be paralleled at Cove (Haslam 1975, fig 10, no 114). It has a second drip-tray above the broad main tray, and a prominent bulging cordon above this, and below the socket. Including the socket, therefore, it has four tiers or stages above the pedestal base. A second, incomplete, candlestick is comparable in form (No 352). The provision of a second drip-tray, half-way up the stem rather than at the base, was made necessary by the use of messy tallow candles (Hornsby *et al.* 1989, 38). Only one of the ornamental candlesticks has yellow glaze; the rest are green-glazed externally, from the rim to just below the main drip-tray. This type has close affinities with contemporaneous metal candlesticks (ibid., figs 53–4; Caspall 1987, figs 163–6).

Saucer candlesticks

Fig 14; Fig 42, Nos 358–65; Fig 43, No 366

Variously known as 'chamber' candlesticks or 'chambersticks' (Caspall 1987, 138ff.), or as 'small hand lamps' (Moorhouse 1970, 45–6, fig 10, nos 16–14), this form consists of a simple socket set in the centre of a saucer. Eighteen are recorded in the corpus. The diameter of the socket rim ranges from 32–40 mm, the base of the saucer from 64–105 mm, the saucer rim from 96–136 mm, and the overall height from 47–76 mm. Although generally well smoothed into the saucer, sockets appear

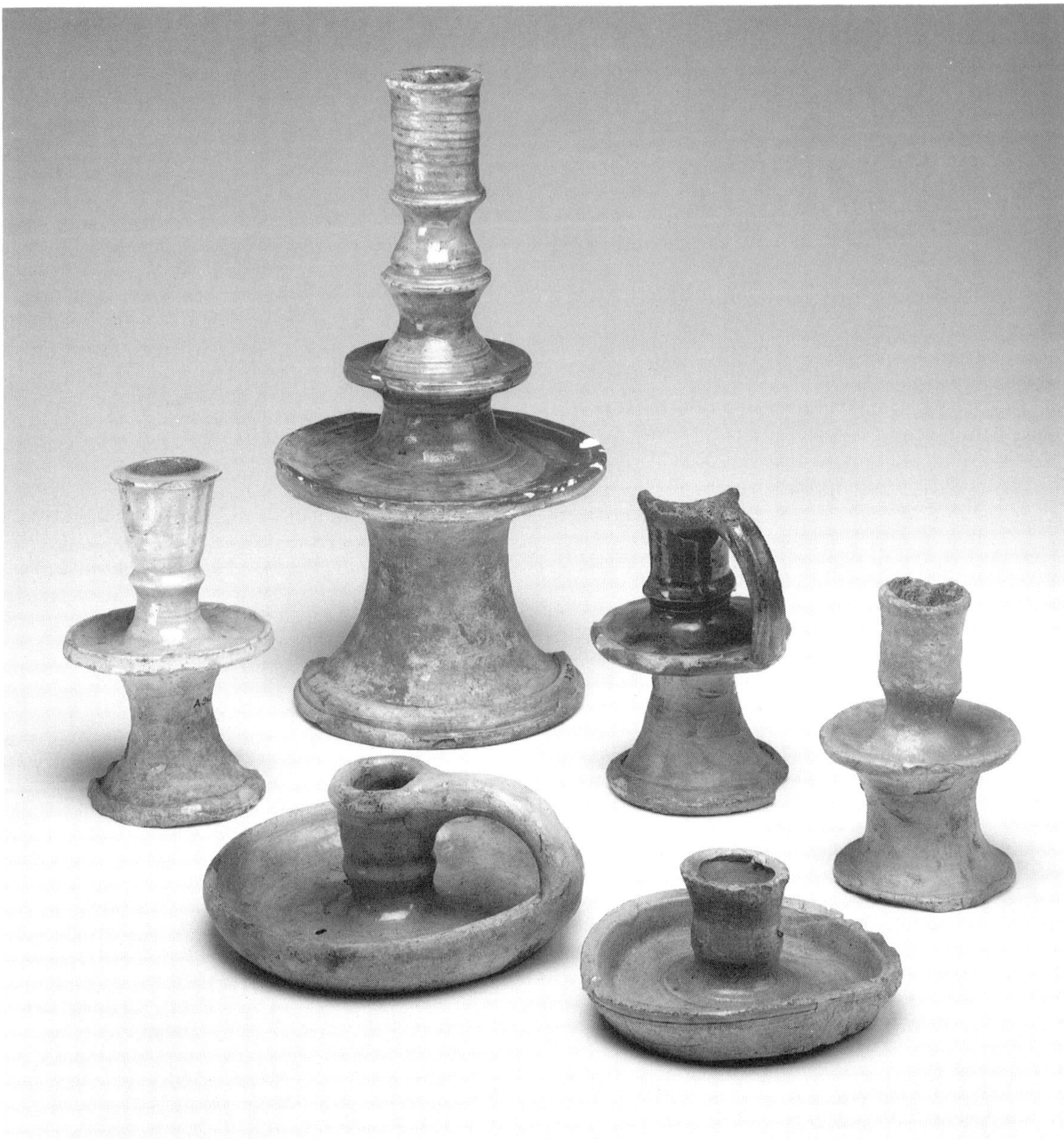

Fig 14 *Candlesticks. From left to right, back row, 17th century: upright type, yellow-glazed (height 124 mm); green-glazed ornamental (height 240 mm); green-glazed (114 mm); yellow-glazed (height 110 mm). Front row, late 16th/early 17th century: saucer type, yellow-glazed (height 55 mm); yellow-glazed (height 47 mm)*

(from broken examples) to have been thrown separately and applied while the saucer was still on the wheel. They have a similar range of rim forms to the upright candlesticks, and may also have light ribbing or rilling, or one or two cordons (e.g. Nos 360–1). The saucer rim is generally not thickened, although two have a flanged rim with an external bevel (e.g. No 358). The base of the saucer may be slightly indented in the centre, underneath the socket, but is more often flat.

Many saucers are also quite warped through handling. Six of the London candlesticks have a single vertical loop handle (e.g. Nos 362–6), sub-rectangular or oval in section, attached at the top either over the rim or just below it on the socket. At the lower end, the handle is attached to the rim of the saucer, with one exception (No 366), where the rather misshapen and pinched handle is folded inside the saucer to join the base of the socket (cf. No 352). None of the London saucer candlesticks are decorated, but are strictly utilitarian. They are glazed inside the socket, and outside as far as the rim of the saucer, or just over. Green and yellow glaze are equally represented; a total of 66%. Only one olive-glazed candlestick was recorded and 28% are in Red Border ware.

Saucer candlesticks are of limited occurrence in the kiln material (Holling 1971, fig 5, N2a). They were found in the earlier pottery at Hawley, and also at Cove (Haslam 1975, fig 10, no 117). They are, therefore, dated at the kiln sites to the second quarter of the 17th century. A group of at least 14 saucer candlesticks, eight of which were given two corpus numbers (Nos 358–9), were found in a late 16th-century London context, and include two in Red Border ware which is otherwise unknown in London at this date. Their close similarities suggest that they may have been bought together as a batch, and were also probably disposed of at the same time. None were found in London in mid- to late 17th-century contexts.

Lantern

Fig 43, No 367

A unique Border ware vessel has been included here because it incorporates features common to candlesticks. Although it is incomplete, the remaining lower part of the body is of jar shape, with a flat base, and reasonably straight sides. In the centre of the base, inside the jar, a candle socket has been attached. Above the rim of this socket, a number of square or rectangular openings have been roughly cut in the walls of the jar. None of these is now complete, and knife-marks are clearly visible at the lower corners of each. The vessel has yellow glaze inside and out, almost down to the base. It cannot be paralleled in any of the published kiln material, and was probably used as lantern.

Money-Boxes

Fig 43, Nos 368–89

There are 27 money-boxes in the corpus, two of which come from dated contexts. Many more sherds are found in excavations than this figure implies, but because of their fragile construction, and because they were generally already broken when discarded, it is seldom possible to reconstruct them sufficiently to assign them a corpus number.

Border ware money-boxes continue the tradition established in the Surrey whiteware industries, in particular Kingston-type ware (Pearce and Vince 1988, 48–9, fig 99, nos 373–83). They were thrown as an enclosed form, with a bulbous or globular body and moulded knop. In this respect the post-medieval form differs from the medieval, which most commonly resembled a bishop's mitre in shape, without a knop. Base diameters range from 35–75 mm (the majority are between 40 and 50 mm), heights from 73–108 mm. The base is either slightly splayed or thickened (e.g. Nos 368–73), or lightly shaved to remove any thickening at the base-angle (Nos 374, 379). The distinctive fan-shaped markings associated with drawing a straight wire under the base in a slightly curved motion are common (Fig 50). Diagonal twisting marks are invariably seen inside the upper part of the body, where the clay was drawn in to close the form. Although the body of one money-box (No 376) was quite badly damaged in throwing or handling, it was still usable.

All Border ware money-boxes have an ornamental knop. The commonest shape is rounded, or slightly pointed at the top, with a saucer-like collar below and a narrow constriction or neck just above the top of the body. Occasionally, the central knop is quite tall (e.g. No 386), or squat and flat-topped (No 384). In all cases, a fine trimming-tool was used to finish it. The coin-slit is always vertical, with one exception, and positioned in the upper half of the body, below the knop. The length of slit varies from 24–44 mm, and all are narrow. In some cases it is hard to see how anything but paper could have been inserted (e.g. No 379). The one exception (No 387) is unique both in London and in the kiln material. In shape, it is a typical money-box, but it has no coin-slit in the body. Instead, a slit was cut across the diameter of the base. A large part of the base was subsequently broken around the slit, probably by the frustrated owner since the form is otherwise intact.

Money-boxes are glazed externally only, on the upper half of the body. The majority found in London (81%) have green glaze. One of those illustrated (No 381) is made in 'Tudor Green'. The remaining forms have yellow glaze, but green was obviously the preferred colour, following the medieval tradition established by Kingston-type ware.

One very unusual money-box from London (No 389) has a prominent ridge or cordon running around the body at the maximum girth, giving it a carinated profile. Another illustrated example has a distinct central groove running around the body (No 388). Sherds from similar vessels have been found in excavated contexts from London dating to the late 16th century, as well as to the mid- to late 17th century. Body sherds, and knops from money-boxes without a central groove come from late 16th- to late 17th century contexts and fragments of at least one 'Tudor Green' money-box were found in early 16th-century material. Money-boxes were found at Farnborough Hill, Hawley and Ash in a fragmentary state, but exhibit little change over time (Holling 1971, 81, fig 5, Q1). They were also made at Cove (Haslam 1975, fig 9, no 111).

Condiment Dishes

Fig 43, Nos 390–3

Three different shapes of double condiment dish have been found in London. None of them has a rim diameter greater than 80 mm, or height above 40 mm. The simplest form of individual dish has straight sides (No 391). It is green-glazed and comes from a late 16th-century context. A number of complete condiment dishes, in Red Border ware as well as in whiteware, are represented by No 390. This is again straight-sided, but with a carination near the base and an unthickened rounded rim. The two dishes in the illustrated example are yellow glazed, joined by a strip of clay well smoothed into each, and have a small, vertical loop handle on one side. A more enclosed form with inverted rim is illustrated by No 392, the other half of which is missing. It comes from an early 17th-century context and has green glaze. All three forms are glazed inside and partly over the outside, up to half the height.

Double condiment dishes were made from at least the mid-14th century in Kingston-type ware (Pearce and Vince 1988, fig 99, nos 367–72). Their form does not appear to have evolved or been changed noticeably by the Border ware potters and examples are known from Cove, dated to the second quarter of the 17th century (Haslam 1975, fig 9, no 113).

Pedestal Dishes or Cups

Fig 44, Nos 394–402

The corpus includes nine shallow dishes set on a pedestal base. Three are quite small, with a rim diameter between 70 and 80 mm, and are 56 to 73 mm in height (Nos 394–6). The pedestals are solid and smooth outside, with a turned foot; underneath they are hollowed out with a knife or trimming-tool, leaving a rough and uneven surface. They all have rounded, unthickened rims, with either a carinated, more or less straight-sided body (Nos 394–5, 400), or a gently curved dish profile (No 396). A pedestal sherd from an early 17th-century context (No 397) probably comes from this form. All have yellow glaze inside the dish and outside as far as the top of the pedestal. Similar forms described as 'cup salts' were found in the Inns of Court and were given a probable date in the late 16th or early 17th century (Matthews and Green 1969, 9, fig 3, no 49). Fragments of pedestal dishes were also found at Basing House (Moorhouse 1970, 48, fig 11, nos 31–3) where they were termed 'sweetmeat dishes' and compared with sherds found at Hawley, but not illustrated in Holling's type-series.

A vessel related to the above in form and probably in function is illustrated by No 400. The body is more cup-like, with an externally thickened rim, and the overall height is greater than that of the above examples. The pedestal was deeply hollowed underneath after throwing, and has a central ridge or step. It is green-glazed inside and out as far as the top of the pedestal.

Four larger pedestal dishes with handles (Nos 398–9, 401–2) cannot be precisely paralleled by any of the published kiln material, and may have been used as salt cellars or sweetmeat dishes, or even as cups. The dishes are shallow, with rim diameters between 110 and 115 mm. Three have a solid pedestal, hollowed underneath. The other (No 398) is more unusual, although similar in shape and size. It has an open pedestal under a separately applied base, in the same manner as chafing dishes (q.v.), although the pedestal has no aperture and there are no lugs on the rim. It may well have had a different function from the other vessels included here. All four dishes have a single, vertical loop handle of strap or oval section. In two cases, the handle is attached over the rim and at the carination (Nos 398–9). The handles of the other two spring from the carination or just below it and are attached at the lower end to the pedestal or foot (Nos 401–2). They are all glazed inside and partly outside, at least as far as the top of the pedestal. One (No 399) has yellow glaze, the other three green.

Jars

There are 26 vessels in the Reserve Collection which can broadly be defined as jars, or containers without handles, at least as tall as they are wide and with similar base and rim diameters. They can be divided into two main forms on the basis of shape. More specific terminology related to function has been avoided since they were probably used to contain a variety of substances, and no clear evidence for usage has survived.

Small rounded jars

Fig 44, Nos 403–13, 417

There are 14 small, globular or rounded jars in the corpus, most of which can be compared with the vessels described as 'ink pots' at the Inns of Court (Matthews and Green 1969, 9, fig 3, nos 40–1). The majority have a narrow mouth, with rim diameters ranging from 30–45 mm. There is one exception (No 413) whose rim is twice the base diameter, although in profile and size it resembles the other jars included here. All have a constricted neck just below the rim. Base diameters range from 30–50 mm, and heights from 48–80 mm. No capacities were measured. Rims are everted, generally with a distinct internal bevel (Nos 405–8), or a slight external thickening (Nos 403–4, 410). Bases are usually slightly indented. Two examples (Nos 413, 417) have a thickened base, one (No 413) with a turned bevel. Another jar (No 403) has been trimmed to give a slightly convex base.

With one exception (No 403), which is glazed entirely inside and out, small rounded jars are glazed externally only, from the rim to just below the maximum girth. The majority have green glaze (78%); the rest are yellow-glazed. None of the jars included here is obviously stained inside, as might be expected if they were used to hold ink. One vessel (No 412) has a lightly incised cross underneath the base, which may have served as a batch or order mark.

No small rounded jars were recorded at any of the kiln sites, nor have any been recognised in excavated material from London.

Straight-sided jars

Fig 44, Nos 414–16, 418–25; Fig 45, Nos 426–7

The term straight-sided is used here in the broadest sense, to describe jars whose profile is more straight than rounded. There are 12 such vessels in the corpus, all but one (No 421) from the Reserve Collection. Within these a distinct range of small straight-sided jars can be recognised (Nos 414–16, 418, 420), ranging in height from 50–90 mm. Rim diameters range from 30–56 mm, and bases from 40–64 mm. There are slight variations in profile, as with the tall jars described below. They include simple straight-sided jars without constrictions (No 414), jars with a constricted neck (Nos 416, 420) and jars of *albarello* shape (Nos 415, 418) with constrictions at the neck and above the base. One vessel (No 416) is unusual in having a small hole neatly drilled through the centre of the base.

The remaining straight-sided jars in the corpus (Nos 419, 421–7) are at least twice as tall as their maximum girth, with one exception (No 419) which is wider in relation to its height than the others. Heights range from 116–228 mm, rim diameters from 60–100 mm, and bases from 48–96 mm. The profiles include the same variations found in small straight-sided jars, with *albarello*-shaped vessels (Nos 419, 421, 423) and vessels with constricted neck only (Nos 422, 424, 426, 427). The sides may be vertical (Nos 421, 426), taper slightly inwards to the base (Nos 422–3), or flare slightly outwards to the base (Nos 424, 425). Rims are generally everted (Nos 419, 423) and may be externally thickened and bevelled internally (No 422) or externally (No 424), or squared (No 425). Bases are slightly indented or kicked and may also be thickened and turned, particularly where there is a constriction above the base-angle (Nos 419, 421, 423). Those jars which more closely resemble *albarelli* have distinct, close-set throwing marks visible inside, but are smooth externally (Nos 419, 421, 423). One tall jar (No 425) has three cordons running around the upper half of the body and a series of horizontal, incised grooves at intervals below them. The tallest jar (No 426) has a single cordon around the lower constriction, just above the base.

The extent of glaze cover varies from a narrow band around the shoulder, with plentiful splashes and dribbles externally (Nos 421–3), to complete external cover from rim to base (Nos 424–6). Only one jar is glazed inside as well as out (No 419), and it follows a pattern set by mugs (e.g. Fig 36, No 273) in having two different colour glazes, yellow inside and green out. One jar has olive glaze (No 425) and the rest are green or yellow-glazed.

Number 427, from the Reserve Collection may well be a butter pot, although it is quite small, with a capacity of only 170 ml. Butter pots with lids were found at Farnborough Hill, Hawley and Cove (Holling 1971, 77, fig 4, H1-H2; Haslam 1975, fig 9, nos 98–101). Apart from a few accidental spots on the body, the London vessel is unglazed and has prominent throwing marks inside, in common with vessels of Holling's late 16th-century phase. It is possible that other jars included here (e.g. Nos 422–3) may also have been intended as butter pots.

The only straight-sided jar from an excavated context (No 421) is dated to the early 16th century. Apart from butter pots and large storage vessels, which are not found in London, jars are not recorded at the various kiln sites.

Whistles

Fig 45, Nos 428–9

There are two whistles in the Reserve Collection. In shape, they resemble small rounded jars, no taller than 64 mm, with a splayed foot and narrow neck. A long, tubular spout was applied over a small hole cut in the body just above the maximum girth. Only one is complete (No 428), and has a small hole cut in its upper surface to produce the sound. Both whistles are green-glazed externally.

Whistles, particularly in the form of birds, were made in north-west Europe and France during the late medieval and post-medieval periods, for example in redware in the Low Countries and in German whiteware (Hurst *et al.* 1986, 142, fig 64; 236, fig 112, nos 354–5). Imported bird whistles are found in London and elsewhere in Britain, but are quite rare. Plain whistles are even more unusual and no parallels have yet been recognised for these Border ware examples.

Fuming Pots

Plate 5; Fig 45, Nos 430–5

Six vessels belong to the form variously known as fuming pots, perfume jars, or 'stink pots'. Three are complete, the others substantially so. They consist essentially of a narrow-necked jar-shaped body with pierced apertures, on a pedestal base. Four of the fuming pots (Nos 430–3) have a straight-sided body, carinated at the shoulder and above the pedestal. The profile may be quite angular, with a prominent ridge or cordon at each of these changes of angle. The rim is either folded or beaded (Nos 432–3), slightly thickened and internally bevelled (No 430), or unthickened and rounded (No 431). A thick disc of clay was applied separately inside the base of the jar, dividing it from the pedestal, and was pierced with circular holes. This is similar to the construction of chafing dishes (q.v.), as is the form of the pedestal base with its single, large cut-out aperture. Each of the complete fuming pots has a roughly triangular pedestal aperture. The apertures in the jar body are of various shapes. The simplest are circular holes pierced in a rather random pattern from shoulder to base (No 431). Two fuming pots have a combination of circular holes and arrow-slit-type vertical openings (Plate 5; Nos 432–3). The fourth combines circular holes with rectangular apertures (No 430). In all vessels, the excess clay left inside after the aperture was made was not cleared away. One fuming pot (No 433) has, in addition, a band of notched decoration around the shoulder. Each vessel has two diametrically opposed, horizontal loop handles, attached at the lower body carination. They are all glazed just inside the rim, and outside at least as far as the top of the pedestal. Patches of glaze inside are the result of seepage through the body apertures. Of the four fuming pots with straight-sided bodies, two have yellow glaze, one is green-glazed and the other brown.

Two unusual fuming pots from London are unfortunately incomplete and have both the top of the body and the base missing (Nos 434–5). One (No 434) probably resembles the above vessels in shape, although its body is not straight-sided. Part of a triangular opening in the pedestal remains, and above this, around the shoulder of the jar, a series of narrow and slightly wider flattened-oval, vertical slits were cut above a closely spaced band of diagonal knife-slits which pierced through the body. The pot is green-glazed externally over the upper part of the body and has two handles. The other form illustrated here (No 435) has the main characteristics of a fuming pot, with a separately applied jar base, not pierced, and originally had at least one handle. The jar body is more rounded in shape, with a cordon at the maximum girth, and is pierced with small closely spaced, circular holes. It is green-glazed externally. Only one of the pots described here has any sign of burning or soot inside the base (No 431).

Fuming pots are not common in Border ware. Fragments which may have come from a fuming pot were found at Cove, dated to the second quarter of the 17th century (Haslam 1975, 183, fig 9, no 112). The only datable illustrated vessel from London comes from a late 16th-century context, although small sherds were found in mid 17th-century material.

Lids

Plate 6; Fig 45, Nos 436–42

Certain forms are provided with an internal or external lid-seating. Cooking vessels, in particular tripod pipkins, are the commonest class for which lids were made. Eight complete or nearly complete lids are recorded in the corpus and six of these are of a size and form which would have been suitable for covering such vessels. Their rim diameters are between 116 and 240 mm, and all fall within the range measured for tripod pipkins. They were made as shallow dishes, inverted in use, and with a central knop for a handle. The flat-topped form is the commonest (Nos 436–9), with a rounded or angular carination above the more or less straight sides. The rims of all but two are rounded and unthickened, the exceptions having a beaded rim (e.g. No 437). Surviving knops are either solid, with a slight indentation at the top and folded rim (No 439), or hollow with a thickened or folded rim (Nos 436, 438). They were probably applied separately. No great care was lavished in the manufacture of lids and No 438 has clumsy trimming marks over the entire interior. One lid (No 440) is more domed in shape than the others, its knop clearly thrown in one with the rest of the form. Only one lid is yellow-glazed externally (No 437). The rest are unglazed, and one is made in Red Border ware.

Lids of the shallow, flat-topped form were made at Farnborough Hill and Ash (Holling 1971, fig 5, R1) and show no great change over time. They were also made at Cove, so their production continued throughout the 17th century (Haslam 1975, fig 10, nos 123–5). All the London examples come from contexts dating to the mid- to late 17th century. The domed form (No 440), which came from a late 17th-century deposit, has also been found in Red Border ware in late 16th-century pottery from Farnborough Hill (unpublished material in Castle Arch Museum, Guildford) and Cove (Haslam 1975, fig 10, no 126).

A small, green-glazed lid in the Reserve Collection (No 441) is as yet unparalleled. It has a solid, domed knop thrown in one with the lid, and is liberally pierced with square holes. It is not certain what form this was made to cover. Far more unusual, but not unique, is a large, highly ornamental lid made in two pieces (Plate 6; No 442). The body and knop were thrown as one, and a broad band of clay forming an upright flange or collar was applied around the rim. This flange was cut in a series of crenellations around the top. The whole body, including the two-tiered knop and flange, was covered at random with ring-and-dot stamps. A number of arrow-like motifs were also incised around the flange. The lid has green glaze over the entire outer surface, and yellow glaze inside. It is not known for what form it was intended. However, a remarkably similar, but not identical, lid was found at Cove (ibid., no 127), dated to the second quarter of the 17th century.

Bottles

Fig 45, Nos 443–4

The rim and neck of a yellow-glazed bottle or flask was found in a context given a broad 17th-century date. The rim is beaded, and the neck has three shallow ribs or raised cordons directly below this. Twisting marks are visible inside the neck and the scar of the upper handle attachment remains, just below the rim. A complete yellow-glazed bottle in the Reserve Collection has a similar neck and rim, but no cordons, and a bulbous rounded body. The base is thickened and turned. The form differs from bottle-shaped costrels only in the type of handle and is not common in Border ware. Two comparable jugs with applied face masks were found at Cove (Haslam 1975, 183, fig 10, no 118). There is little doubt that they were made in imitation of contemporaneous German stoneware Bellarmines or Bartmann jugs.

Bedpans

Fig 15; Fig 45, No 445; Fig 46, No 446

Substantial remains of three bedpans in the Reserve Collection have no parallel in any of the published kiln material. They were made as large, deep dishes with rims inverted to such an extent as to provide a seat, either with a flat flange fitted at an angle (No 445) or more rounded profile (No 446). They are thick-walled and very heavy, as befits such a form, with a single, wide, tubular handle applied over a circular hole cut from the side of the body below the level of the rim-flange. Only one still has its handle, which is nearly complete (Fig 15; No 446). This handle was thrown as a long tube, flaring slightly at the end with three or more raised cordons behind the rim. It served the dual function of enabling the bedpan to be carried around conveniently, and to be emptied without spilling the contents. All the bedpans are poorly finished, and trimmed heavily underneath the base and around the lower sides. They are glazed completely, inside and out and underneath the base. Two have green glaze and one is in Red Border ware, with clear glaze. Sherds of a yellow-glazed bedpan were found in a mid-17th-century context.

Double Dishes

Fig 16; Fig 46, Nos 447–8

There are three double dishes in the Reserve Collection. One further very fine example made in 'Tudor Green' and comparable to No 447 is not illustrated. They are all deep, straight-sided dishes, wheel-thrown and altered to give a sub-rectangular shape in plan. One (Fig 16; No 448) has a folded, beaded rim; the other illustrated example (No 447) has a thickened rim with internal bevel that could have accommodated a lid. The process of altering the basic thrown shape is obscured by subsequent treatment, and is somewhat unclear. The dishes may have had an oval section cut from the base, with the remaining halves folded across each other and smoothed together. Alternatively, they could have been thrown as an open-ended ring, folded in at the bottom to make a base, and smoothed over inside and out. It is difficult to see exactly how they were made without sectioning the complete forms. A slightly shallower compartment was then attached to one long side of the main dish. This could well have been half a thrown ring, which was wrapped underneath to meet the base. The base was then smoothed across the two portions of the dish, obscuring the join. Incised horizontal grooves, numbering from two to six, run around the whole body and encompass both compartments. The two illustrated dishes have a number of circular holes pierced through the base of the secondary compartment. Two (No 447 and one not illustrated) have two vertical loop handles attached to the narrow ends of the main dish; the third has two horizontal loop handles attached in a similar position. They are all green-glazed over the base inside both compartments and over the upper half of the body outside. No parallels are known from the kiln sites, although parts of three double dishes were found at Basing House (Moorhouse 1970, 50–1, fig 11, no 51). Similar forms in the Reserve Collection are made in Guy's ware and other 16th-century redwares from London. However, the precise purpose for which this specialised form was originally made remains a matter of speculation.

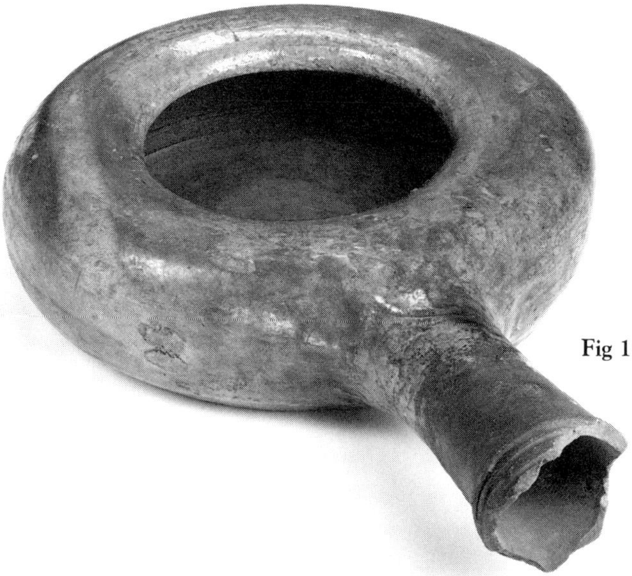

Fig 15 *Green-glazed bedpan (height 72 mm)*

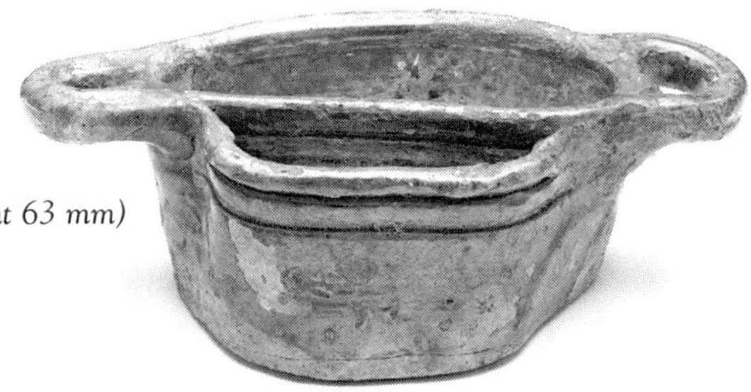

Fig 16 *Green-glazed double dish (height 63 mm)*

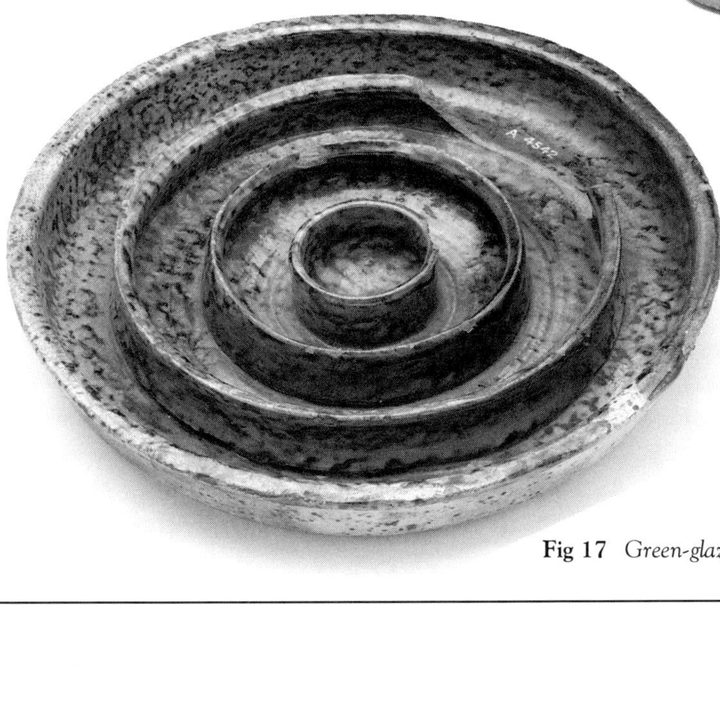

Fig 17 *Green-glazed 'chicken feeder' (diameter 200 mm)*

'Chicken Feeders'

Fig 17; Fig 46, No 449

There are seven complete or nearly complete shallow dishes in the Reserve Collection, of the form generally known as 'chicken feeders'. Although this function is open to question, the dishes are all similar in shape and construction, and only one is illustrated. They were thrown as a shallow, wide dish, with rim diameters ranging from 180–230 mm and height from 30–35 mm. The base and lower sides are trimmed, sometimes heavily and clumsily, and the rim is rounded and unthickened. Within the main dish, additional thrown rings were applied at regular intervals, forming a series of concentric rims of more or less the same height. In all but one of the dishes, three rings were added; the exception (not illustrated) is incomplete and had at least four additional rings. They are all glazed internally and just over the outermost rim. Two have yellow glaze, two green, and three are in Red Border ware.

Miscellaneous Strainers

Fig 46, Nos 450–2

A fragment of a shallow, slab-built dish with a perforated base (No 452) comes from a mid-17th-century context in London. The original shape of the complete vessel is unclear, but it may have been oval or sub-rectangular with pointed ends, in the manner of a dripping dish. The walls were applied separately and smoothed into the base, which has a number of circular holes pierced through it. The vessel has a patchy green glaze inside. No similar vessels are illustrated in the published kiln material.

A virtually complete, perforated tripod dish (No 450) comes from the Reserve Collection. It is straight-sided, with an externally thickened rim and kicked base. A single raised cordon runs around the body just under the rim, and one small horizontal loop handle is attached at the rim. Three short, stubby feet were smoothed neatly into the base around the circumference. A large number of small circular holes were pierced through the lower 2/3 of the body and base. The vessel is green-glazed inside and out. It must have been used for straining substances of one sort or another, and is thus related in function to colanders (q.v.). However, in form it is noticeably different from the larger dish- or bowl-shaped vessels and is not at all common. Part of a perforated dish of a similar form, but without its base (No 451), comes from an early 17th-century context. It has green glaze inside which has seeped through the holes to the outside. The holes are diamond-shaped and very numerous. The base of a tripod strainer with yellow glaze was found at Basing House (Moorhouse 1970, fig 10, no 26), but there are no published parallels from the kiln sites.

Warming Pan

Fig 46, No 453

Part of the body of an almost enclosed perforated vessel in the Reserve Collection probably comes from a warming pan. It was thrown as a large, wide-bodied, jar-like form with a comparatively small rim diameter. The body has a gently carinated profile, accentuated by knife-trimming. The base is lost, and the form originally had a handle which is now missing. Circular holes were pierced through the upper half of the body from rim to maximum girth, and were not trimmed or cleaned inside. The vessel has yellow glaze on the outside surface, but not inside, apart from seepage through the holes. No comparable vessels were found in the kiln material, but sherds of a yellow-glazed warming pan were found in London in a mid-17th-century context.

Lobed Dish

Fig 18; Fig 46, No 454

Part of a lobed dish in the Reserve Collection is paralleled by fragments of similar dishes from mid- to late 17th century contexts. The illustrated dish was slab-built with straight sides and a flat base cut to a lobed shape – there were originally six lobes. The base is trimmed untidily underneath in several directions, but is quite smooth; the sides are also trimmed to at least half their height from the base. Cracks around the joins between base and sides are visible both inside and out. The rim is decorated all around with shallow, closely-spaced nicks or notches. Both the illustrated dish

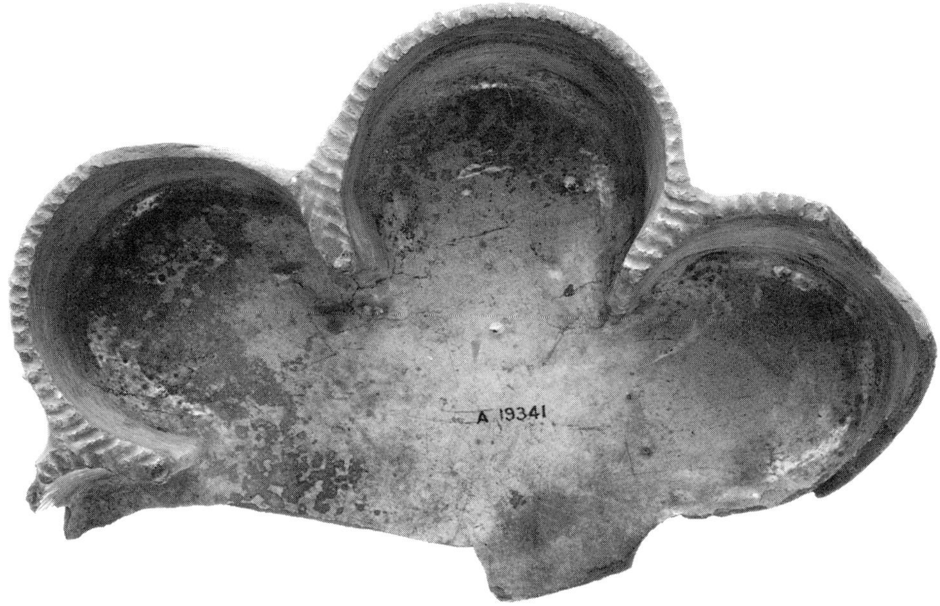

Fig 18 *Yellow-glazed lobed dish (diameter 220 mm)*

and the excavated parallel have yellow glaze inside and out, but not under the base.

Crucibles

Fig 46, Nos 455–6

Two virtually complete Border ware crucibles were found in London in a late 16th-century context. They have straight sides, slightly flared from base to rounded rim. Both are wheelthrown, and one (No 456) was subsequently given an almost triangular shape in plan by the addition of three pinched and pulled pouring lips. The other crucible has only one lip. This vessel has in addition two small circular holes drilled through its thick base. The rims are unthickened and rounded and neither is glazed nor shows any sign of burning. No kiln parallels are recorded.

Unidentified Forms

Plate 7; Fig 46, Nos 457–60

There are a number of vessels in the Reserve Collection which are related to each other in form, but which cannot be paralleled at the kiln sites or elsewhere. They all have a stepped profile with a narrow, generally straight-sided base, separated by a pronounced cordon from a wider body section that is also more or less straight-sided. The rim is flanged and turned up at the edge, so could have accommodated a lid. A single, solid and stubby horizontal handle is attached at or just below the rim. They are partially glazed inside the rim and over the top half of the body outside, leaving the narrow base section unglazed. Only one has yellow glaze; the rest are green. One of the illustrated vessels is burnt around the base, but none of the others shows any sign of having been heated. They were apparently made for a specific purpose, which remains unknown.

Figures 19 to 46

These figures illustrate Border ware vessels by class and form

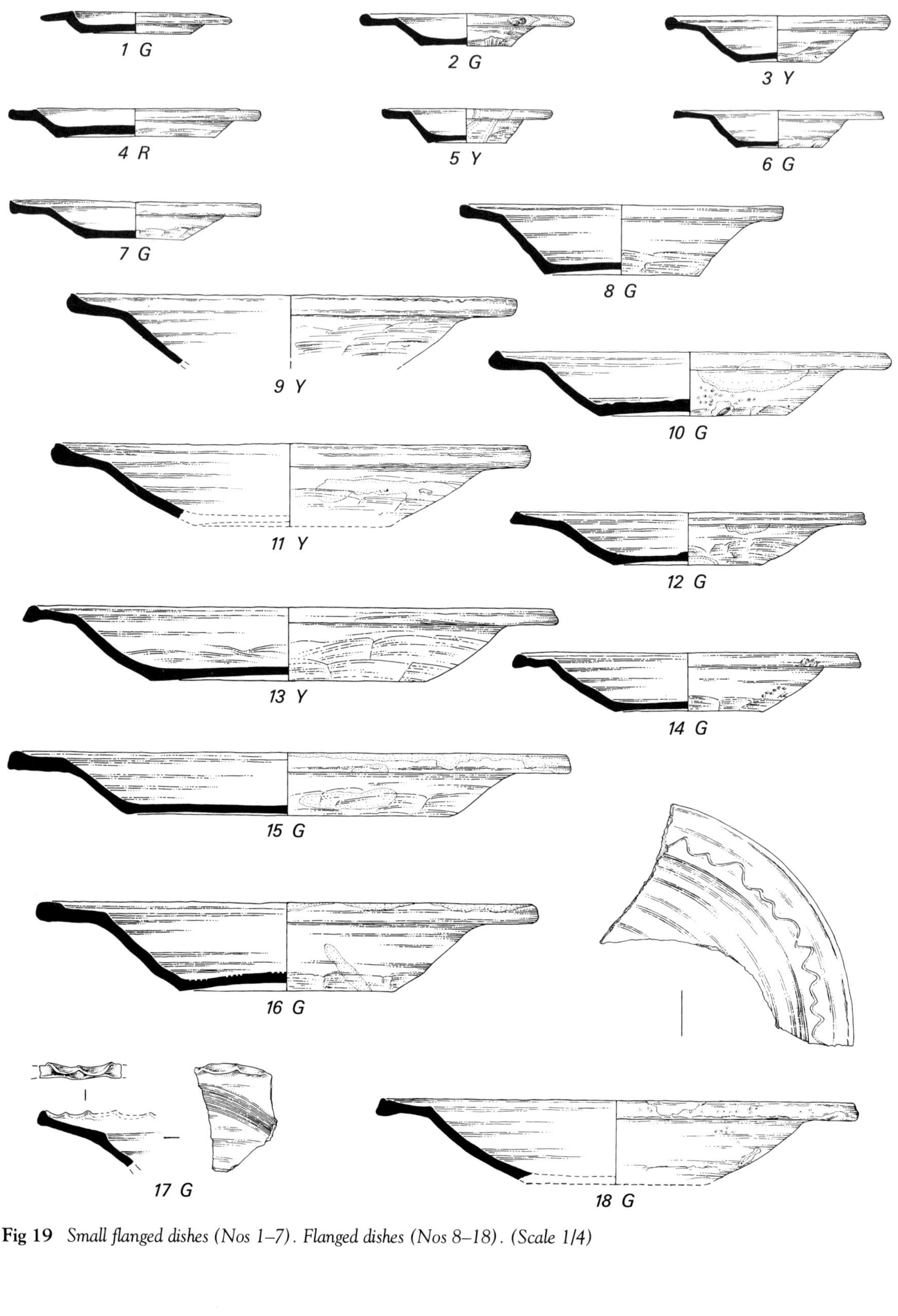

Fig 19 *Small flanged dishes (Nos 1–7). Flanged dishes (Nos 8–18). (Scale 1/4)*

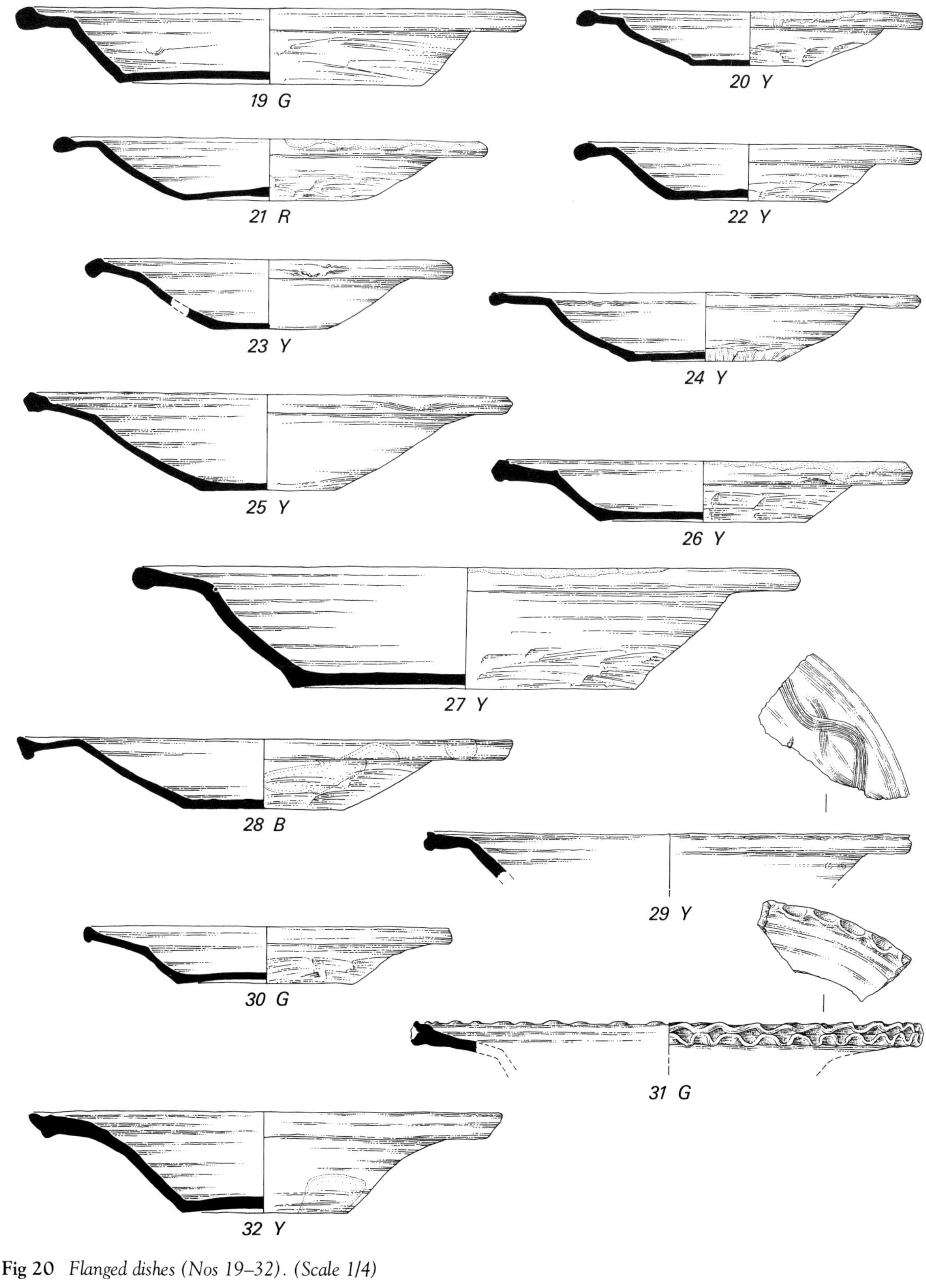

Fig 20 *Flanged dishes (Nos 19–32). (Scale 1/4)*

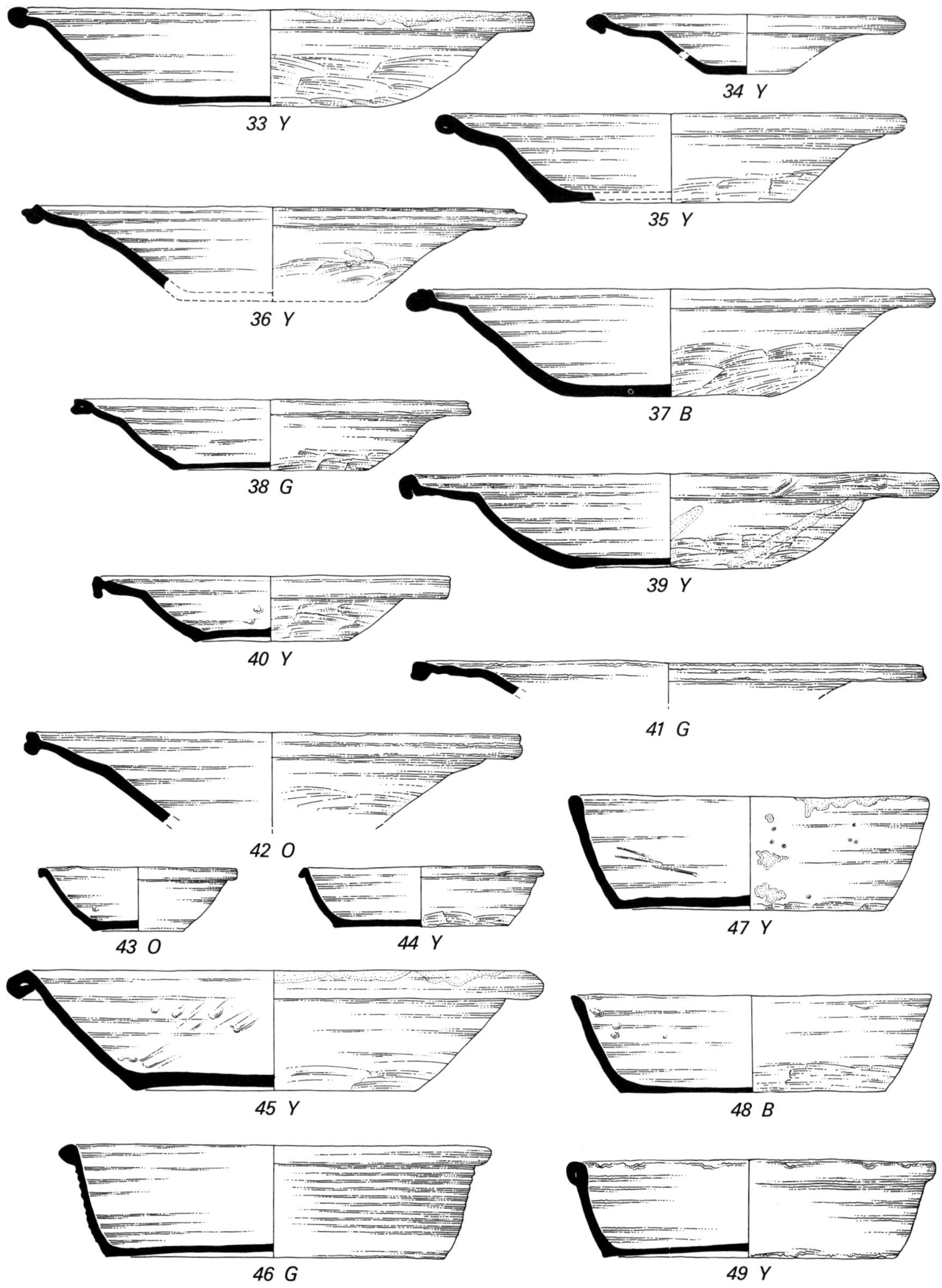

Fig 21 *Flanged dishes (Nos 33–42). Deep dishes (Nos 43–9). (Scale 1/4)*

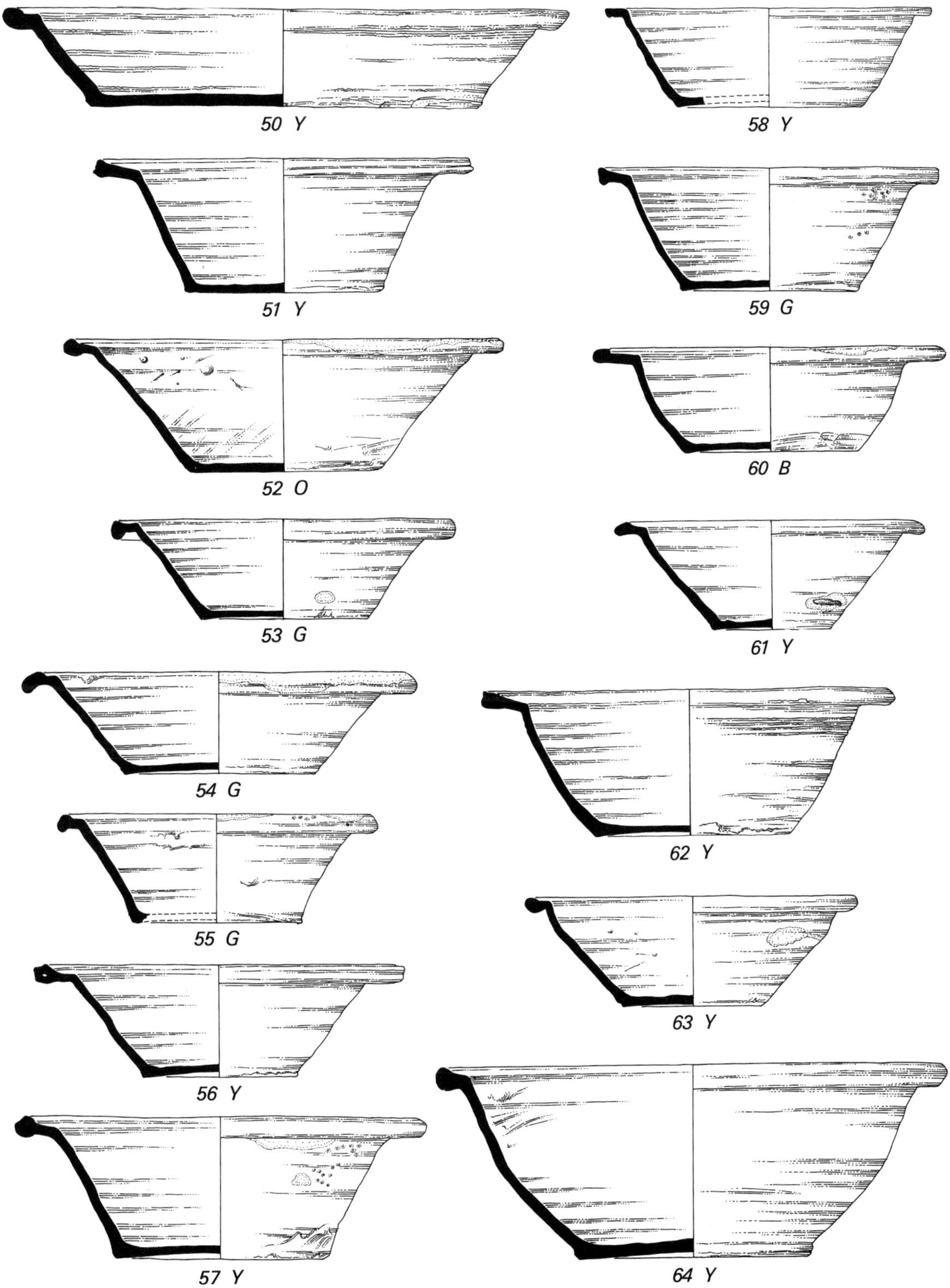

Fig 22 *Deep dish (No 50). Wide bowls (Nos 51–64). (Scale 1/4)*

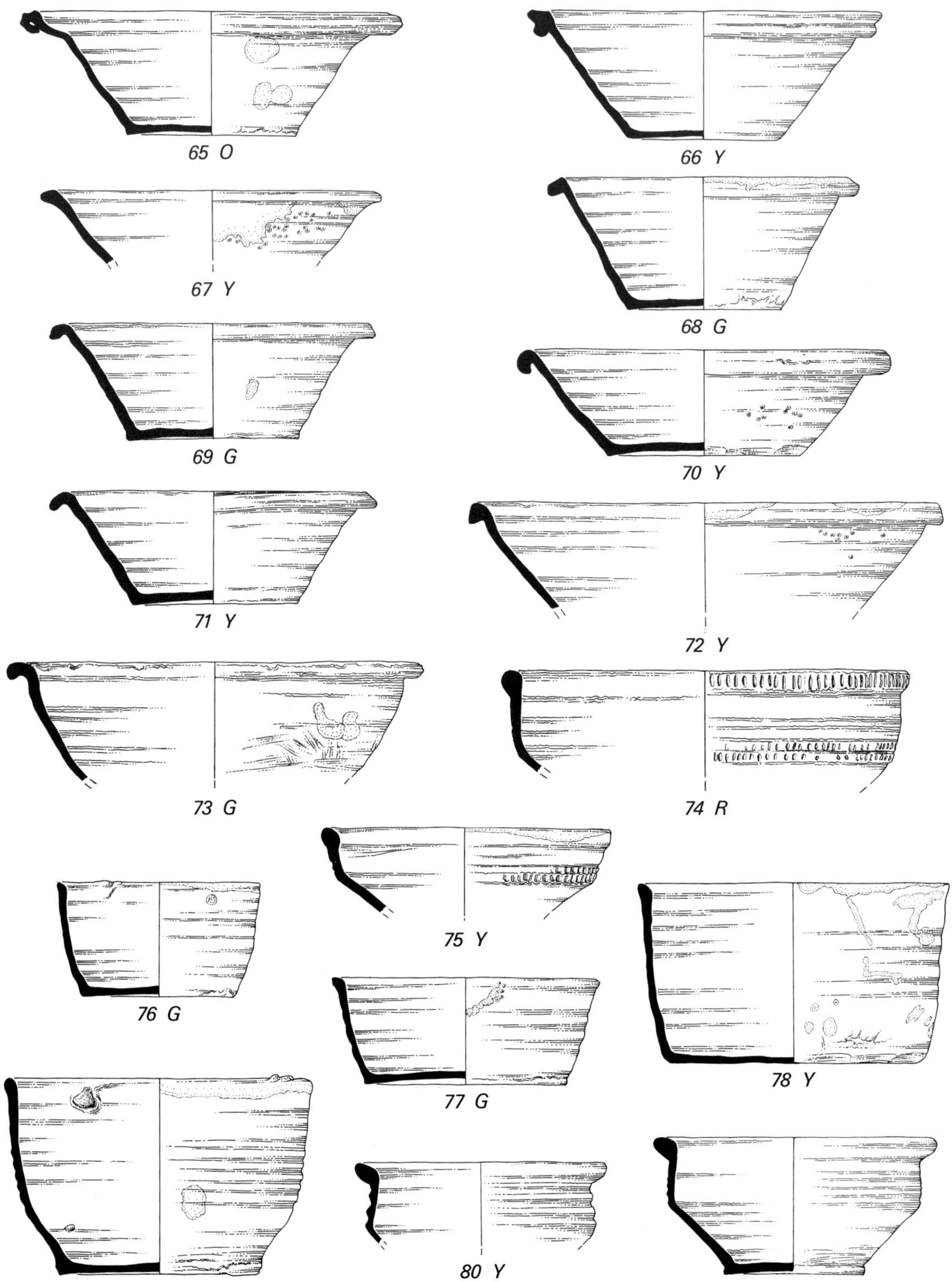

Fig 23 *Wide bowls (Nos 65–73). Deep bowls Type 1 (Nos 76–9). Deep bowls Type 2 (Nos 74–5, 80–1). (Scale 1/4)*

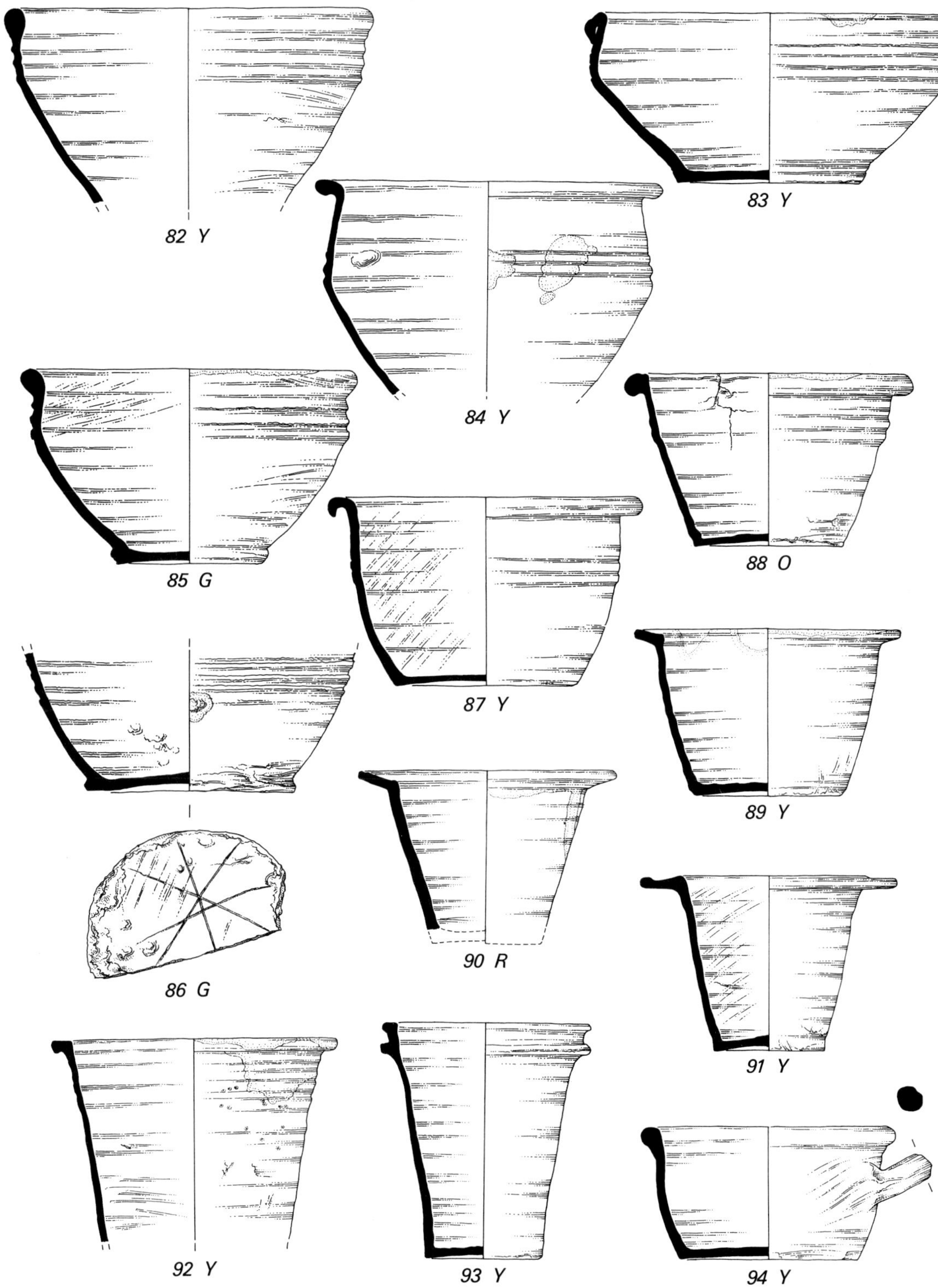

Fig 24 *Deep bowls Type 2 (Nos 82–6). Deep bowls Type 3 (Nos 87–93). Handled bowl (No 94). (Scale 1/4)*

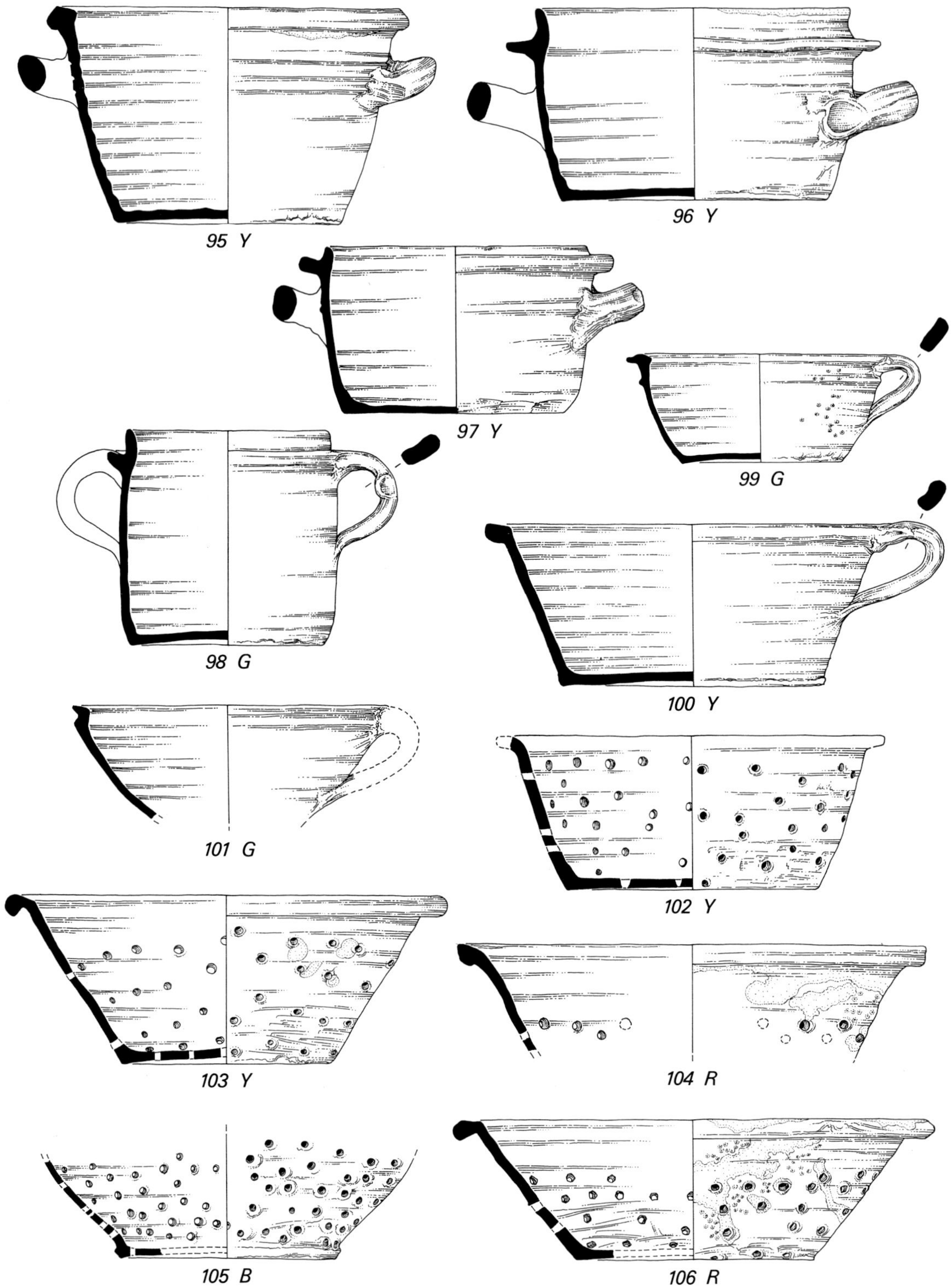

Fig 25 *Handled bowls (Nos 95–101). Colanders (Nos 102–6). (Scale 1/4)*

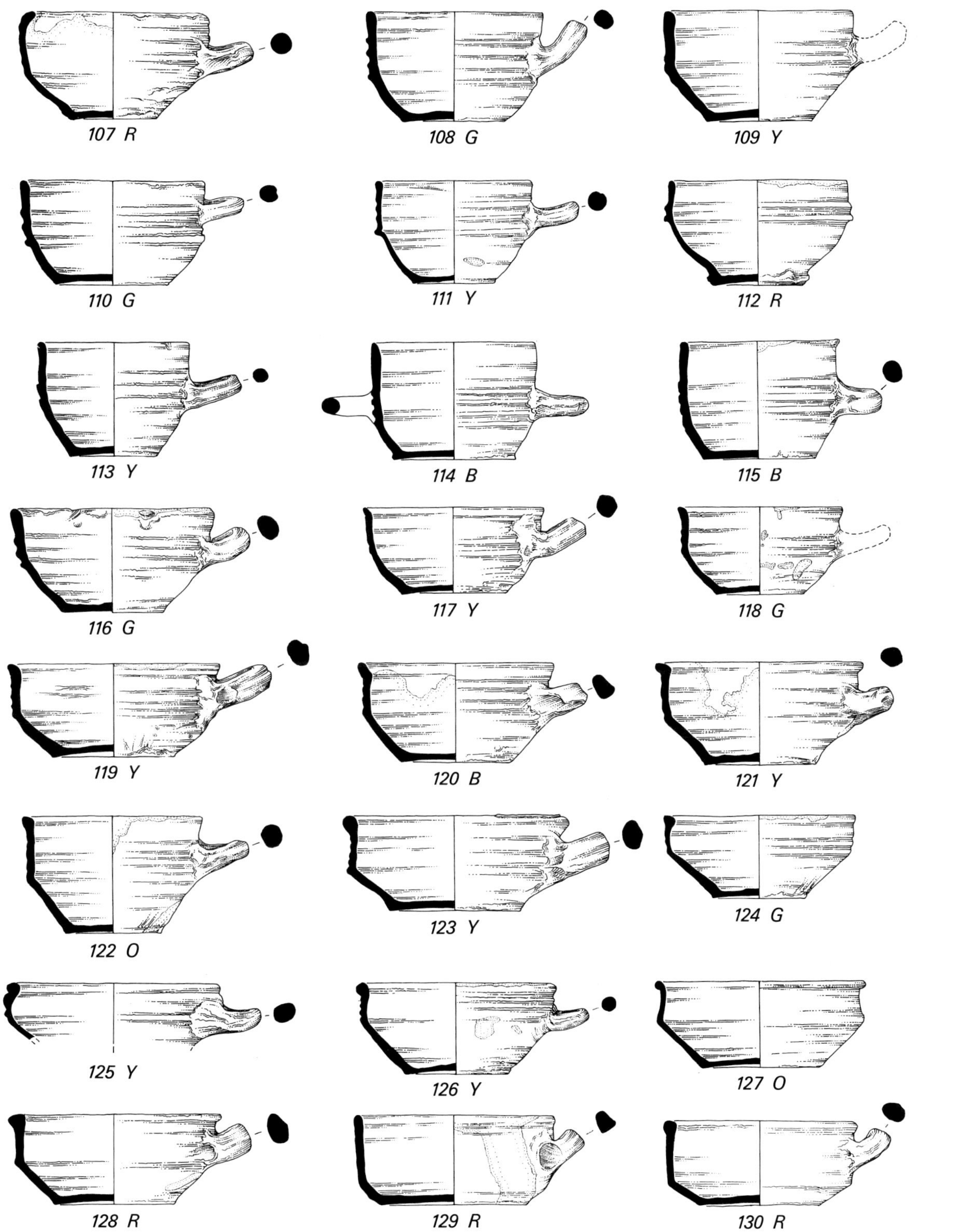

Fig 26 *Porringers (Nos 107–30). (Scale 1/4)*

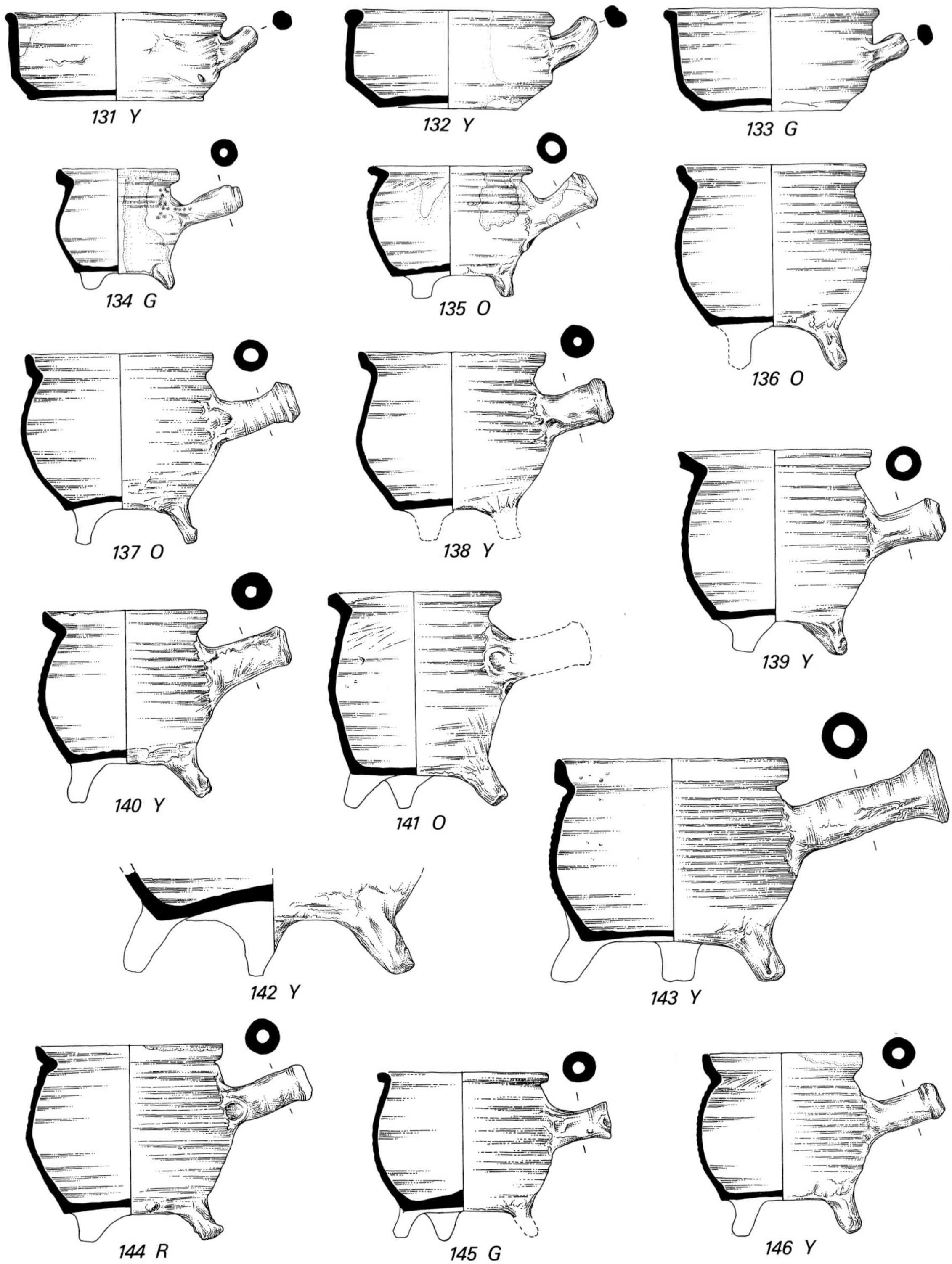

Fig 27 *Porringers (Nos 131–3). Tripod pipkins (Nos 134–46). (Scale 1/4)*

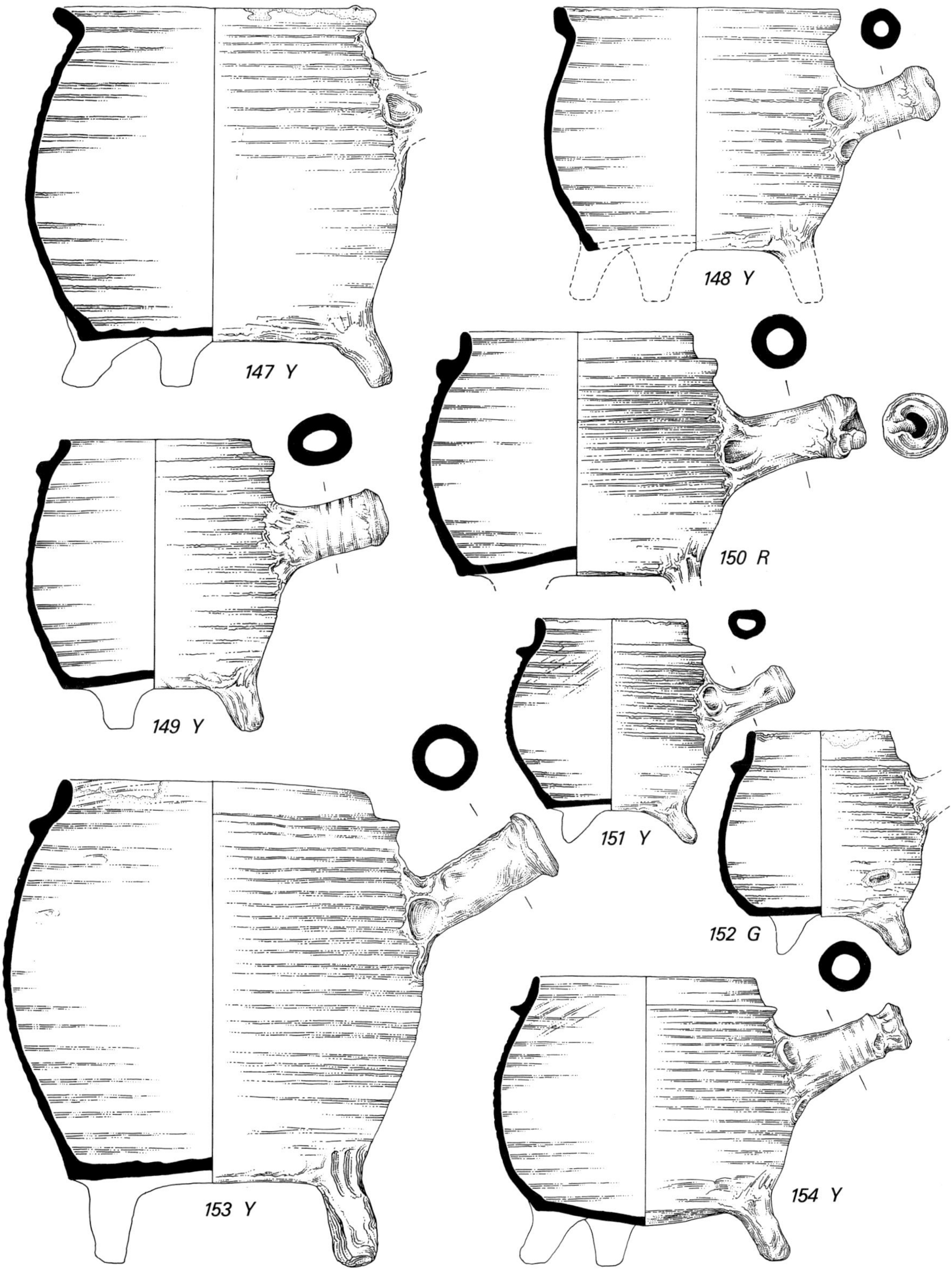

Fig 28 *Tripod pipkins (Nos 147–54). (Scale 1/4)*

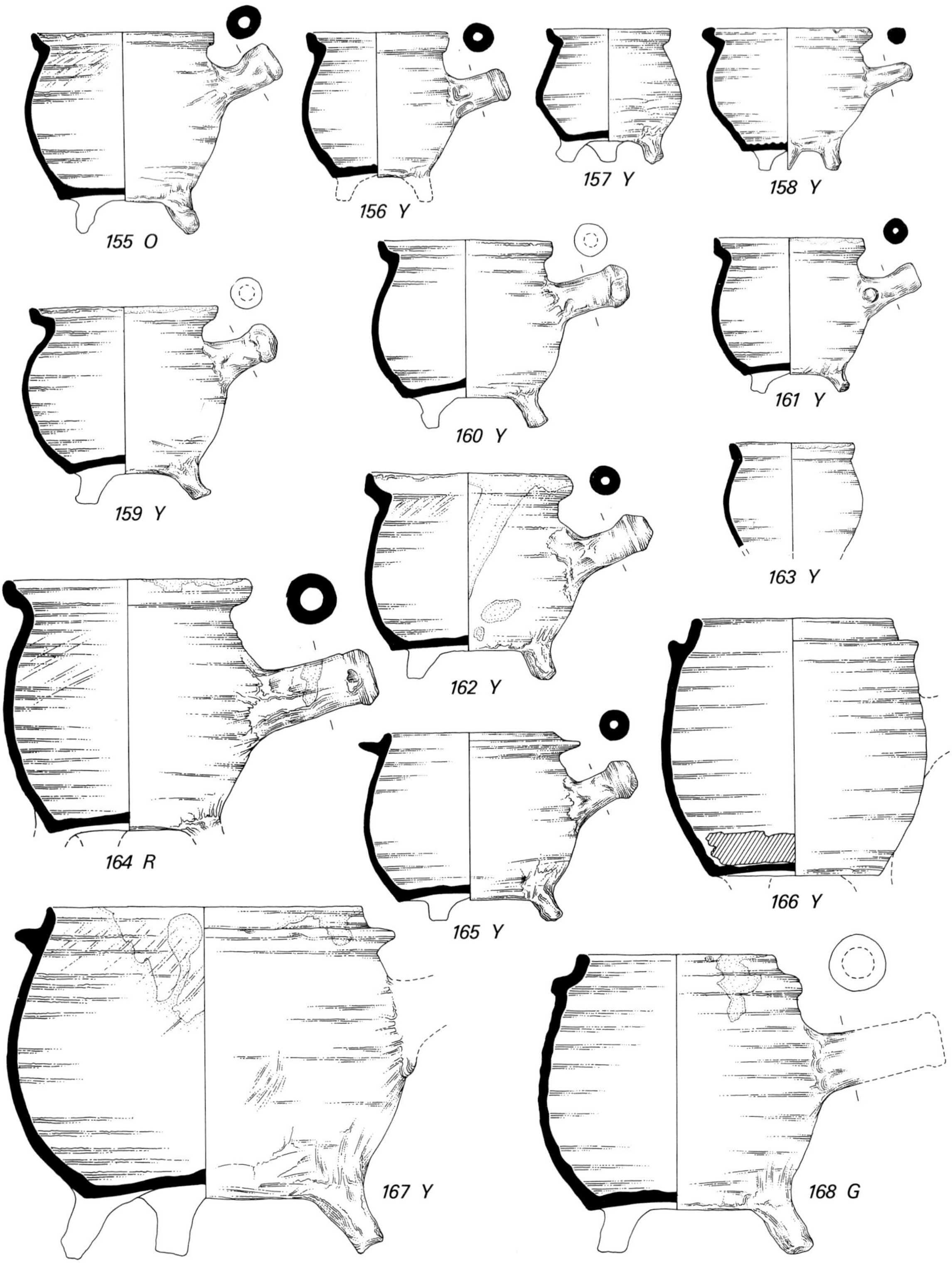

Fig 29 *Tripid pipkins (Nos 155–68). (Scale 1/4)*

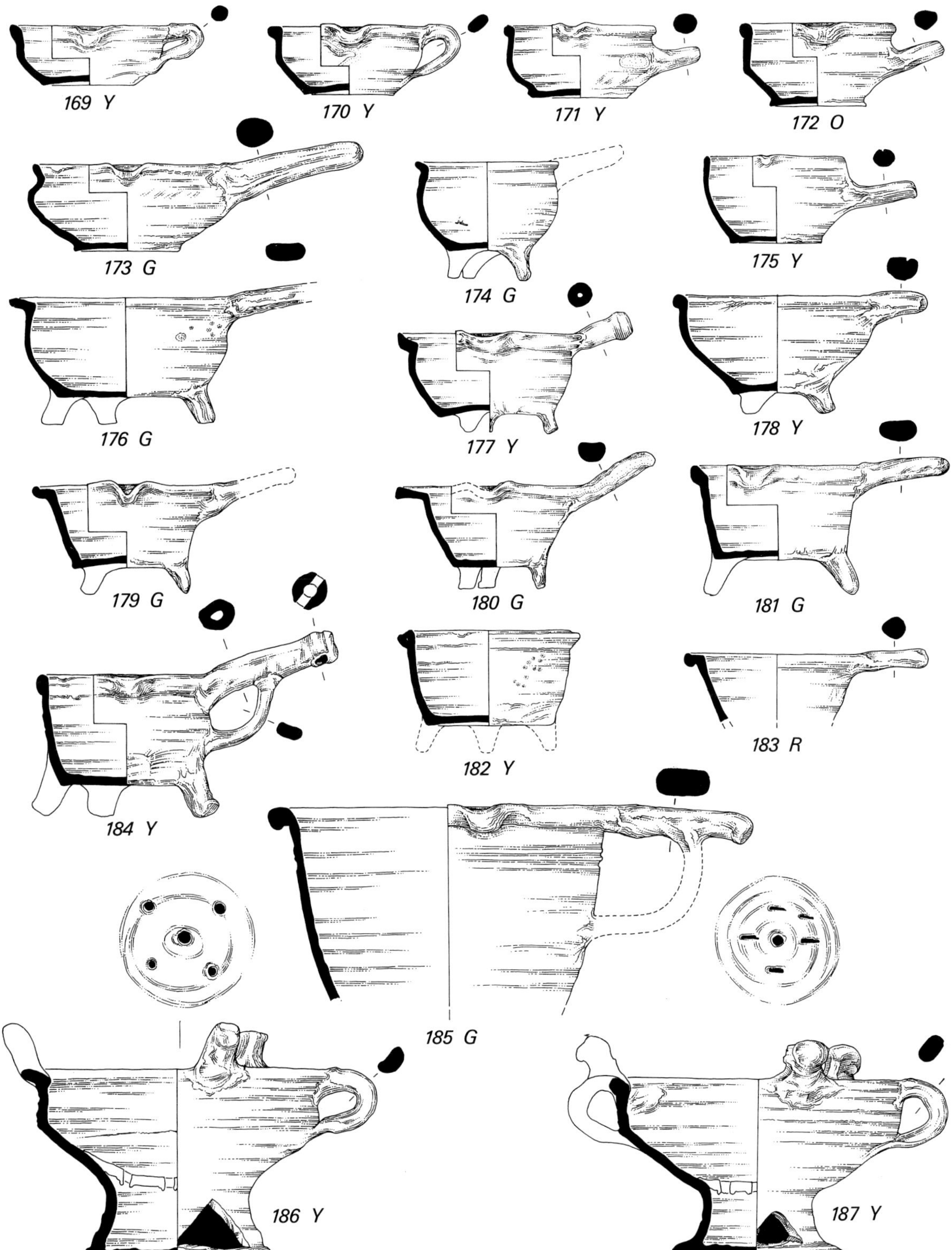

Fig 30 *Skillets (Nos 169–84). Saucepan (No 185). Chafing dishes (Nos 186–7). (Scale 1/4)*

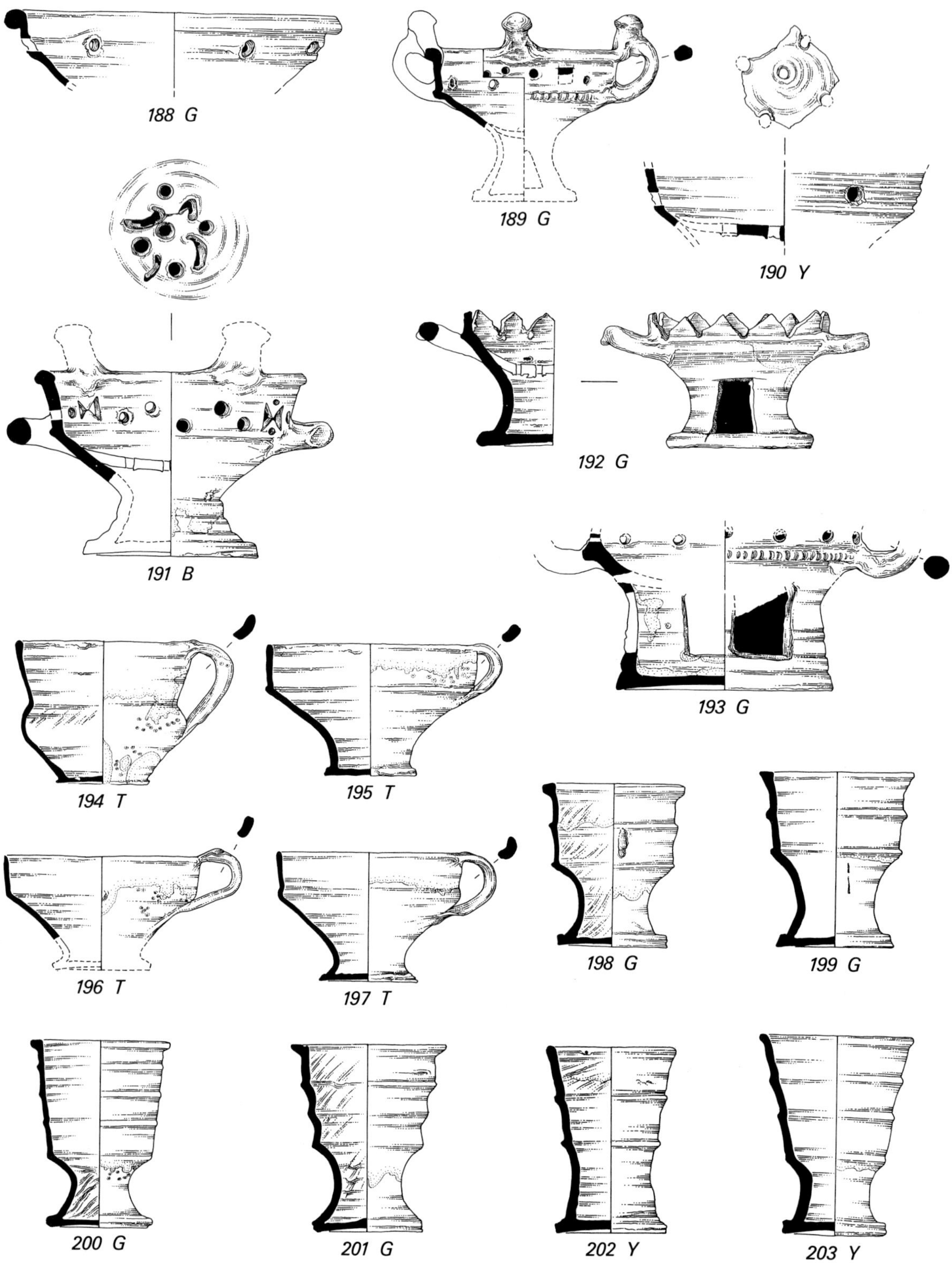

Fig 31 *Chafing dishes (Nos 188–93). Cups (Nos 194–7). Goblets (Nos 198–203). (Scale 1/4)*

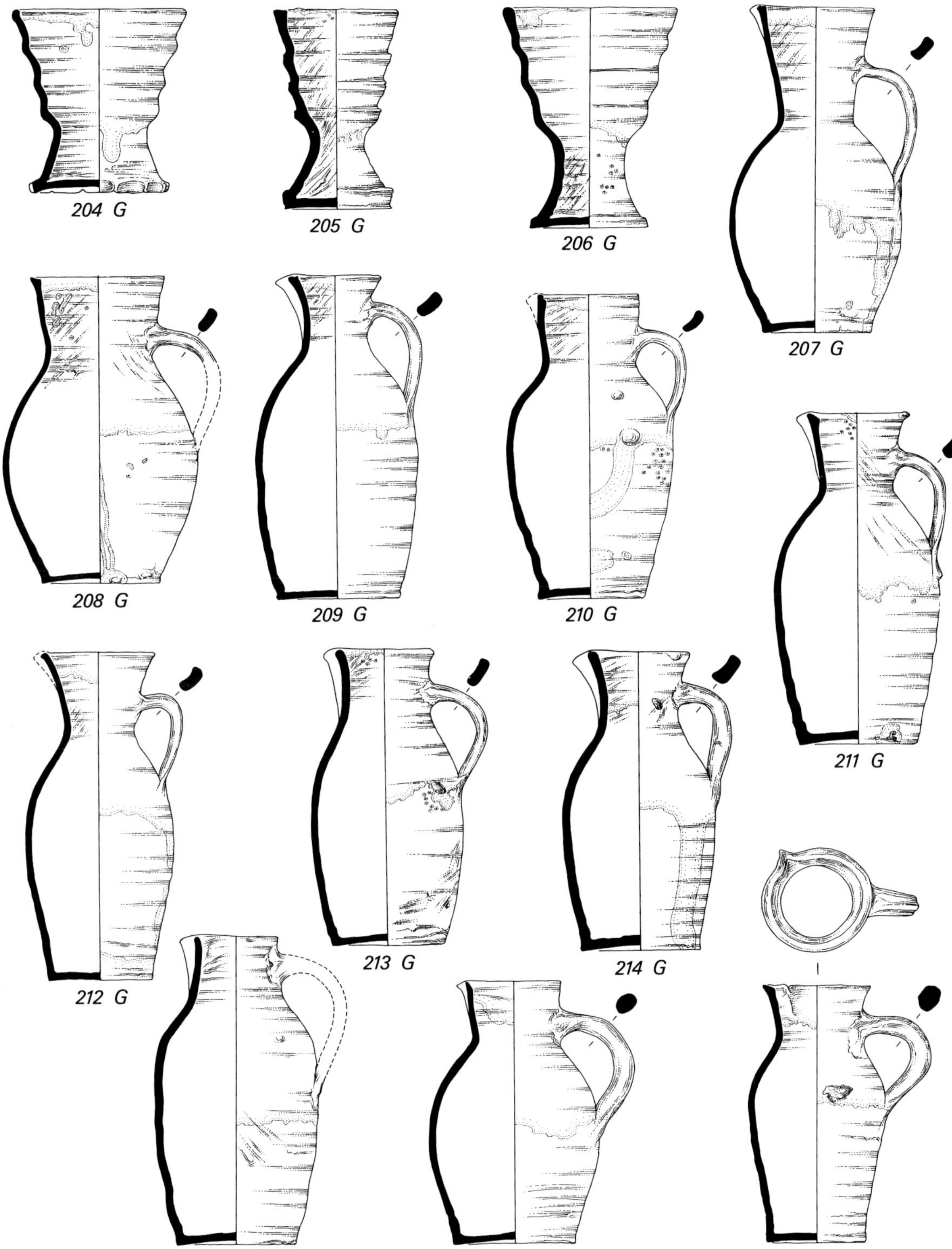

Fig 32 *Goblets (Nos 204–6). Rounded drinking jugs (Nos 207–17). (Scale 1/4)*

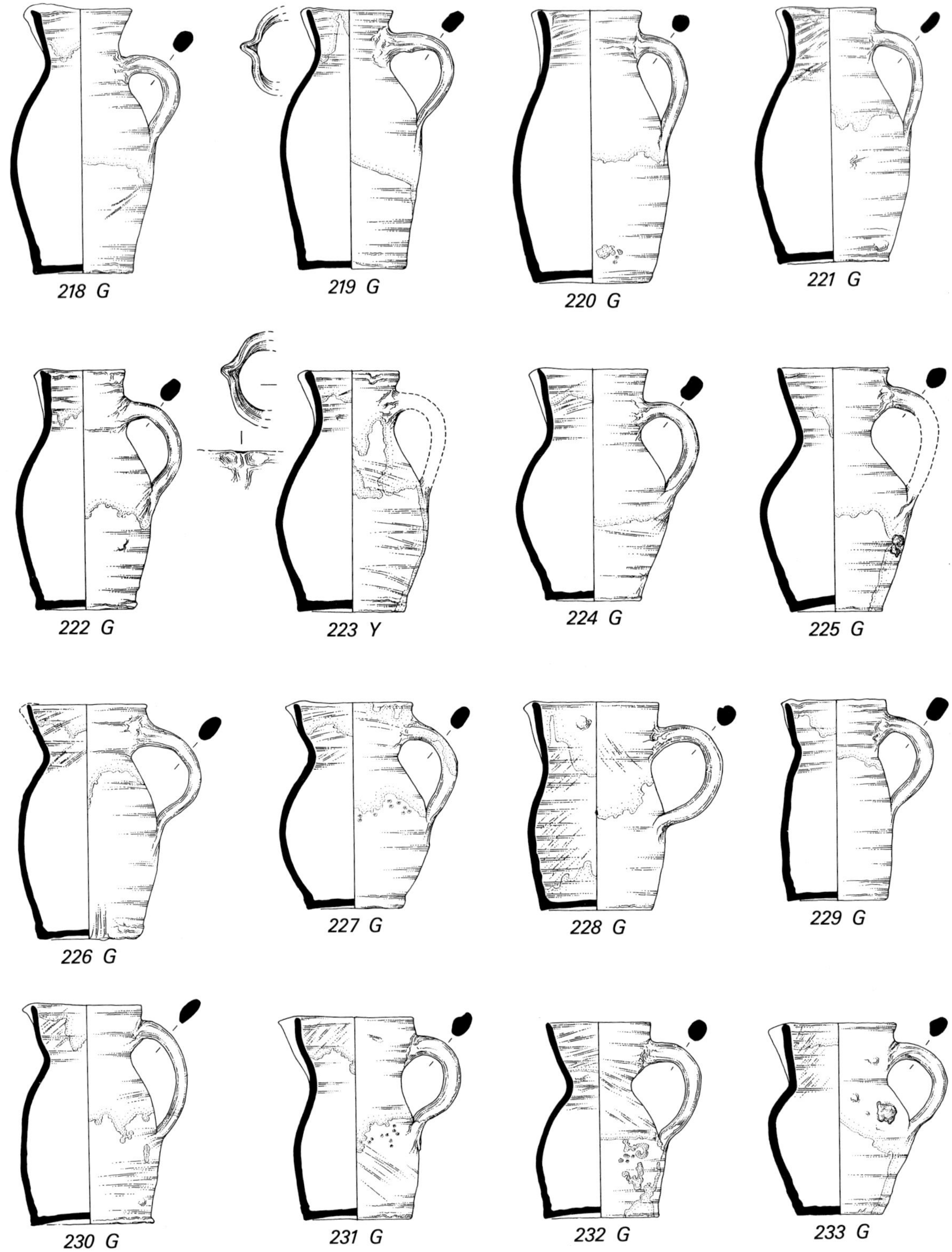

Fig 33 *Rounded drinking jugs (Nos 218–33). (Scale 1/4)*

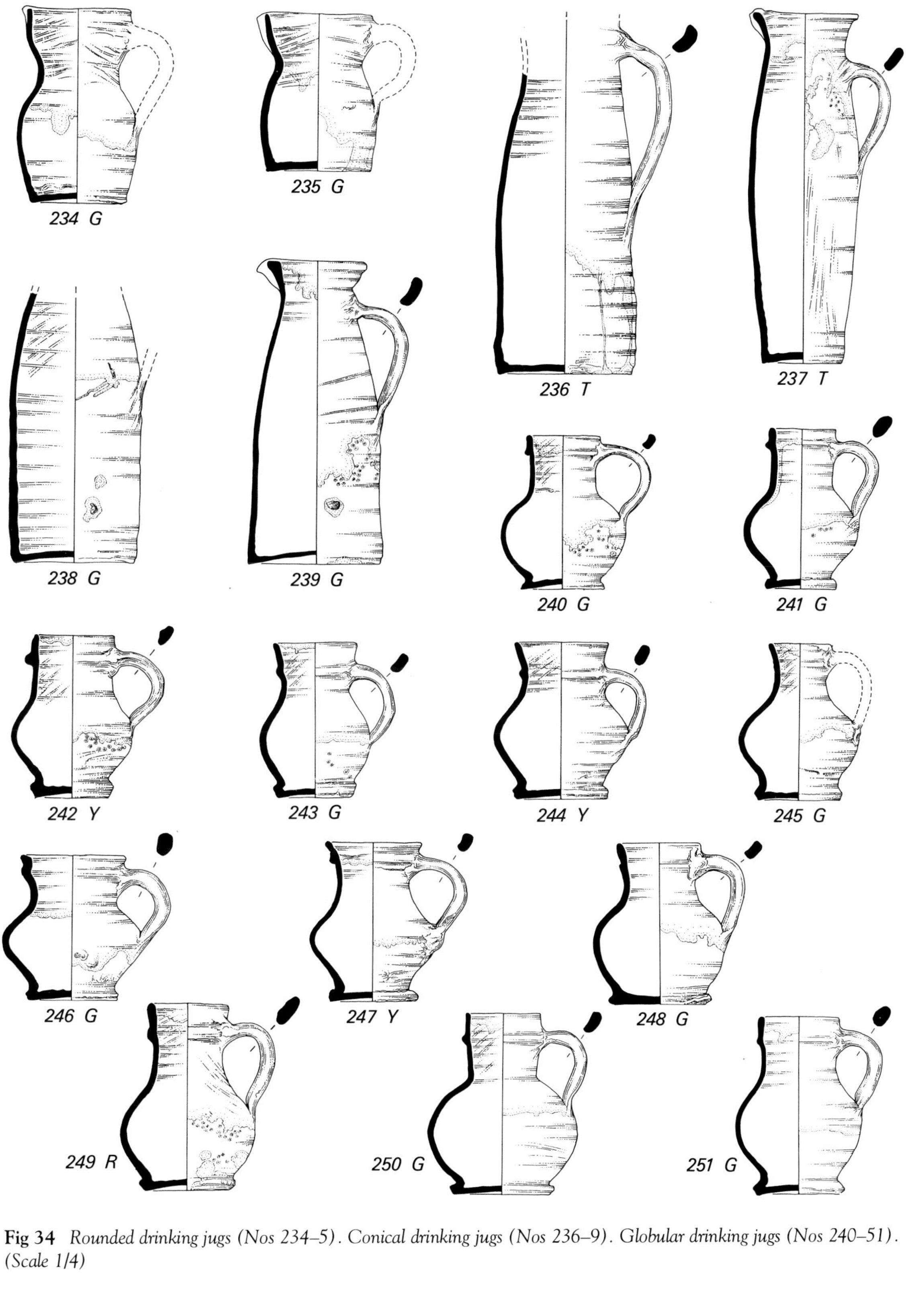

Fig 34 *Rounded drinking jugs (Nos 234–5). Conical drinking jugs (Nos 236–9). Globular drinking jugs (Nos 240–51). (Scale 1/4)*

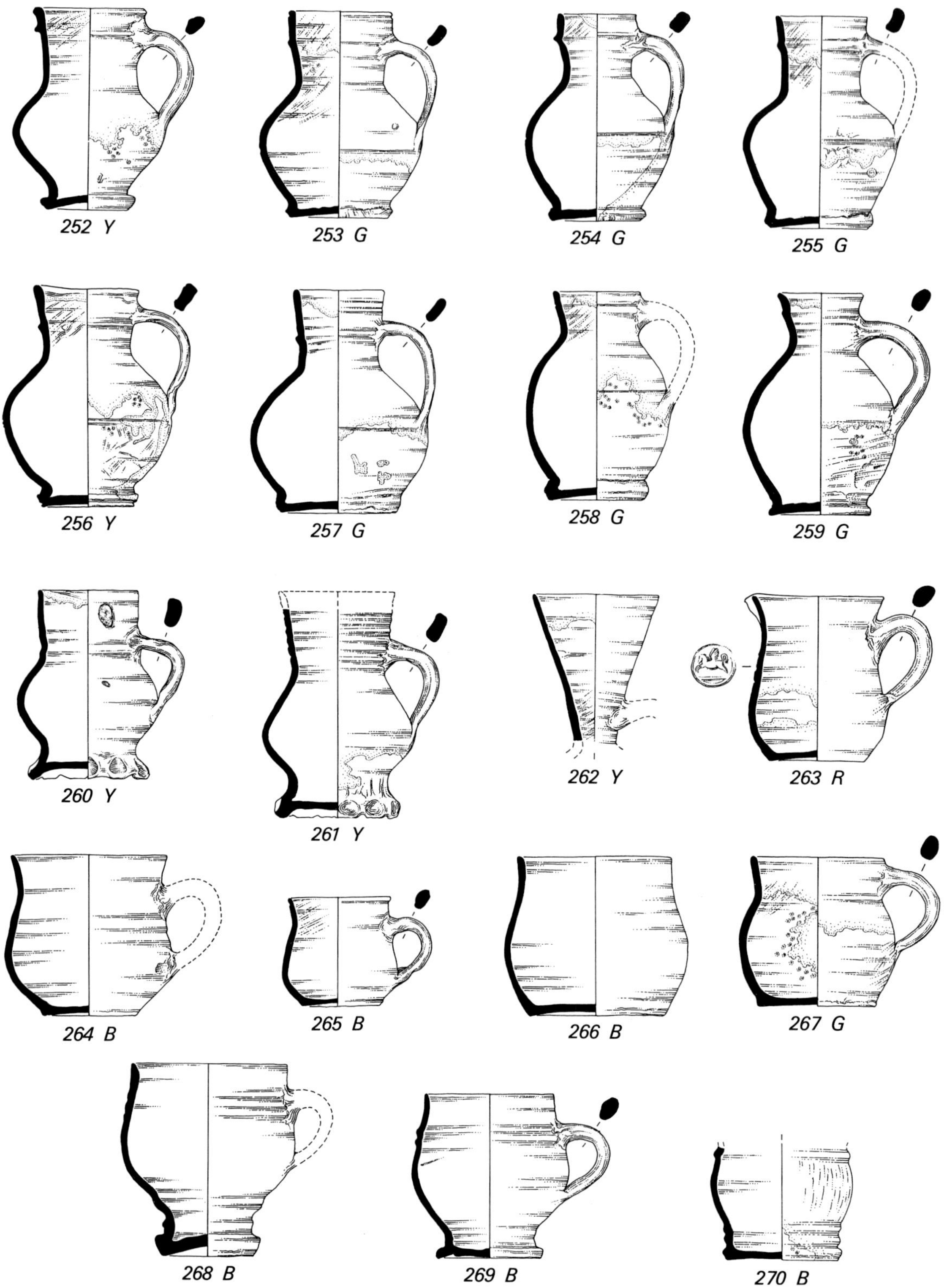

Fig 35 *Globular drinking jugs (Nos 252–62). Mugs Type 1 (Nos 263–70). (Scale 1/4)*

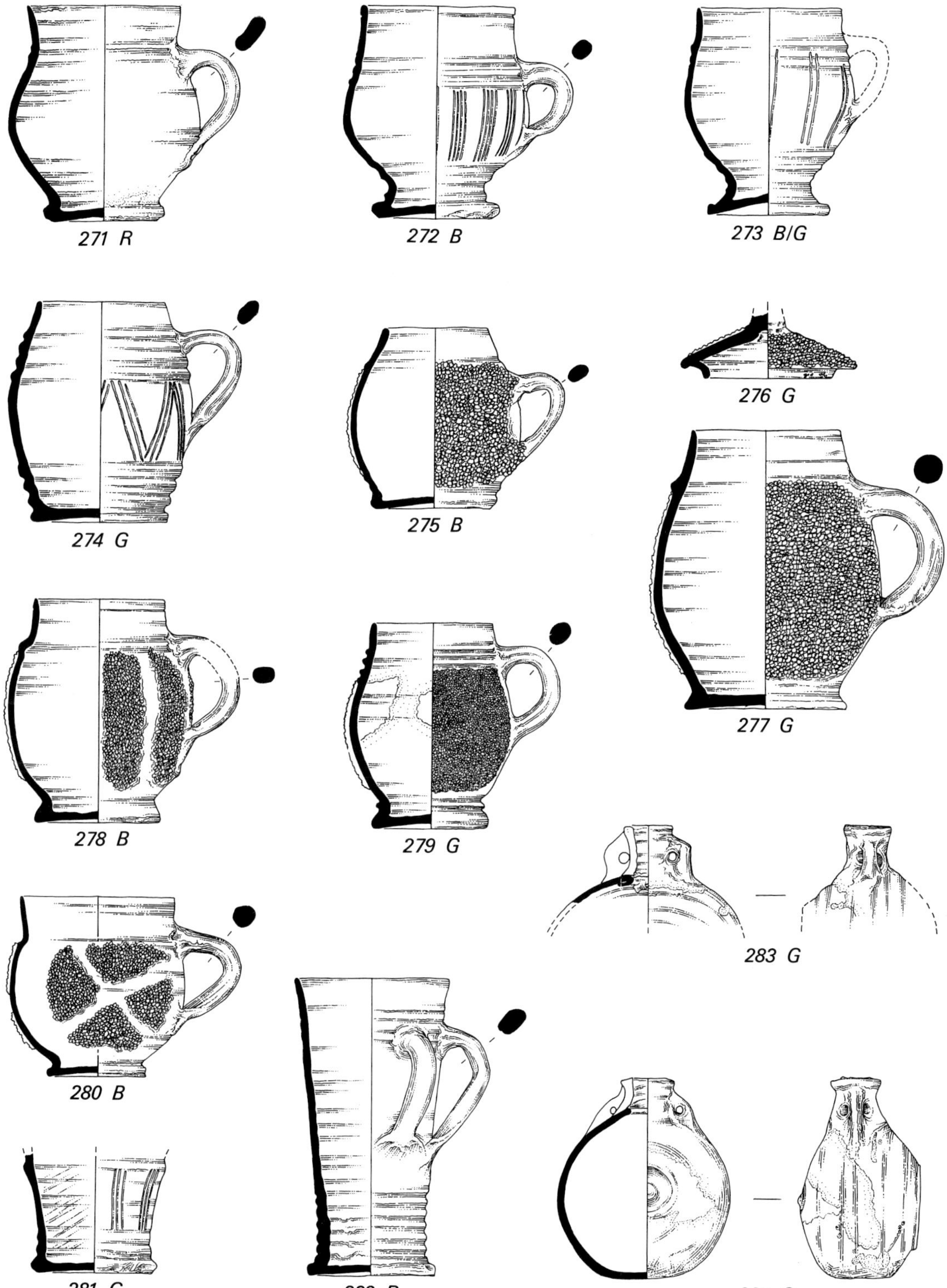

Fig 36 *Mugs Type 1 (Nos 271–4). Mugs Type 2 (Nos 275–80). Mugs Type 3 (Nos 281–2). Mammiform costrels (Nos 283–4). (Scale 1/4)*

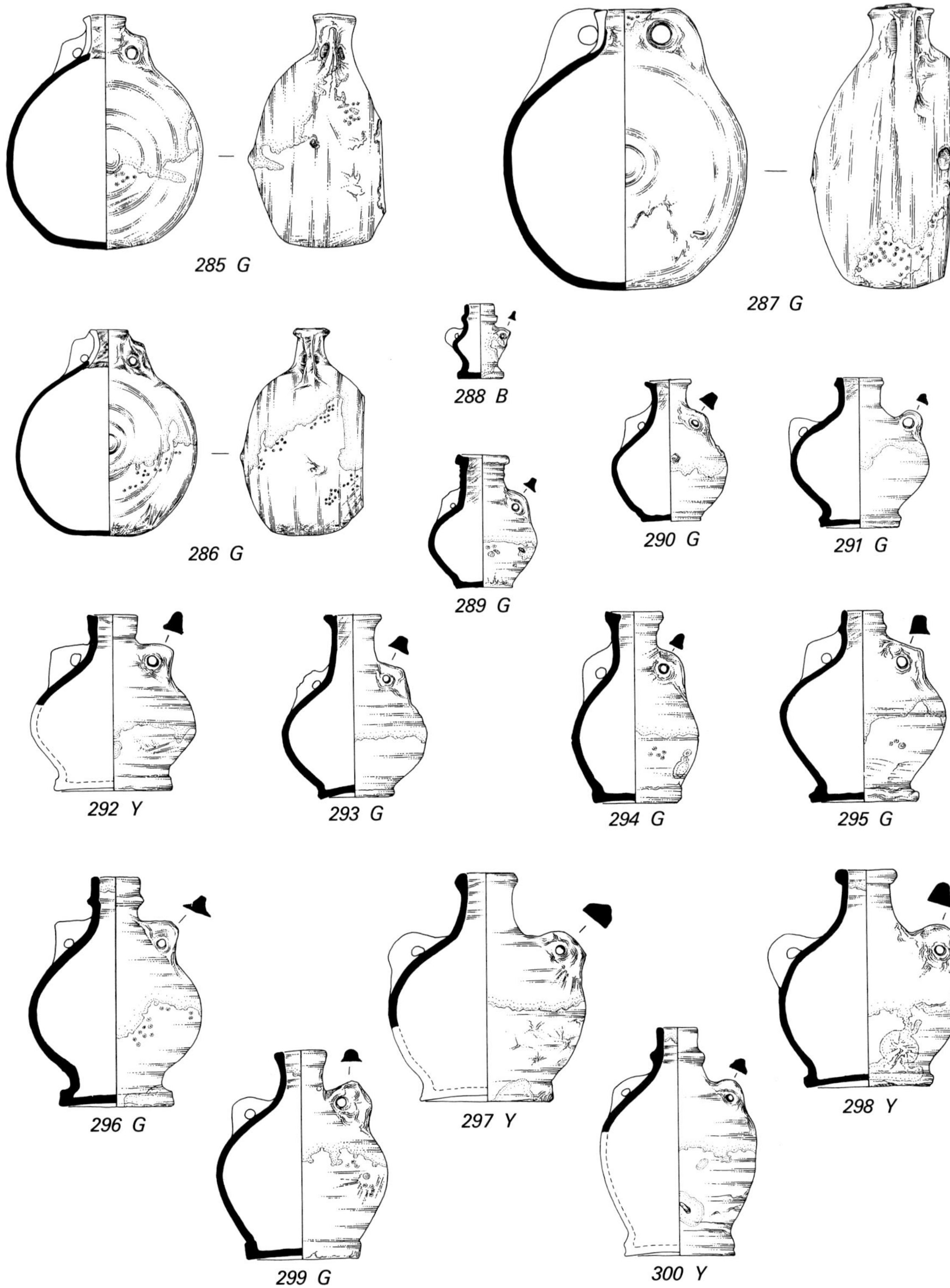

Fig 37 *Mammiform costrels (Nos 285–7). Miniature costrel (No 288). Bottle-shaped costrels (Nos 289–300). (Scale 1/4)*

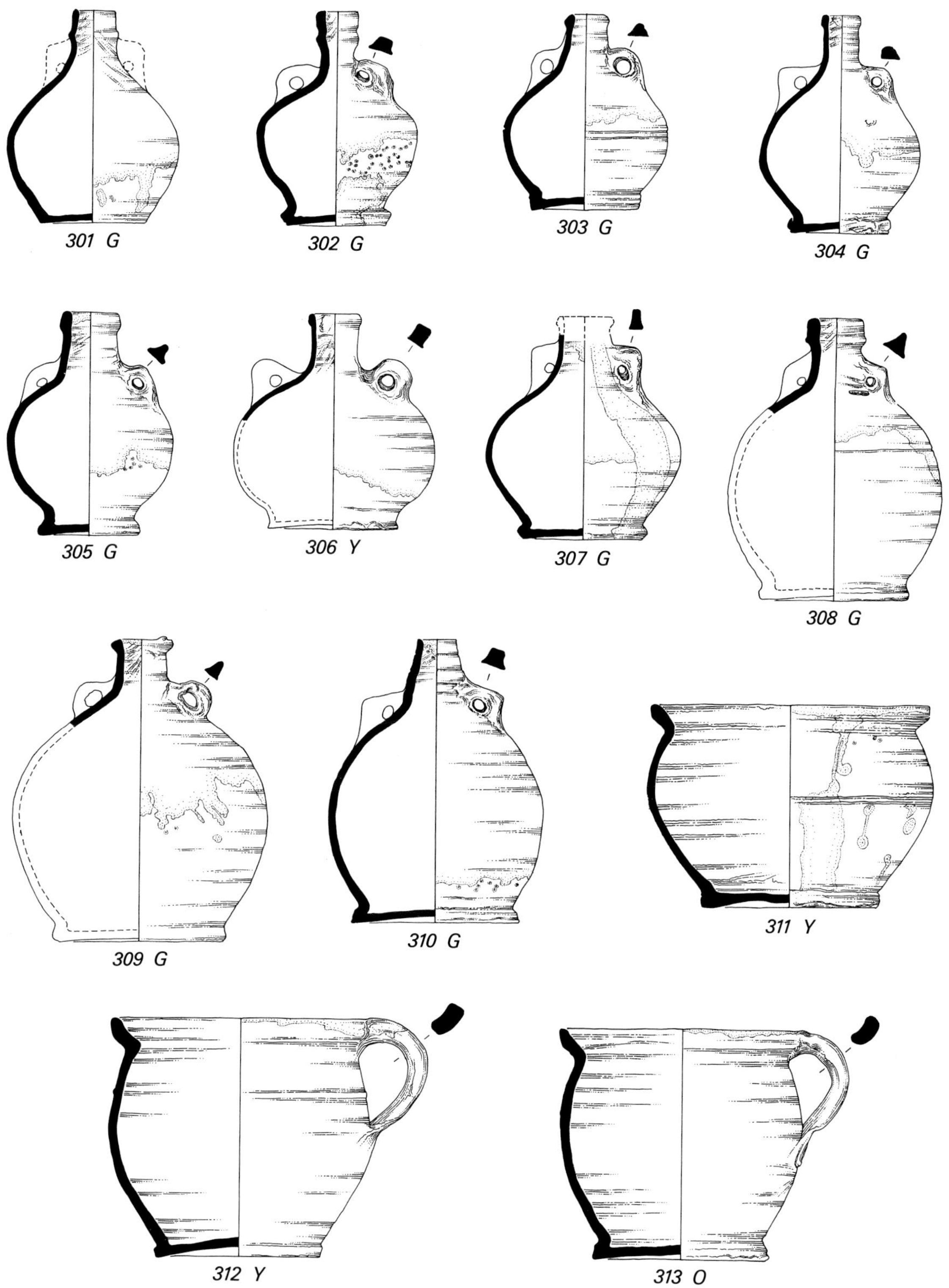

Fig 38 *Bottle-shaped costrels (Nos 301–10). Chamber pots Type 1 (Nos 311–13). (Scale 1/4)*

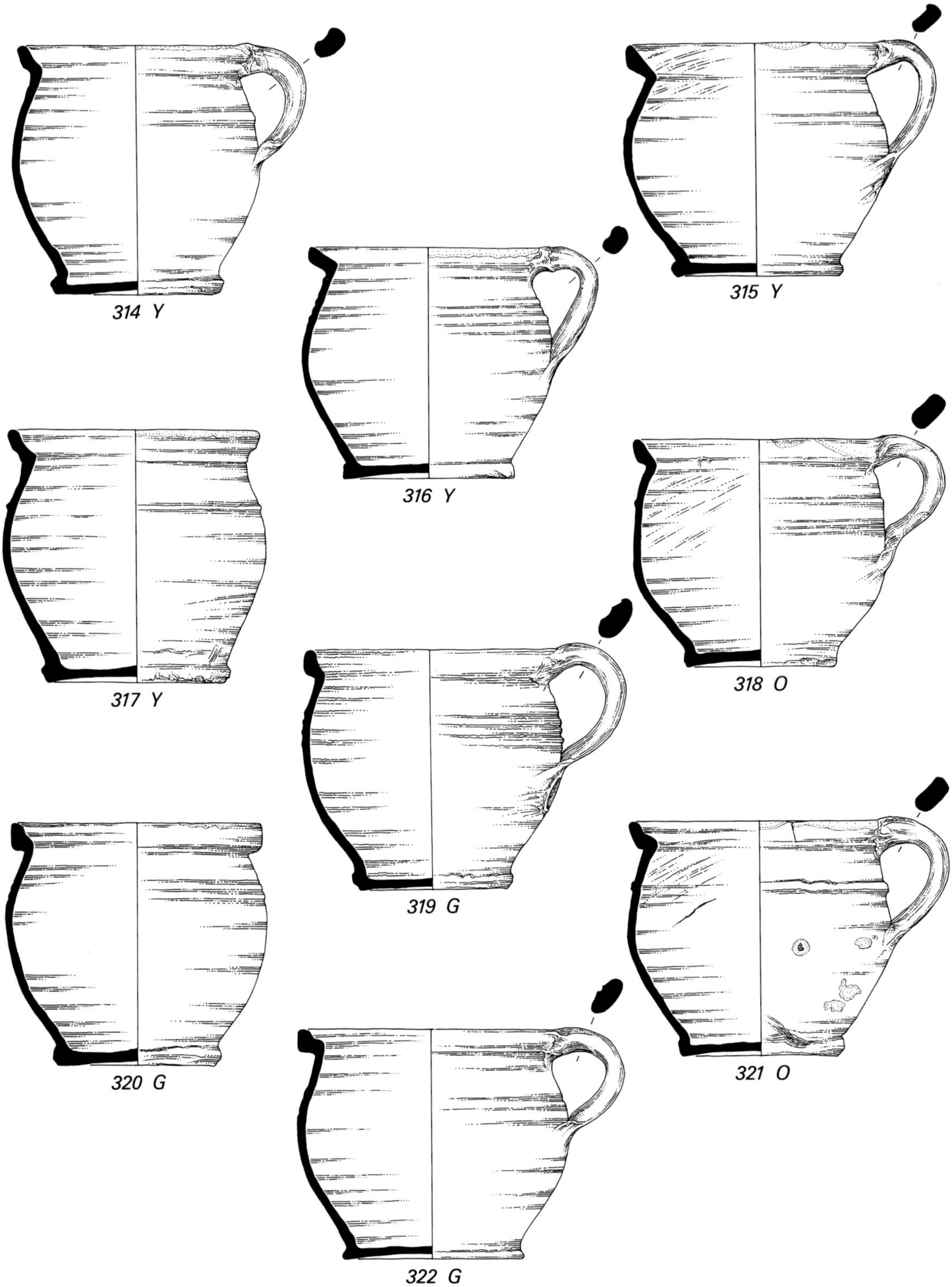

Fig 39 *Chamber pots Type 1 (Nos 314–22). (Scale 1/4)*

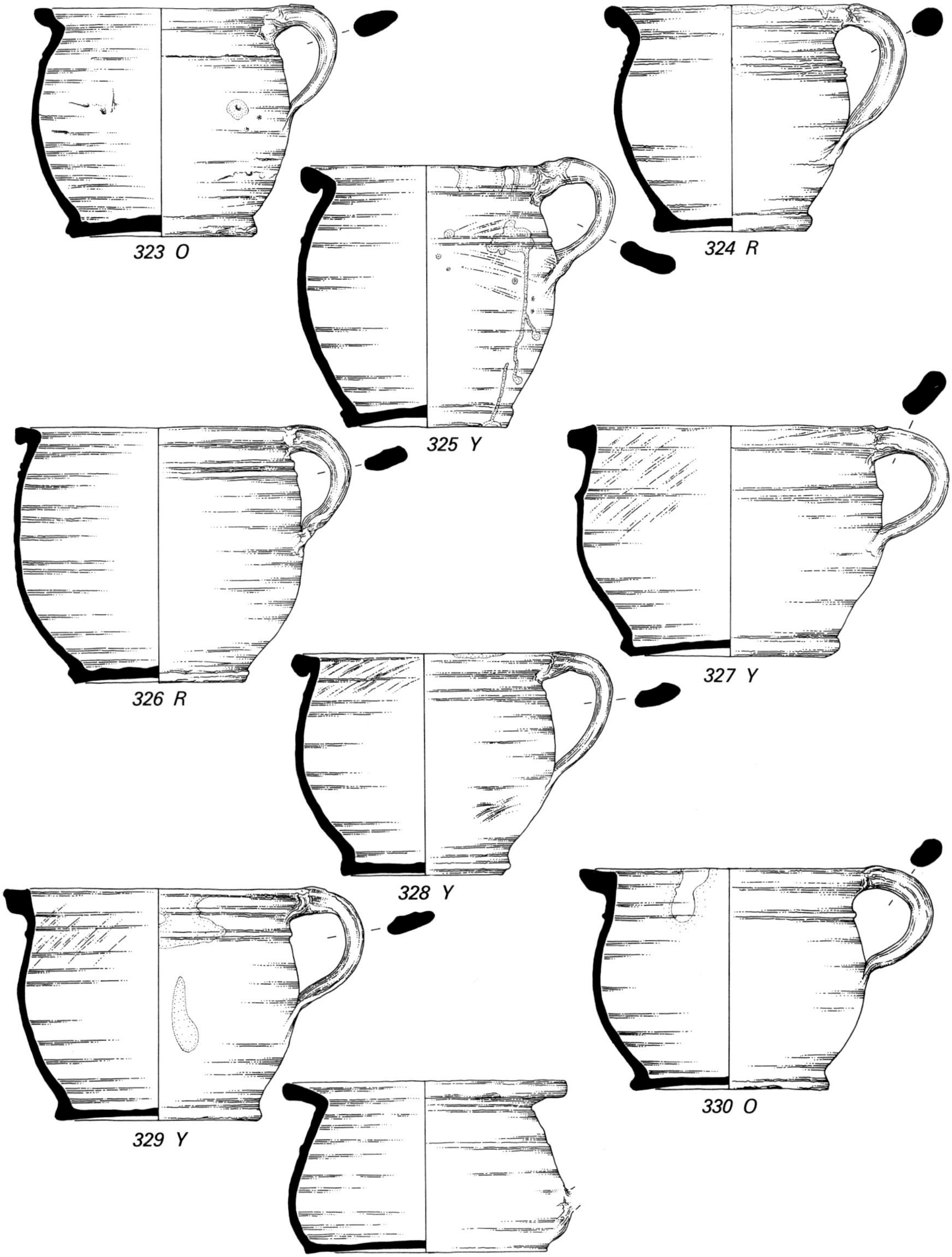

Fig 40 *Chamber pots Type 1 (Nos 323–30). Chamber pot Type 2 (No 331). (Scale 1/4)*

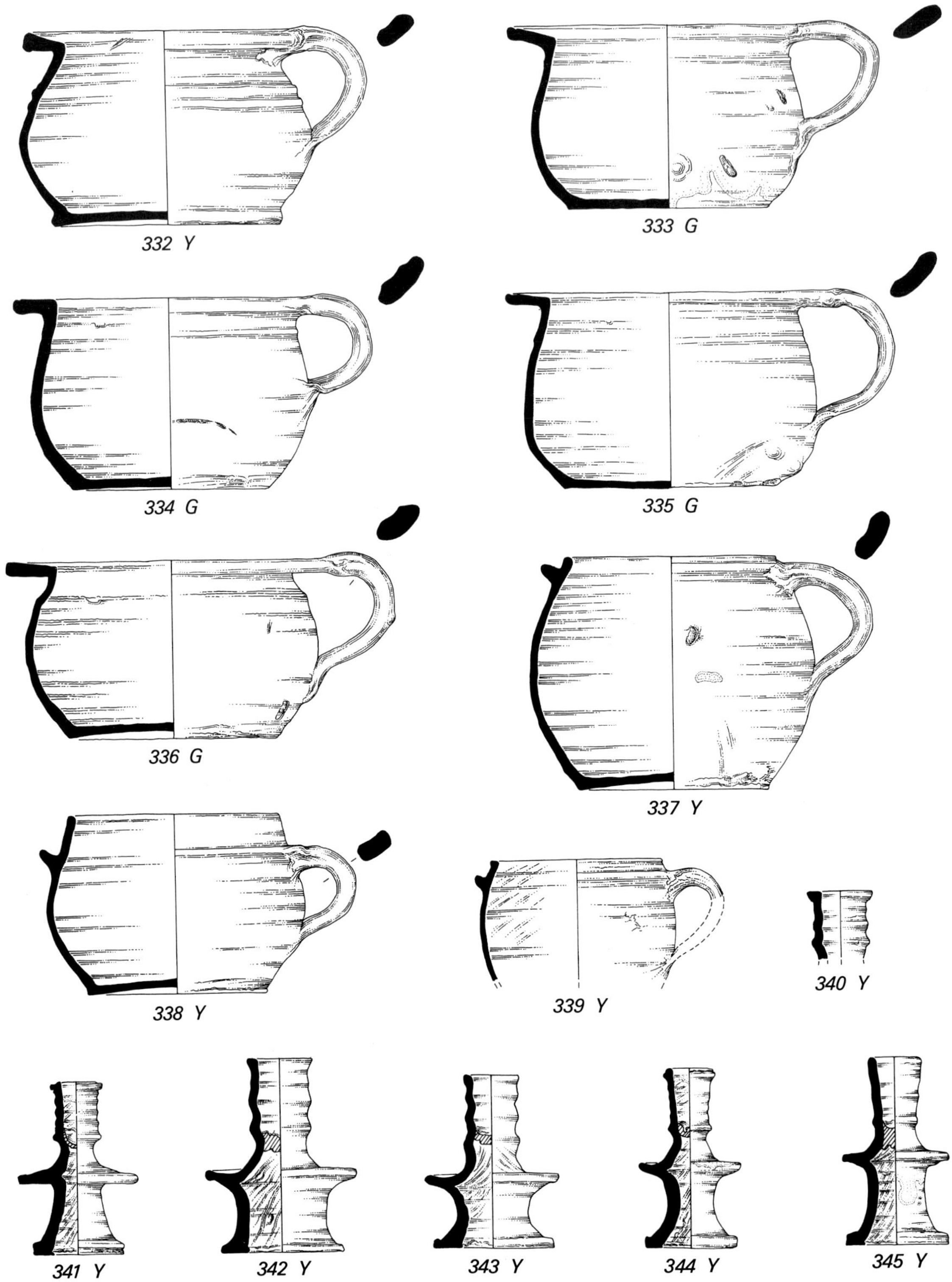

Fig 41 *Chamber pots Type 2 (Nos 332–6). Lid-seated chamber pots (Nos 337–9). Upright candlesticks (Nos 340–5). (Scale 1/4)*

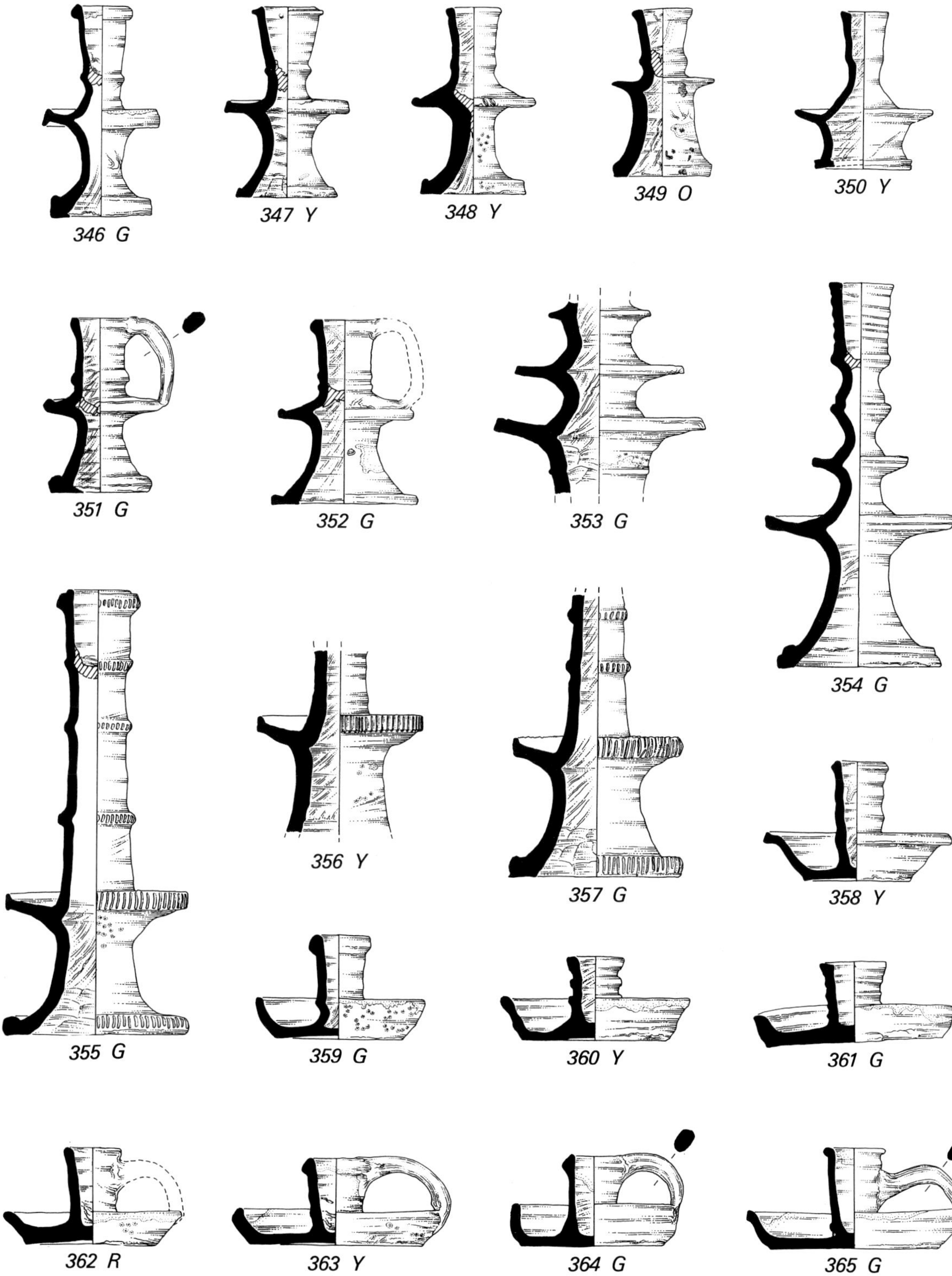

Fig 42 *Upright candlesticks (Nos 346–52). Ornamental candlesticks (Nos 353–7). Saucer candlesticks (Nos 358–65). (Scale 1/4)*

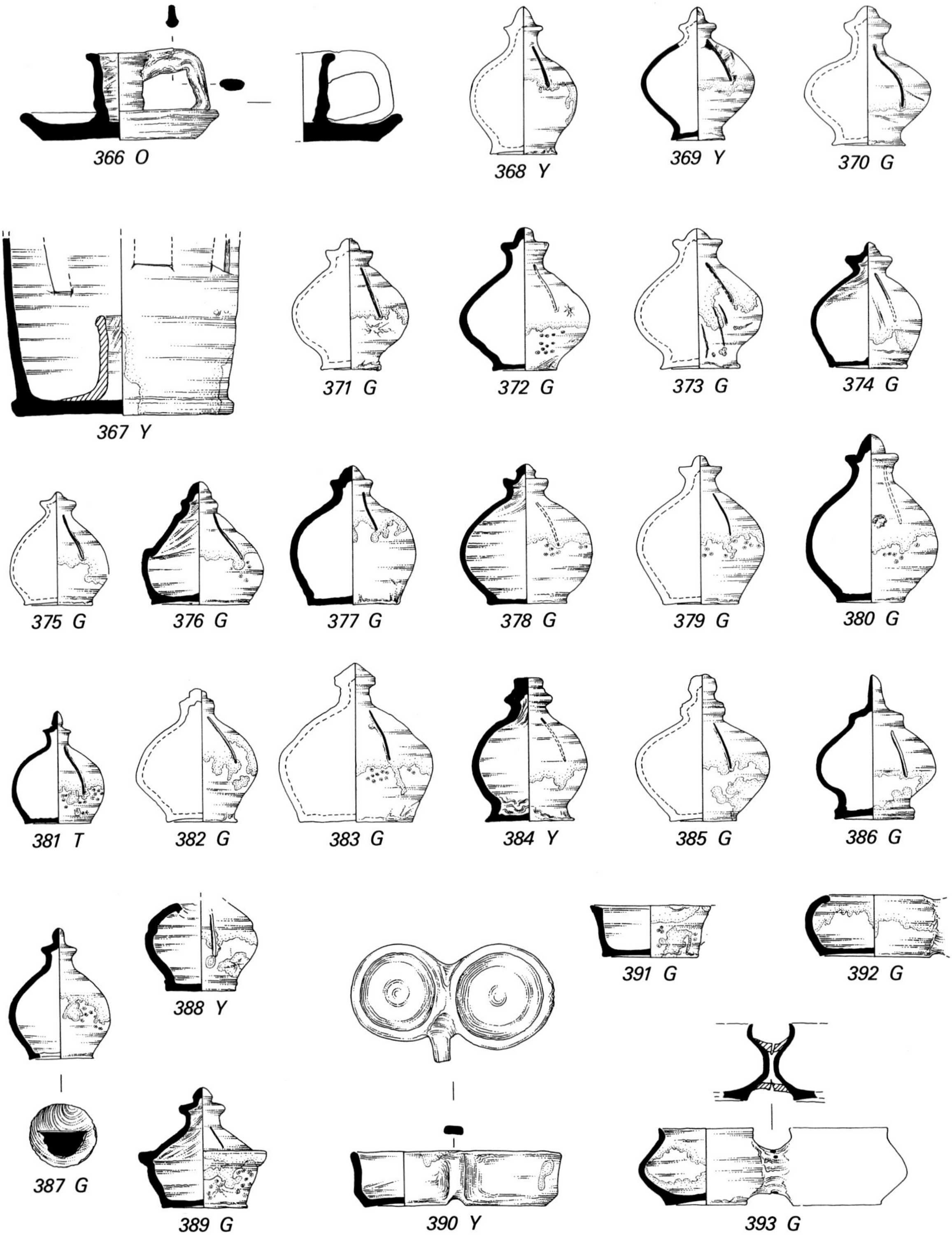

Fig 43 *Saucer candlestick (No 366). Lantern (No 367). Money-boxes (Nos 368–89). Condiment dishes (Nos 390–93). (Scale 1/4)*

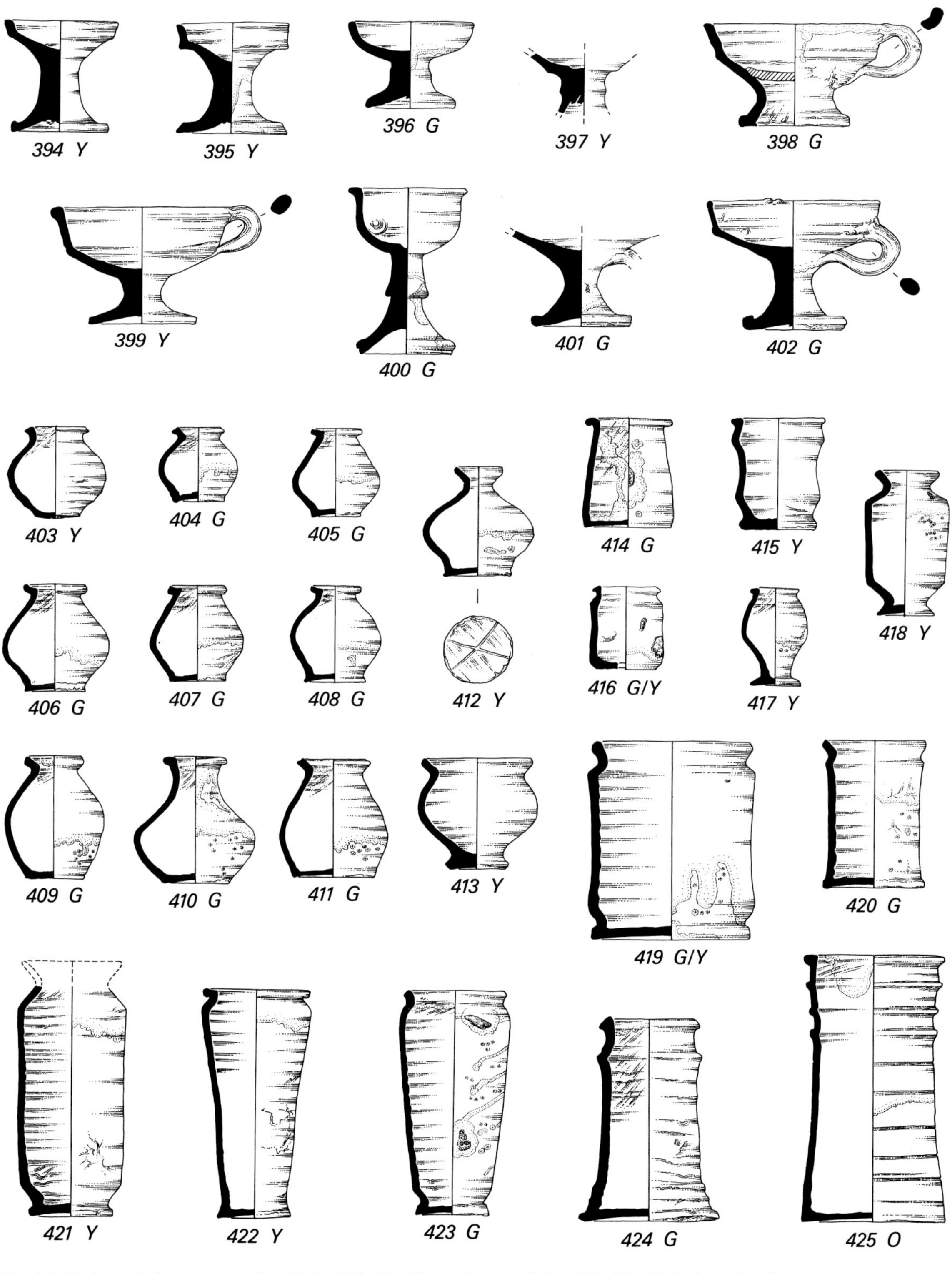

Fig 44 *Pedestal dishes or cups (Nos 394–402). Small rounded jars (Nos 403–13, 417). Straight-sided jars (Nos 414–16, 418–25). (Scale 1/4)*

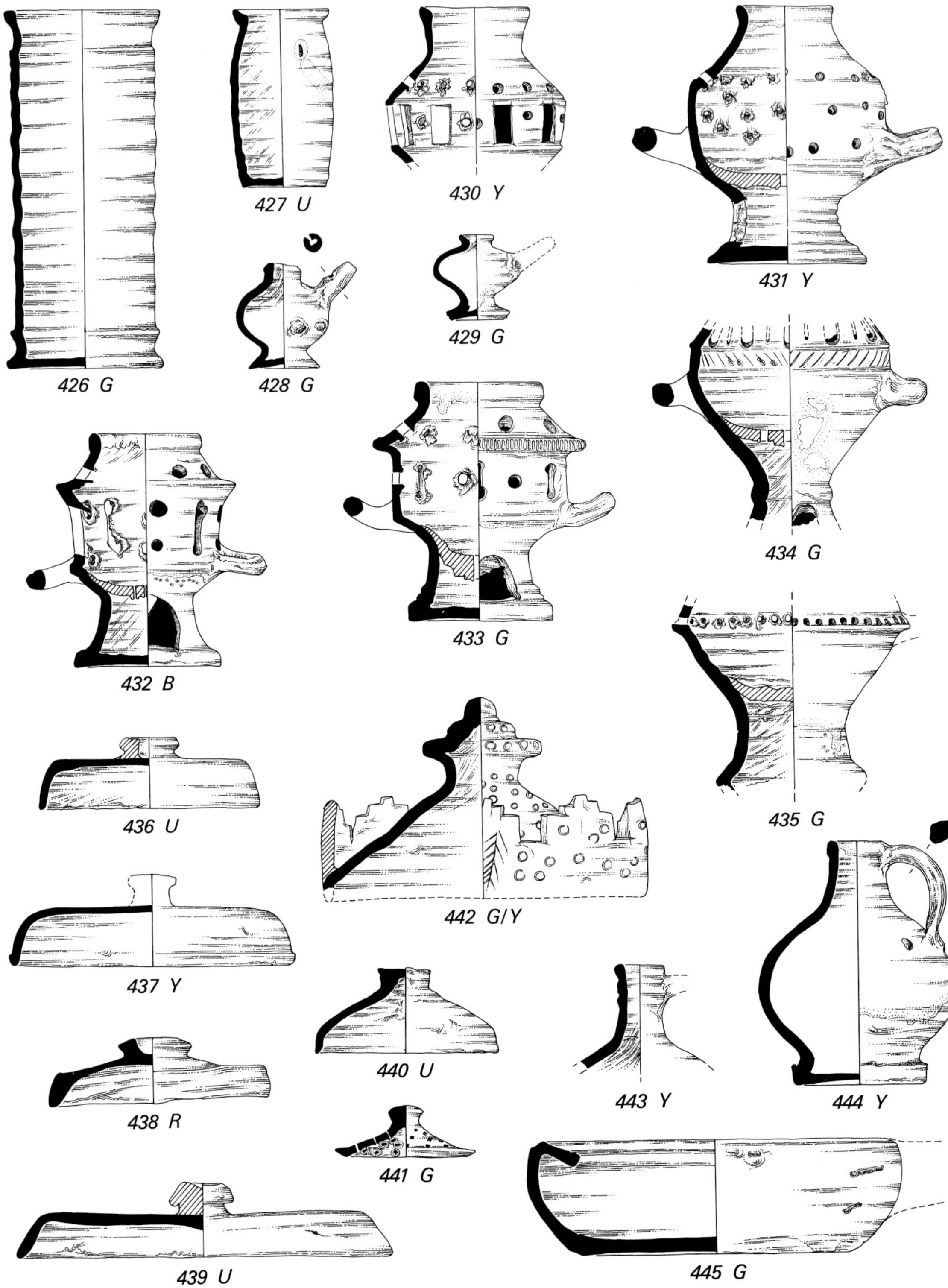

Fig 45 *Straight-sided jars (Nos 426–7). Whistles (Nos 428–9). Fuming pots (Nos 430–5). Lids (Nos 436–42). Bottles (Nos 443–4). Bedpan (No 445). (Scale 1/4)*

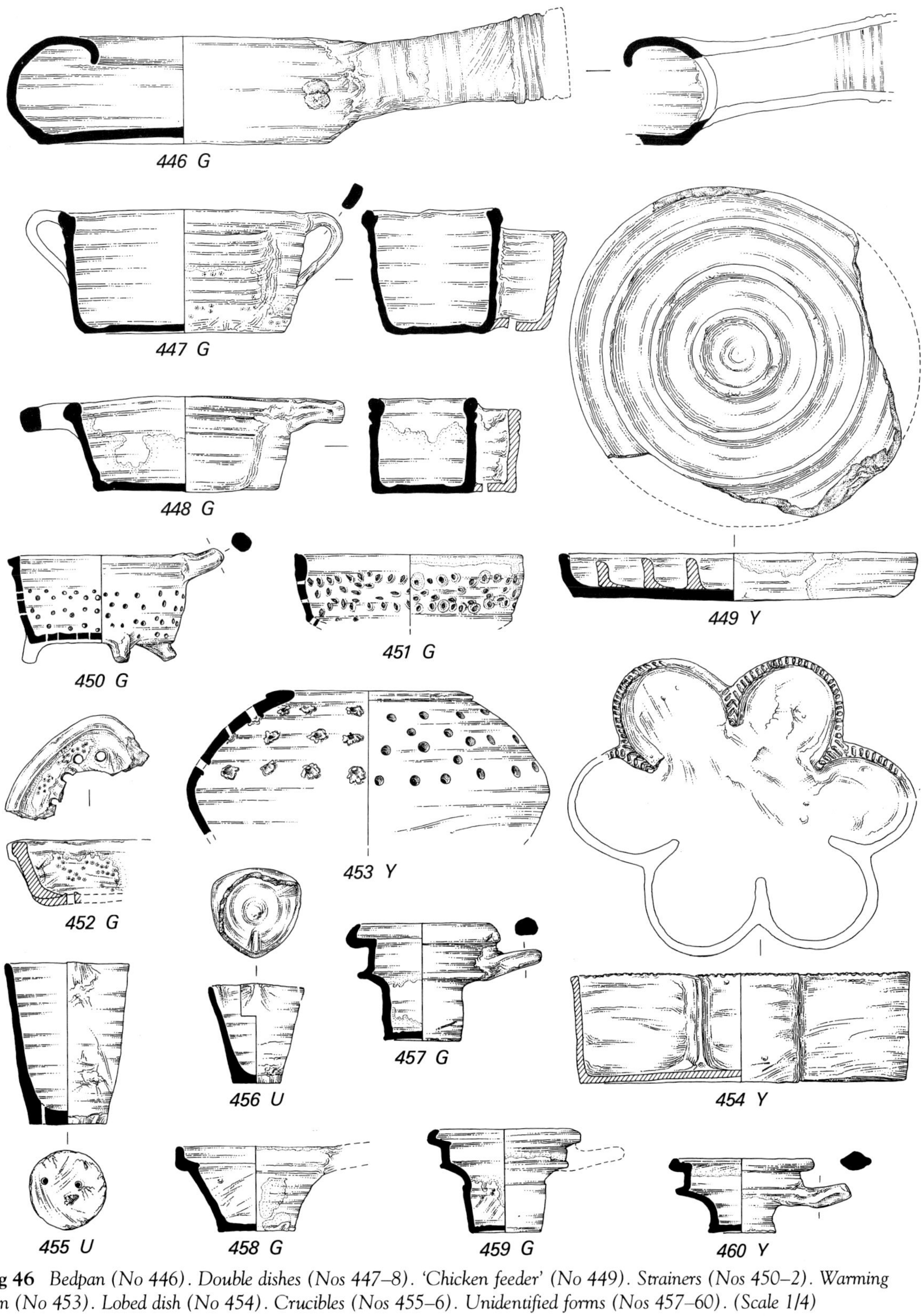

Fig 46 *Bedpan (No 446). Double dishes (Nos 447–8). 'Chicken feeder' (No 449). Strainers (Nos 450–2). Warming pan (No 453). Lobed dish (No 454). Crucibles (Nos 455–6). Unidentified forms (Nos 457–60). (Scale 1/4)*

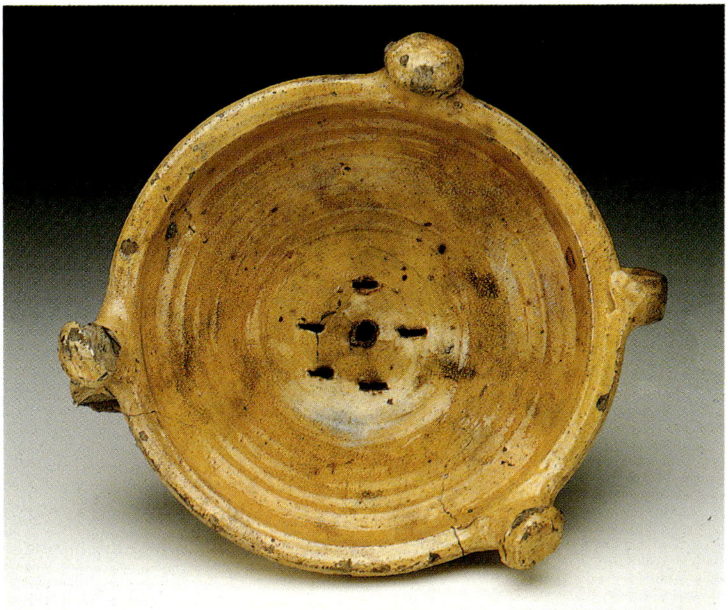

Plate 1 *Chafing dish (overall height 140 mm); (A) plan view, (B) side view*

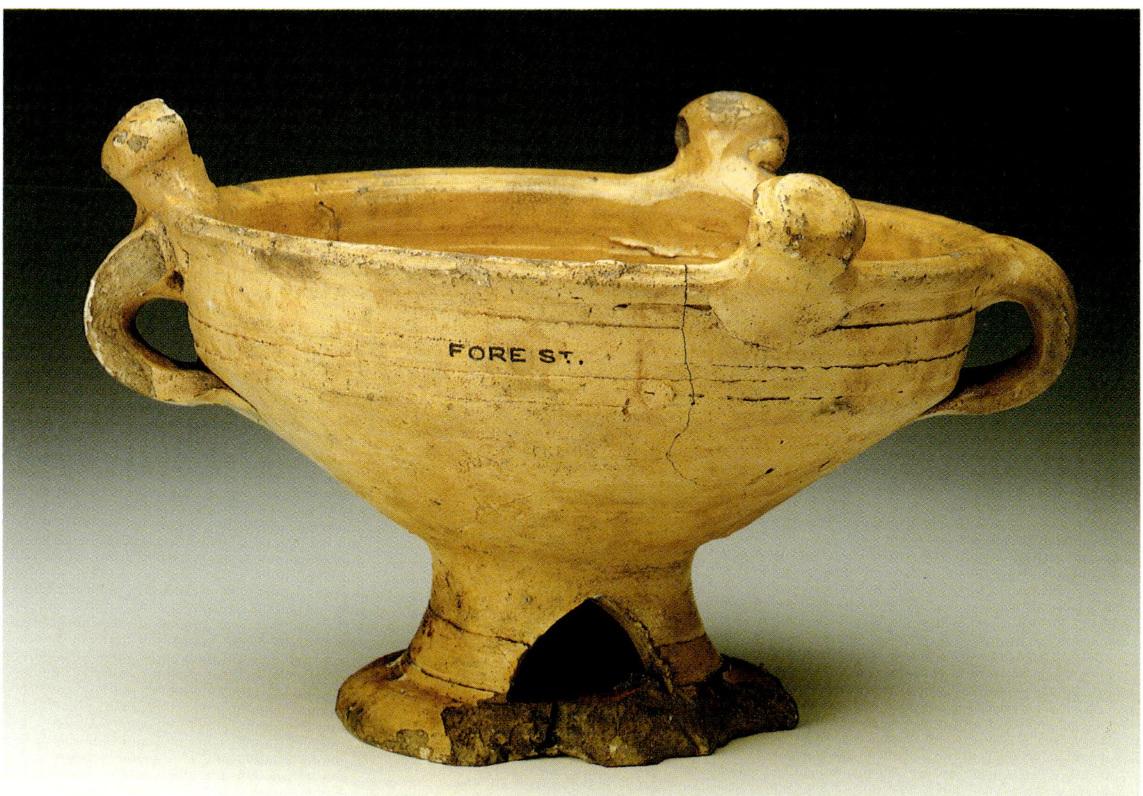

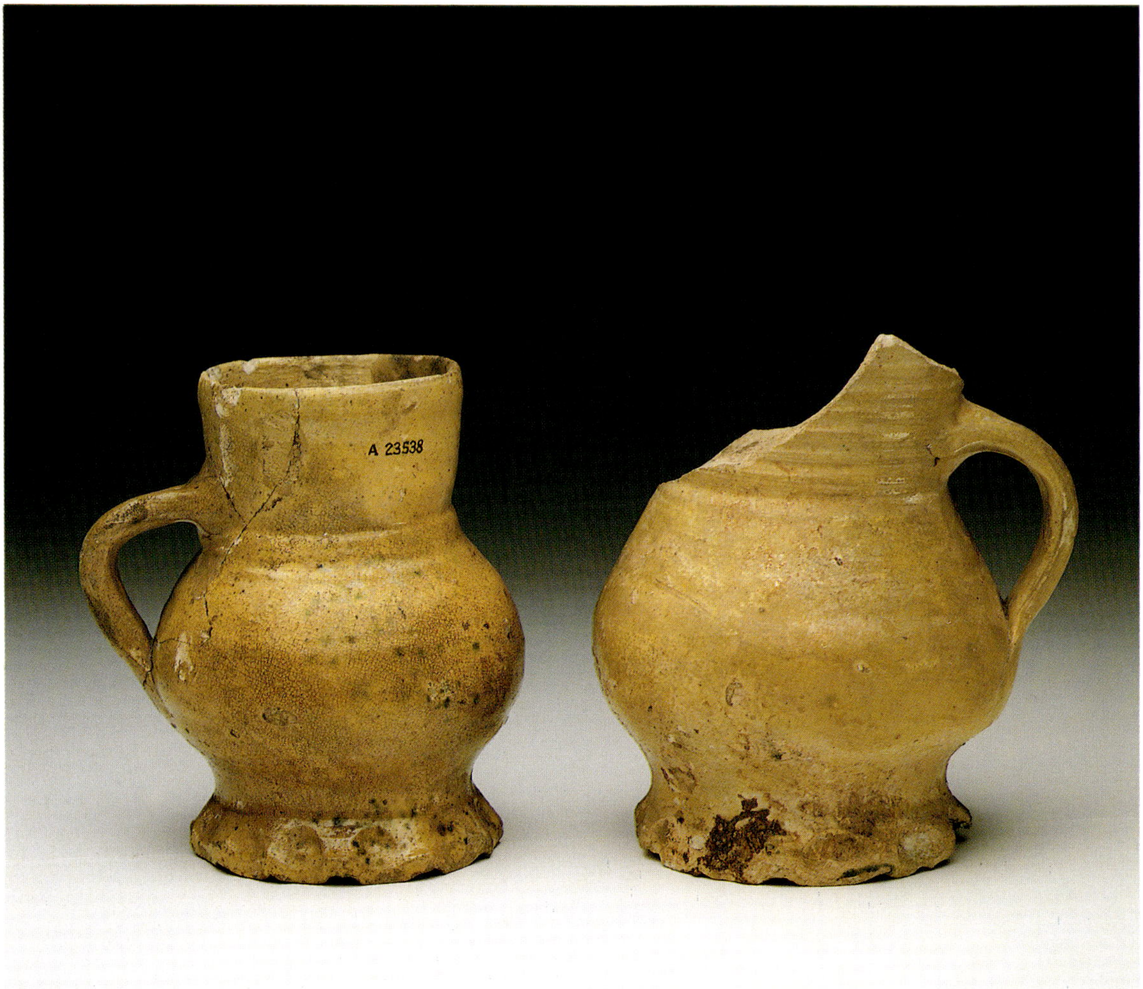

Plate 2 *Drinking jugs made in imitation of Raeren stoneware (vessel on left, height 120 mm)*

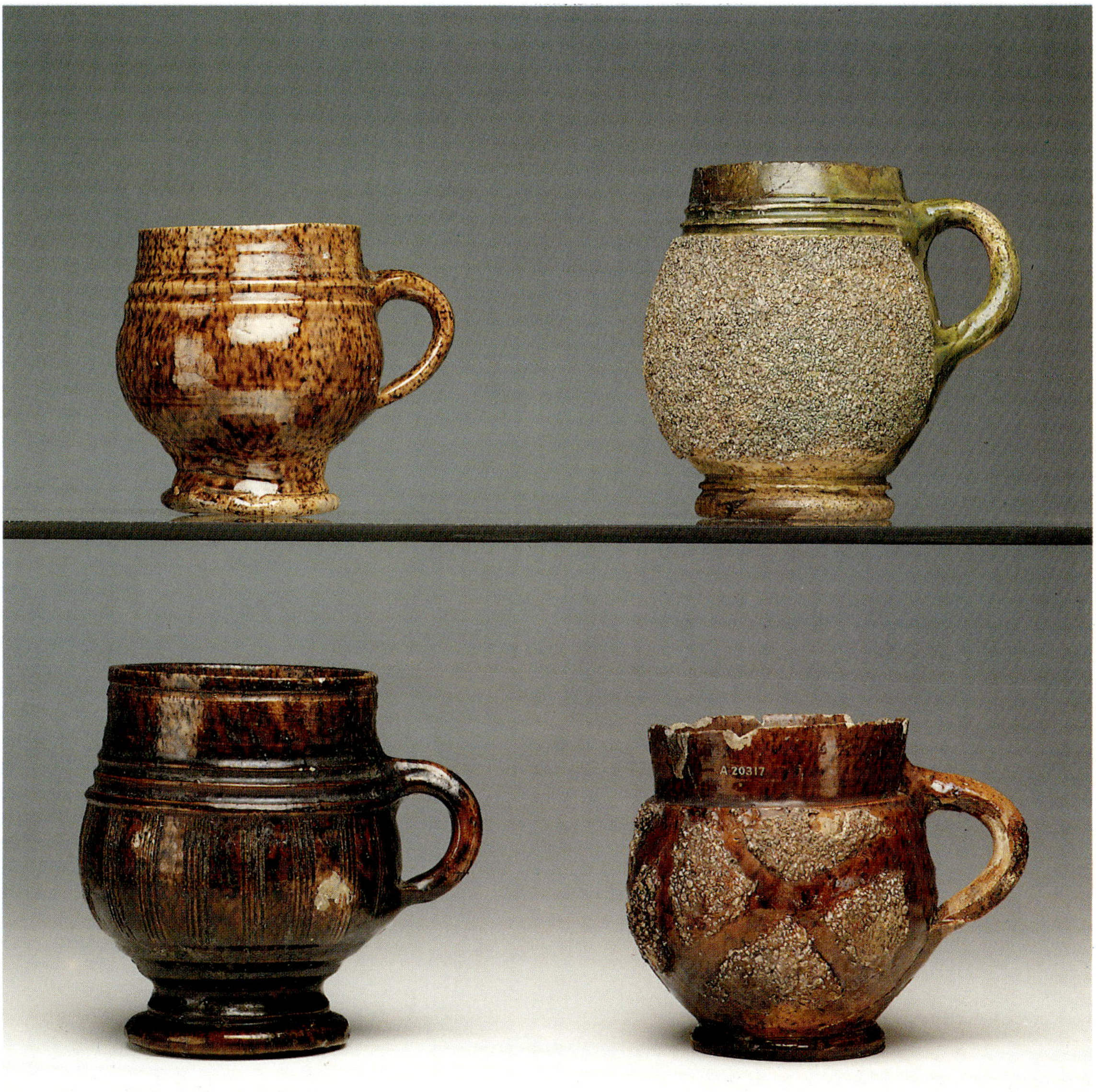

Plate 3 *Mugs with incised and encrusted decoration dated to the mid- to late 17th century (height of vessel top right, 112 mm)*

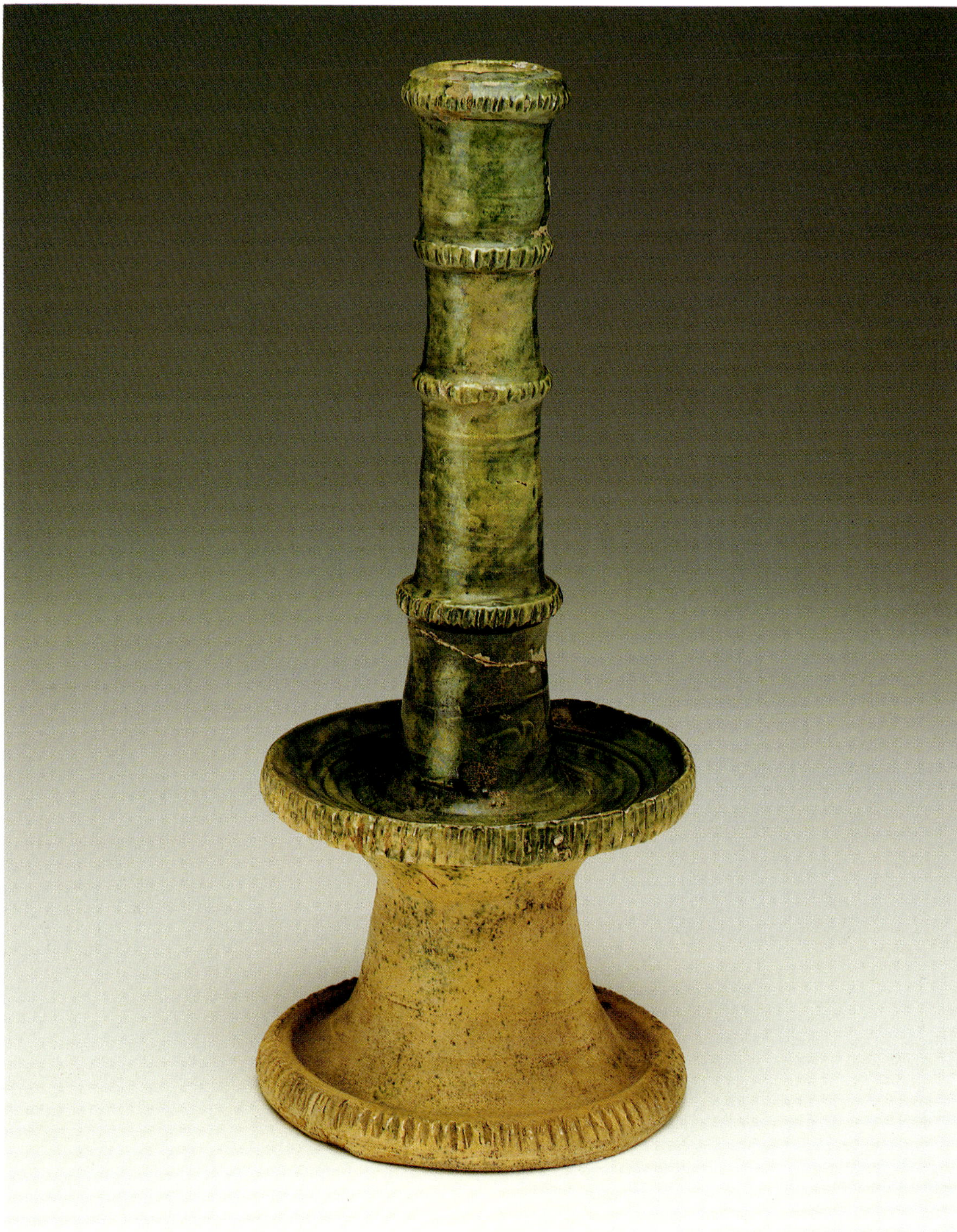

Plate 4 *Tall ornamental candlestick (height 276 mm)*

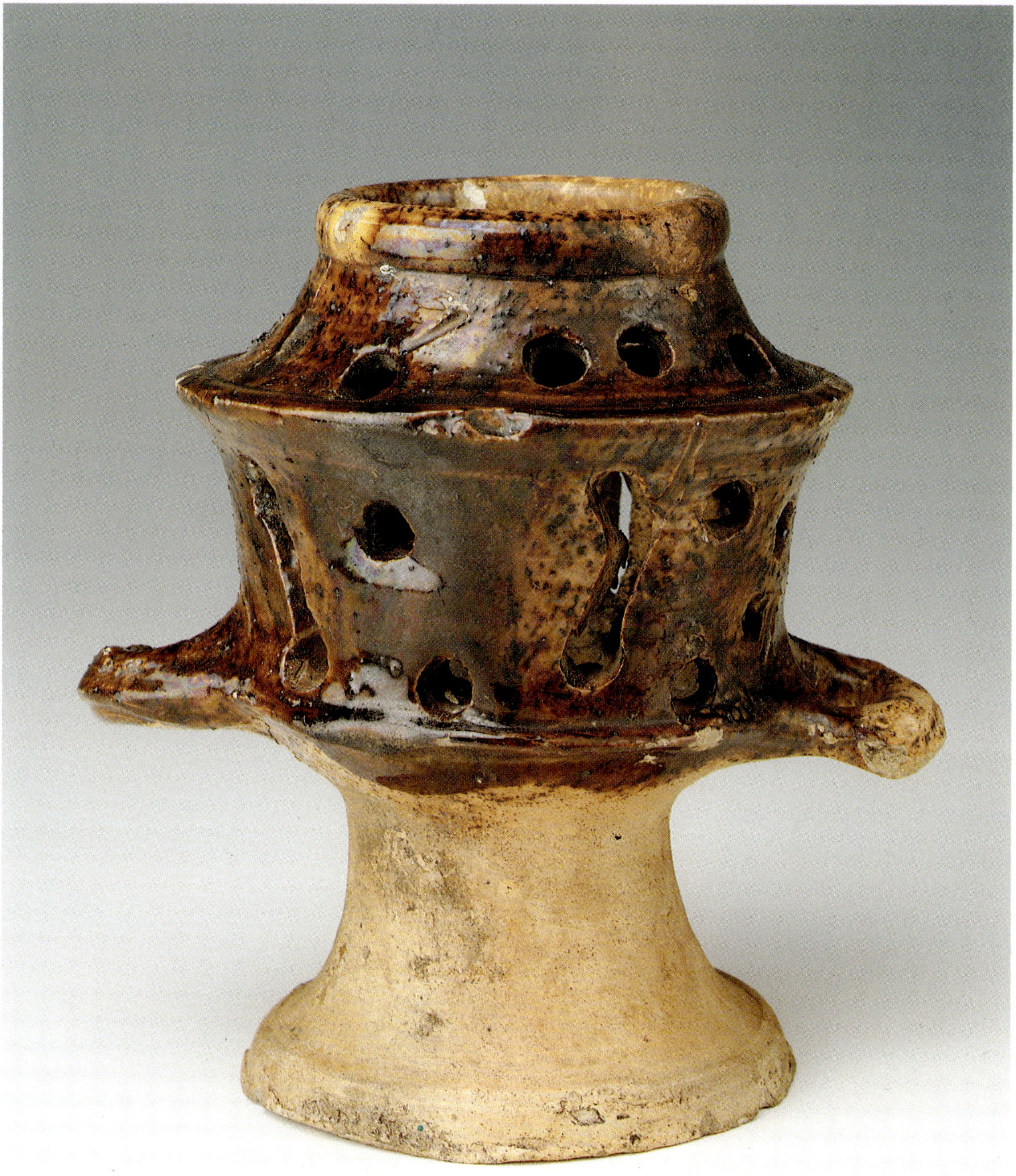

Plate 5 *Fuming pot (height 148 mm)*

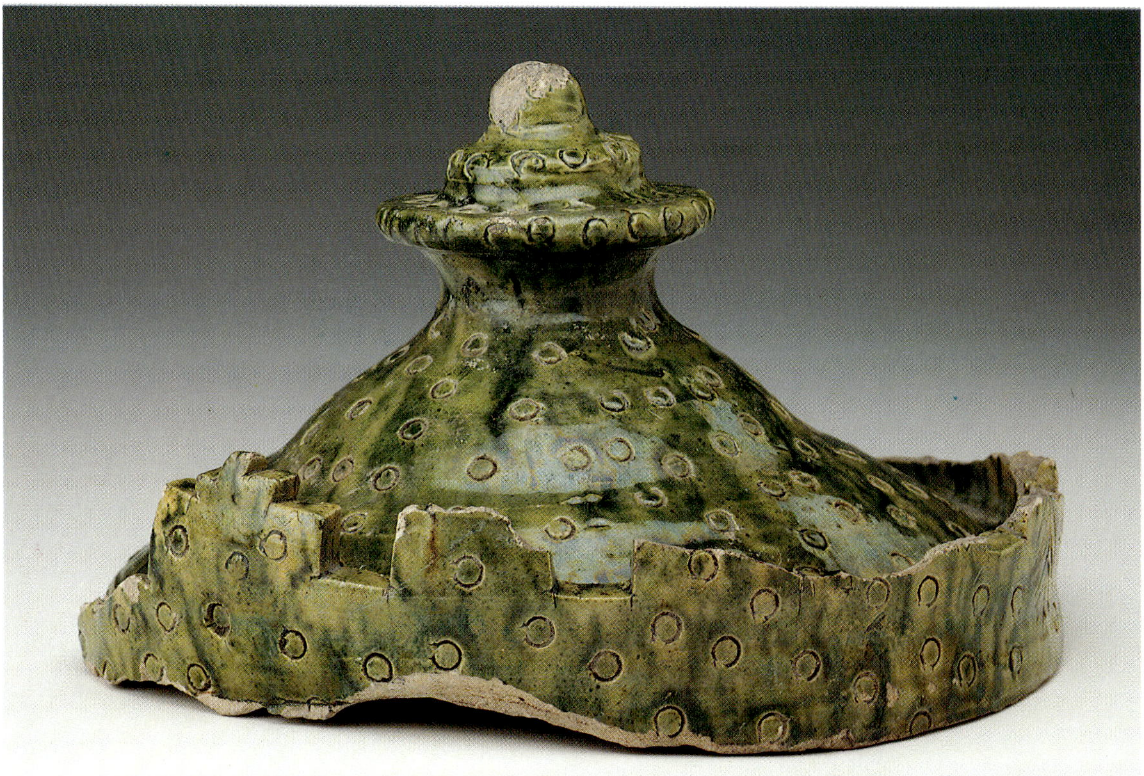

Plate 6 *Large ornamental lid (diameter 200 mm)*

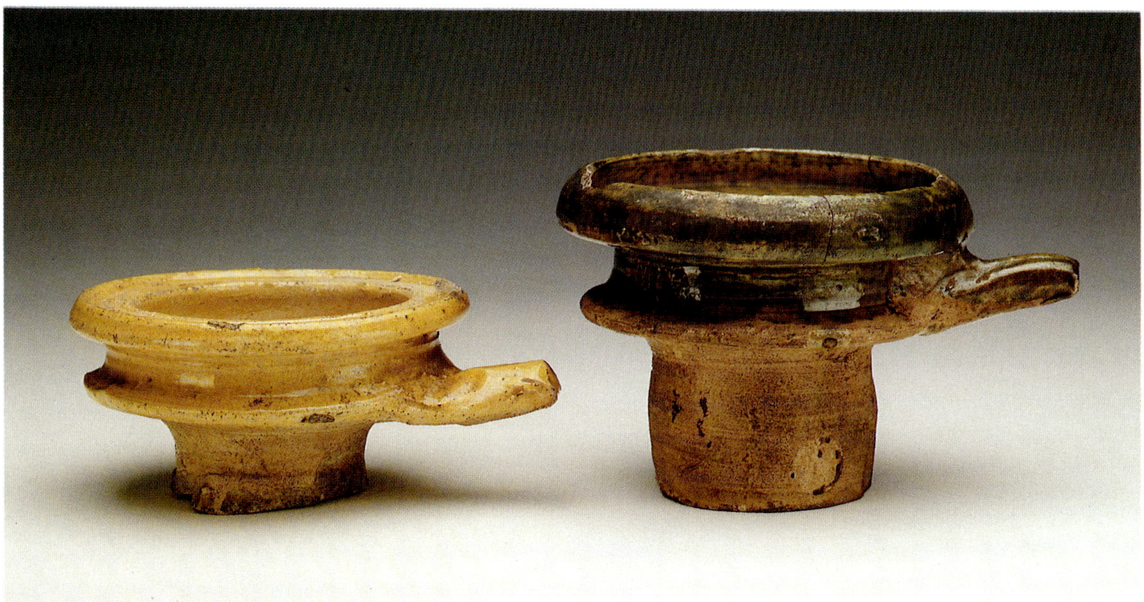

Plate 7 *Unidentified vessels (left, height 48 mm)*

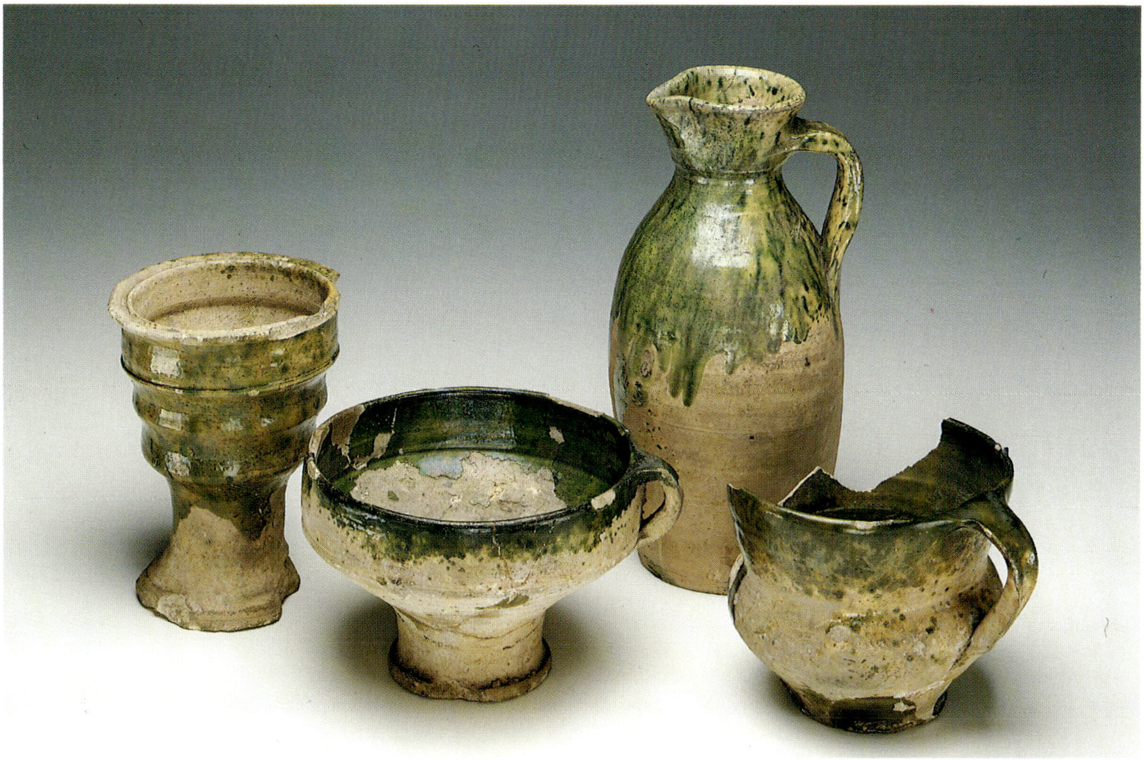

Plate 8 *Early 16th-century 'Tudor Green' ware vessels from London. From left to right: goblet (height 124 mm); cup (height 84 mm); rounded drinking jug; cup (height 92 mm)*

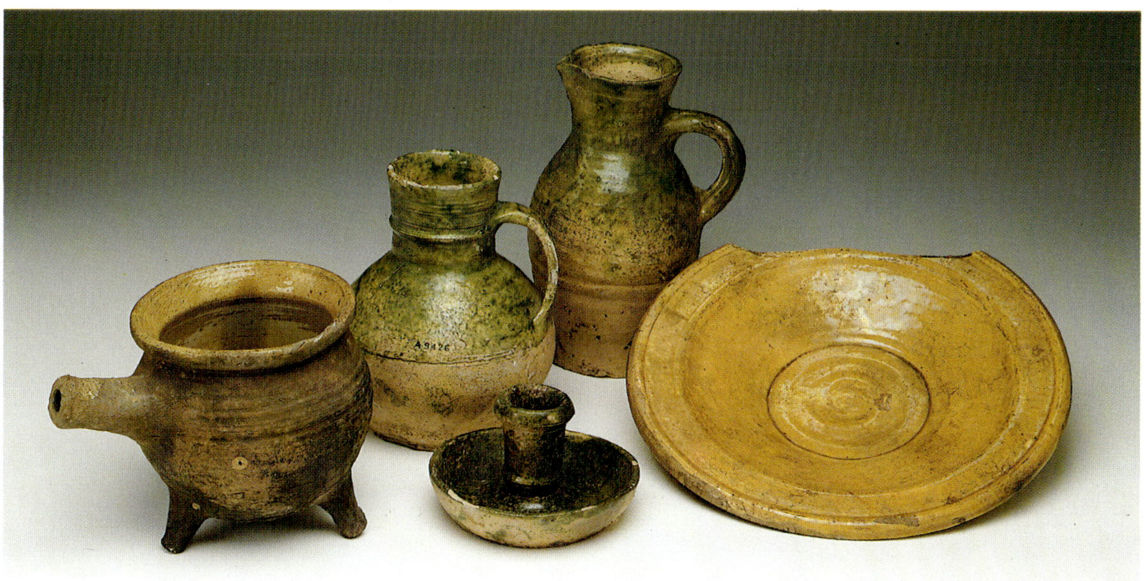

Plate 9 *Late 16th-century Border ware vessels from London. From left to right (clockwise): tripod pipkin (height 120 mm; globular drinking jug; rounded drinking jug; flanged dish (diameter 224 mm); saucer candlestick (height 64 mm)*

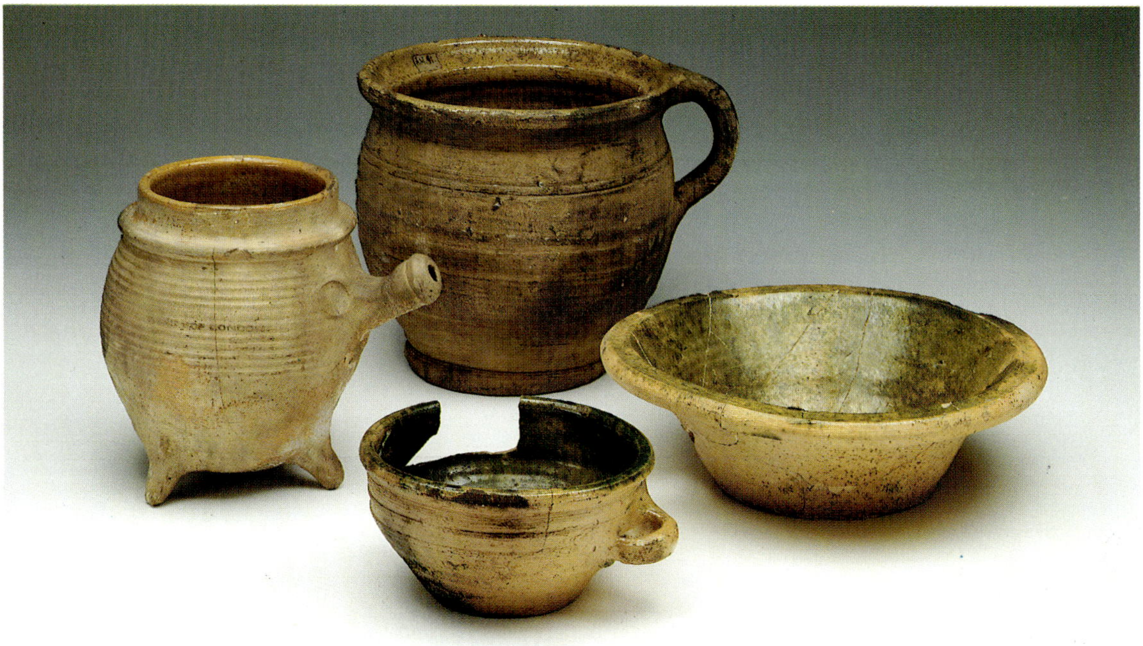

Plate 10 *Mid-17th-century Border ware vessels from London. From left to right (clockwise): tripod pipkin with external lid seating (height 140 mm); Type 1 chamber pot; wide bowl (diameter 216 mm). Front: porringer*

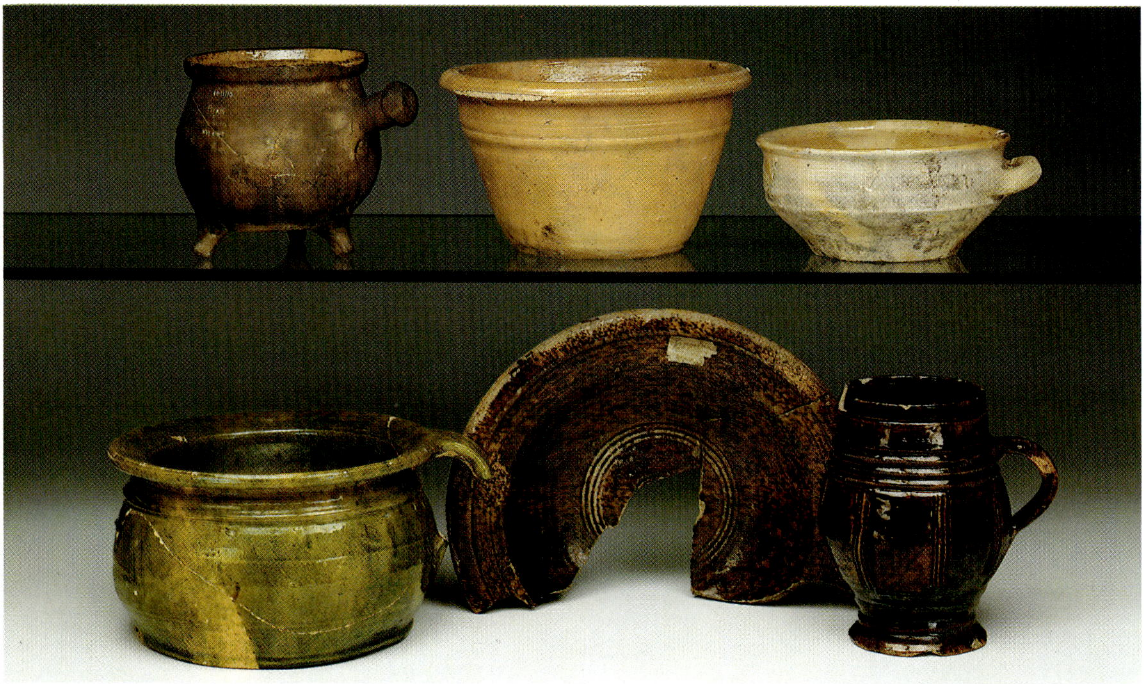

Plate 11 *Late 17th-century Border ware vessels from London. Top row, from left to right: tripod pipkin (height 120 mm); Type 3 deep bowl (height 112 mm); porringer (height 68 mm). Bottom row, from left to right: Type 2 chamber pot; flanged dish; mug*

History and Development

· 6 ·
Technology

Methods of manufacture used by the Border ware potters are described in detail throughout the Description and Type-Series in Chapters 2–5, and it is not necessary to repeat that detailed information here. Rather, the technological scope of the industry is outlined, tracing developments in potting from the medieval Surrey whiteware industries. The range of techniques, from clay preparation to firing, which were widespread within the Border ware tradition, were by no means limited to that tradition; nor were they distinctive in themselves. Future work should concentrate on the kiln material if the 'trademarks' of individual kilns or potters are to be recognised. However, the examination of such a large body of material as has survived in London is valuable in demonstrating the technological repertoire and accomplishments of the industry as a whole.

Clay Preparation

It has already been suggested (Chapter 1) that white- and red-firing clays were mixed to produce the pale orange-red fabric typical of Red Border ware. Holling records this practice at Wrecclesham in Surrey where, until relatively recently, white-firing clay from Farnham Old Park was mixed with Gault Clay to give greater porosity (Holling 1971, 63). The mixing of different clays to improve handling was known to potters in other parts of the country in the late 17th century, as is attested by Dr Robert Plot, in his *Natural History of Staffordshire* of 1686 (Brears 1971, 87–8). There is also documentary evidence for the mixing of clays by London Tin-glazed ware potters in the 17th century (Edwards 1974, 19; Britton 1987, 12). Both cursory examination and petrological analysis of the redwares from Farnborough Hill and Cove suggest that coarser cooking and storage vessels were made from unmixed red-firing clay, while a mixed clay was more often used for finer tablewares such as dishes and porringers, which tend to have a paler fabric colour. The clay was not always mixed very thoroughly, as is shown by off-white or buff streaks and patches within the fabric. Moreover, although the process of clay preparation and cleaning generally succeeded in removing coarser inclusions, some vessels survived firing with large quartz inclusions still in their fabric. Evidence for the presence in the clay of organic matter, which burnt out in firing, may also occasionally be seen in the form of small blackened holes, grooves and impressions on the surface. A number of whiteware pots, found in London and in the kiln groups, have smears and small lumps of red clay, other than kiln scars, which suggests that both clays were used in the potting area at the same time.

Manufacture

All but a few Border ware forms (see below) were thrown on a fast wheel. This is shown by the close-set, parallel, horizontal throwing-marks which are clearly visible inside, if not outside, almost all thrown vessels. Subsequent treatment of the external surfaces often obscured any throwing-marks, which would in any case have been undesirable, particularly for finer tablewares. Throwing-marks also tend to be more prominent, or ridged, inside relatively tall, narrow, or more enclosed forms, such as drinking jugs or straight-sided jars, in which there was less room for the potter to work. Spiral marks, left by the potter's thumb as the ball of clay was opened on the wheel, remain inside the base of most pots, and show that the wheel had made several revolutions by the time the sides were drawn up (Fig 47). Evidence for shaving or turning of the base-angle of most forms, rather than knife-trimming, suggests the use of a wheel which could be stopped and started easily and which revolved at some speed (Van Der Leeuw 1975, 75).

Certain forms have fine diagonal stretch-marks

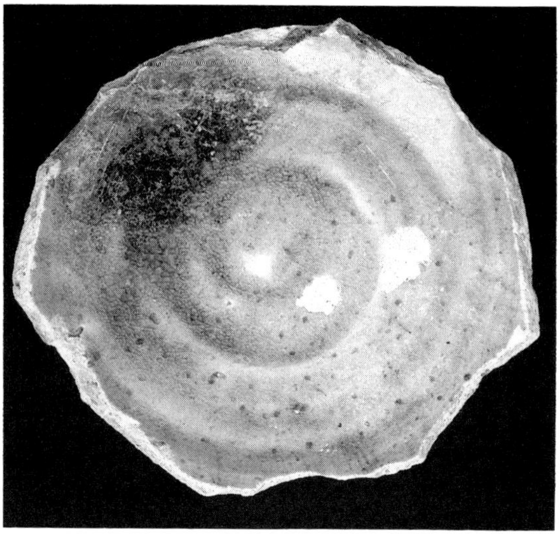

Fig 47 *Detail inside tripod pipkin base showing throwing spiral and collection of glaze*

or striations inside, and sometimes outside on constricted parts of the body (e.g. Fig 31, Nos 198, 201; Fig 33, Nos 228, 232; Fig 41, Nos 341–5). Particularly susceptible were drinking jug necks, money-boxes, mammiform and bottle-shaped costrels, upright candlesticks, forms with a pedestal base, goblets, and even the thrown handles of tripod pipkins. Sometimes faint stretch-marks can also be seen inside larger, more open forms such as chamber pots and tripod pipkins, where the clay has been drawn inwards to the rim to form a neck or constriction. However, the evidence is much clearer when parts of the body have been squeezed more noticeably. Similar stretch-marks, are also known on medieval Surrey whiteware forms such as baluster jugs and money-boxes (Pearce and Vince 1988, 7–8) and may be a particular feature of fine white-firing clays, known to be more temperamental to handle than red clay (Holling 1971, 64–5). Moorhouse (1971a, 184) suggests that stretch-marks or striations were a characteristic of Beauvais jugs from northern France, and were not found on material from Farnborough Hill. However, unpublished pottery from this site (in Castle Arch Museum, Guildford) does include vessels with stretch-marks. Moreover, the wide range of Border ware forms listed above (in addition to drinking jugs) with these markings, clearly shows that the clay used by the Border potters responded in the same way as the ostensibly more plastic French clays. The skill of the Border potters in throwing the white-firing clay of the Reading Beds is especially evident in some of the high quality, top-of-the-range tablewares, particularly drinking vessels made throughout the 16th and 17th centuries.

The number of piece-formed Border ware vessels from London is relatively small. The main range of products were thrown in one piece, but certain forms were finished by the application of secondary thrown parts. The bases of chafing dish and fuming pot bodies, above the pedestal base,

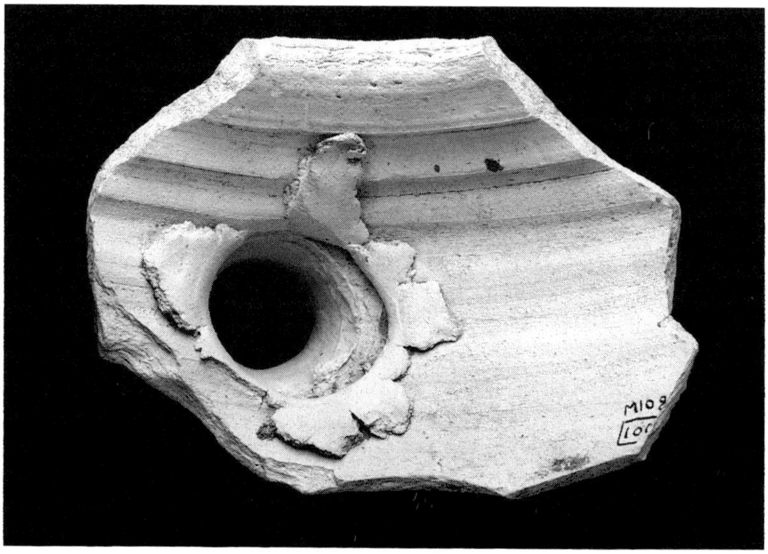

Fig 48 *Detail inside mammiform costrel showing neck attachment*

were formed by discs of clay applied separately while the vessel was being turned. Mammiform costrels were thrown as enclosed forms to which a separate neck was added (Fig 48), and saucer candlesticks appear to have been made in two parts, with the socket joined to the saucer on the wheel. The enigmatic 'chicken feeders' consist of three to four thrown rings inside a shallow dish, again attached while the vessel was being turned on the wheel. The only other piece-formed vessels are the double dishes with their sub-rectangular, main dish and applied secondary compartment. Entirely slab-built vessels are extremely rare in London; the only forms recognised to date are a strainer and the more elaborate, decorative lobed dishes.

The standard Border ware base-form as thrown is either flat or slightly indented or 'kicked'. The only forms which were regularly knife-trimmed are dishes and some bowls. Although it was often necessary to reduce the thickness of clay around the base, this was not easy to achieve on very shallow flatwares by turning or shaving, which was normally used for deeper vessels or hollow forms. Dishes were therefore removed from the wheel-head and the surplus clay pared off by hand with a knife or similar tool, in a series of overlapping arcs. This trimming method was common on medieval pottery from the London area, particularly on sagging or convex bases. In the Surrey whiteware tradition, it can be seen on a wide variety of Kingston-type and Coarse Border ware forms. However, Cheam whiteware vessels were seldom knife-trimmed and many were clearly turned (Pearce and Vince 1988, 8). It is this method of removing the unwanted clay inevitably left around the base-angle which appears to have been used by the Border ware potters, for whom the convex base was an alien form. The pot would have been inverted on the wheel and lightly shaved with a trimming tool. The practice is not always easy to detect, but can often be inferred from a 'clean' base-angle with no sign of knife-trimming by hand. A slightly raised, smooth band just above the base-angle, only a few millimetres in depth, is a further indication of shaving. Externally thickened bases, with a rounded, bevelled or faceted external profile are also found on certain forms, notably goblets, cups, mugs, bottle-shaped costrels, globular drinking jugs, chamber pots and forms with pedestal bases. Sometimes the foot was so widely splayed when

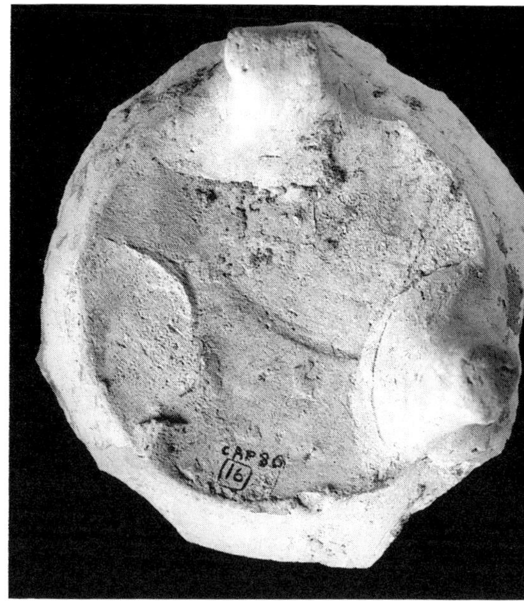

Fig 49 *Detail underneath tripod pipkin base, showing attachment of feet*

thrown that the clay was folded up and inwards around the circumference, rather than removed by trimming or turning. This recalls the method of forming a folded rim, and would have given a more stable, heavier footing to the pot. The thickened, folded base was often shaved as well. Pedestals are either open at the base (for example, on upright candlesticks) or closed, and finished as described above (for example, on chafing dishes, fuming pots and pedestal dishes or cups). In the case of candlesticks, it was often necessary to trim the inside of the pedestal by hand. Some forms, cooking pots for example, were not carefully finished and may not be trimmed or shaved at all, surplus clay around the base simply being wiped up the sides. Tripod bases are almost entirely limited to cooking vessels made to stand directly over embers or coals: that is, tripod pipkins and skillets. In all instances, the feet are relatively short and stubby (Fig 49) as opposed to the long, heavy legs of Kingston-type and Coarse Border ware cauldrons (Pearce and Vince 1988, fig 96, nos 483–9). Thumbed bases are extremely rare in Border ware. The medieval fashion was outmoded by the 16th century, and restricted to drinking jugs copied from an anachronistic Continental tradition which did not otherwise form part of the Border ware repertoire.

Evidence for the methods used to remove pots from the wheel-head may survive as faint marks underneath the base. However, these are often obscured by subsequent treatment, such as knife-trimming or turning, the addition of feet, or by an accumulation of clay waste and rubbish picked up from the floor of the workshop or drying area. The commonest method of removal was to draw a taut wire straight across the wheel-head, under the base when the wheel was stationary or rotating slowly. This left a series of parallel, straight or slightly curved lines in the clay, with shallow drag-marks from inclusions pulled along by the wire (Brears 1974, fig 4a). A second kind of removal mark is fan-shaped, radiating from a single point on the circumference (Figs 50–1). This was probably formed when the potter pulled the wire round as he sliced the pot from the wheel, rather than drawing it straight across. It is similar to but not quite the same as the mark left by slicing with an encircling wire (ibid., fig 4b), in which the wire was looped around the base of the pot and constricted. There are very few bases which show the regular, deep spiral marks which result from the use of a twisted wire (Fig 52), a method which appears to be used rarely before the mid-18th century. Sometimes concentric markings running all the way around the base, and over existing removal marks, indicate that the base as well as the base-angle had been shaved while the pot was inverted on the wheel. Such markings are not common. It was not possible to link any particular method of removal with individual forms, and the one which was used probably depended more on the potter than on the form of the pot.

The range of Border ware rim forms was fairly limited by comparison with medieval Surrey whitewares. Rims tended not to be elaborate, or to require complex forming, and were generally well adapted to the function of the pot. Simple, unthickened, rounded rims were usual for drinking vessels other than goblets, and were ideally suited to this purpose. In this, they contrast with the thickened rims of Kingston-type ware and Cheam whiteware drinking vessels (Pearce and Vince

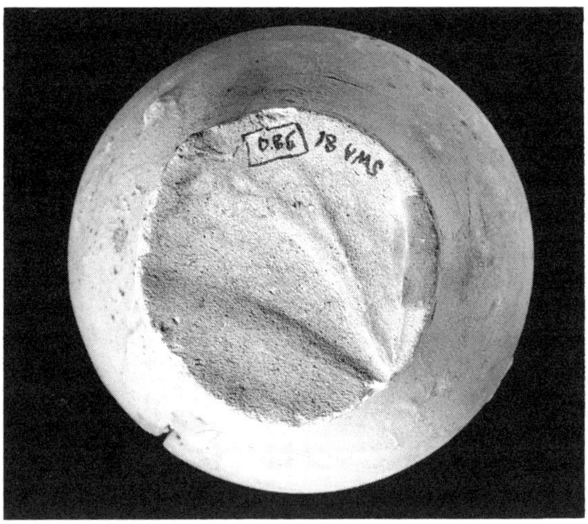

Fig 50 *Detail underneath base of money-box showing marks left by removal from the wheel*

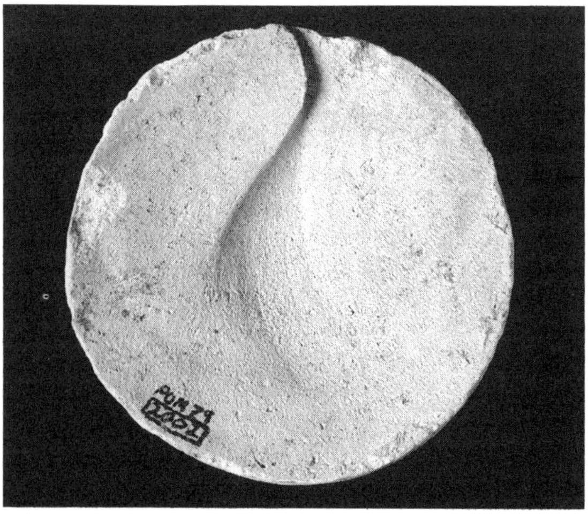

Fig 51 *Detail underneath base of drinking jug showing marks left by removal from the wheel*

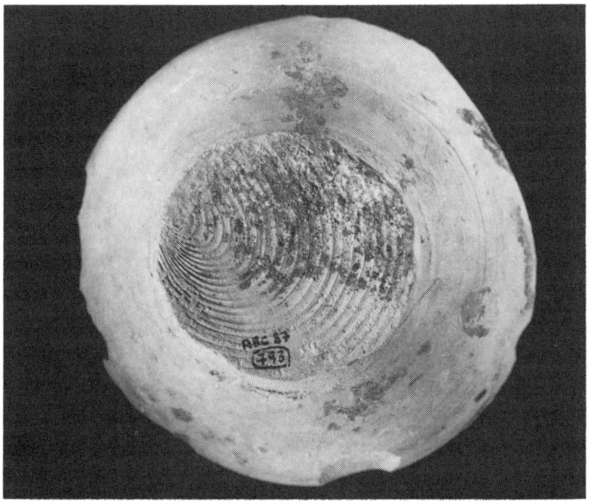

Fig 52 *Detail underneath base of money-box showing marks left by removal from the wheel with a twisted wire*

1988, figs 88, 122). Thickened rims with various profiles – triangular, bevelled, flat-topped, squared – were made on most other forms, and would have required relatively simple finger positions in throwing. Folded rims, beaded or rolled, or shaped with a tool, are also easily and quickly made, and are found on a variety of forms. Broad flanges with a rolled or beaded edge are found only on flanged dishes. Lid-seating, either internal or external, was provided mainly for cooking vessels such as tripod pipkins. However, it was not necessary for vessel rims to have the pronounced internal ledge, step or external flange typical of many of these cooking forms for them to have accommodated a lid. Internally bevelled rims would also have been suitable for a lid where appropriate, and lack of evidence by archaeological association must not rule out the provision of lids for more unlikely forms. For example, some chamber pot rims are well suited to house a lid.

The various methods used to attach handles can be a good indication of the potting tradition to which they belong. There has, to date, been little comparative study of such details of manufacture for the post-medieval pottery of the London area. However, some information is available for the medieval period, and comparison of Border ware handle attachments with methods common between the 13th and 15th centuries reveals some interesting developments. In all the major medieval pottery industries supplying London, that is London-type ware, Mill Green ware and Surrey whitewares, handles were generally secured by some form of disruption or breaking of the vessel wall (Pearce 1984). Handles which are simply luted or pressed on to the body are uncommon and mostly restricted to small or miniature forms, Cheam whiteware small barrel-shaped jugs, for example (Pearce and Vince 1988, 73). Drinking vessels made in 'Tudor Green' could not have withstood any vigorous methods of attachment and their handles were accordingly luted on to the body. By the time the Border ware industry was fully established, this was the only method used for all the main forms of handled vessel. Vertical loop handles, of various sections, were made principally for drinking vessels, chamber pots and certain forms of bowl, chafing dish and candlestick. Horizontal loop handles were preferred for porringers, but are also found on bowls, chafing dishes and fuming pots. Both forms were luted on to the body at one end and smoothed all around the join. At the other end, they were either thumbed, leaving a single impression (Fig 53), or wiped to each side (Fig 54). For all forms, wiped handles are more common than thumbed; indeed, this method may be seen

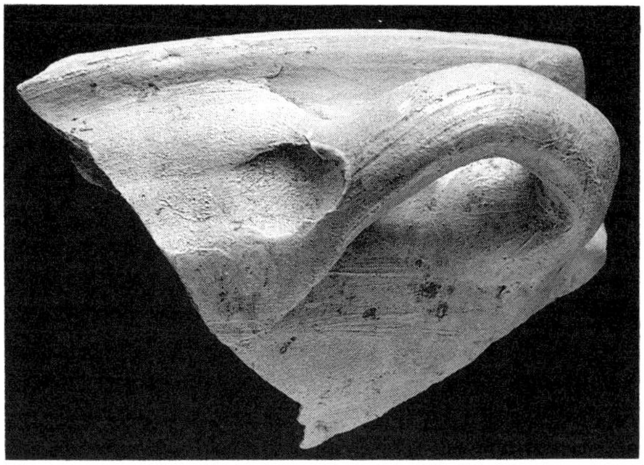

Fig 53 *Detail of porringer handle showing thumbed attachment*

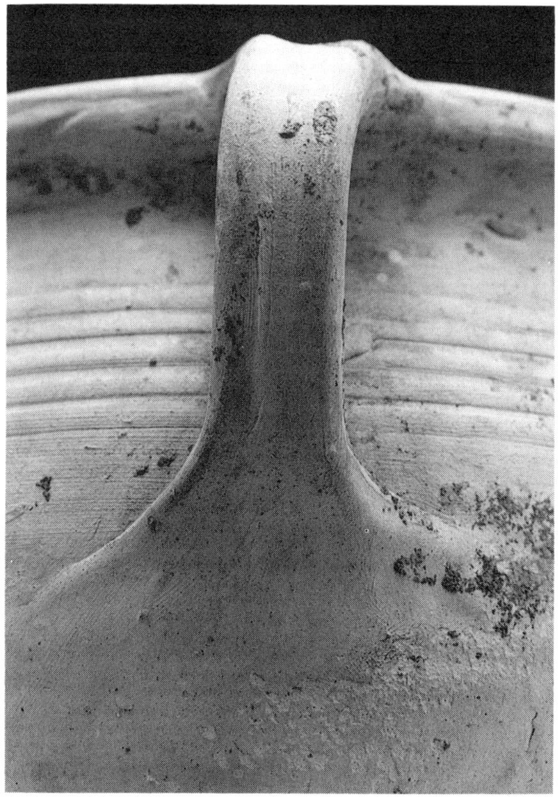

Fig 54 *Detail of chamber pot handle showing wiped attachment*

as characteristic of the industry. There is little evidence that additional pads or strips of clay were used to wrap round, join or fill in the gap between handle and body, as was common on medieval jugs (Pearce 1984, 19). There is also little evidence that the surface of the pot was prepared in any way, although attachment over rilling or grooves and ribs may have made for a more secure join. Simple, solid horizontal handles are restricted to small cooking vessels, such as skillets. Thrown tubular handles were the norm for tripod pipkins and were again attached without breaking the wall of the vessel in any way, in spite of their size. Handmade pierced lugs are found only on costrels.

Finishing

Few Border ware forms were very carefully finished. The greatest care and attention was lavished on the various thin-walled drinking vessels, particularly mugs, whose appearance and aesthetic appeal were obviously important. The delicacy and quality of the very fine 'Tudor Green' cups of the 15th and early 16th centuries remained unsurpassed throughout the life of the industry. However, the major output of the Border potteries, from the late 16th century onwards, was for kitchen and general household use, and quantity rather than quality was the main concern. Knife-trimming and shaving or turning are discussed above, but it is not uncommon for finished vessels to have crumbs, encrustations and lumps of clay picked up from the workshop. Such manufacturing detritus was subsequently liable to be covered in glaze. Greater care was given to the appearance of visible external surfaces, although many handles were applied quickly and were not carefully smoothed around the join. Internal surfaces, when not obviously visible to the user, were not cleaned or tidied after pieces were joined or the walls perforated. Finger- and palm-prints, dents and surface smears are found to some extent on most forms. Lids and saucer candlesticks are often noticeably warped.

Decoration

Following the trend towards utilitarian pottery established by the later medieval Surrey whitewares, there was little call for the purely decorative in the 16th- and 17th-century Border ware industry. Decoration was limited to certain tablewares, and the repertoire of techniques was much narrower than in the high medieval period, characterised by the exuberant ornamentation of many Kingston-type ware jugs (Pearce and Vince 1988, 35–45). Incised or combed decoration in simple linear or curvilinear patterns was used by the Border ware potters on flanged dishes and mugs. Horizontal bands of incised lines or simple grooves may also be seen on drinking jugs and even cooking vessels, but the decorative effect is minimal, and they frequently had the practical purpose of indicating the level of handle attachment. The only other forms of decoration are pinching of dish or bowl rims to produce a piecrust effect; encrustation, which is restricted to mugs; and rouletting, or notched decoration, and ring-and-dot stamping, both of which are extremely rare on vessels from London.

Glaze

The majority of forms were glazed on one surface alone; in the case of externally glazed vessels, this was generally only partially covered in a well-defined zone. There is no evidence for splash-glazing. The control over the area glazed and the even cover achieved suggest that liquid glaze was painted or poured over internal surfaces and swilled round to coat them. The best quality and most completely glazed forms, such as mugs, were probably dipped. Haslam suggested that the glazes used by Border ware potters were fritted in a separate kiln and mixed in powdered form with water (Haslam 1975, 167). There is, however, no evidence from any of the kiln sites for frit or fritting kilns, and it is equally possible that powdered lead or a lead compound was used, mixed with slip. Iron-rich compounds may leave dark brown or red spots and streaks in clear glazes on whitewares, and redwares. Though not widespread, this effect is noticeable on Border wares from the late 16th and early 17th centuries, both from London and the kiln groups. Some forms are quite densely speckled, and individual spots may be up to 2–3 mm across, either with a central pit or pock mark where the lead has reacted with the body of the pot, or else with a minute speck of powdered metal remaining on the surface. Late 17th-century pots from London, and from the kiln site at Ash, tend to have a more even glaze colour, without speckling. This argues for a better mixing of the glaze, and possibly for the use of frit by this date rather than earlier. Green and brown glazes were produced by the addition, respectively, of powdered copper and manganese to the basic lead glaze. There is a tendency for late 16th- and early 17th-century green glazes to be rather uneven, with some mottling, particularly at the margins of the glazed area. By the mid- to late 17th century, on the evidence from London and the kiln sites, a more even green colour was obtained. This may again suggest the use of a frit. If so, the absence of archaeological evidence for its manufacture is hardly surprising, since there are no late 17th-century kilns, and little published kiln waste from this period.

Holling has commented on the relationship between glaze colour and form, suggesting that particular colours were preferred or traditionally used for certain forms (Holling 1971, 83–4). It is appropriate to comment here on how the London material relates to these observations. In London, as at the kiln sites, green glaze was typically, but not exclusively, used for drinking vessels, such as cups, goblets and drinking jugs, which in form are a continuation of late medieval Surrey whitewares in the late 15th century. Only drinking jugs were still in use in the late 17th century. They are still predominantly green-glazed at this period, although a small but not insignificant number from London have yellow glaze. The only other forms which are generally green-glazed are money-boxes and costrels, again, direct descendants of the medieval tradition. Mammiform costrels always have green glaze, but a small proportion of bottle-shaped forms are yellow-glazed. Bowls and dishes and the various forms of cooking vessel – tripod pipkins and skillets – porringers and chamber pots may have yellow or green glaze, or the indeterminate yellow-green glaze described here as 'olive'. In all these forms, the tendency is for yellow to be the principal glaze colour, irrespective of date. Fewer than 1/3 of these vessels have green glaze, with the exception of skillets which are green and yellow in equal proportions. Olive glaze is found chiefly on tripod pipkins and chamber pots, but not to a significant extent on any other forms from London. Holling (ibid.) noted that green instead of yellow glaze was generally used for the most developed form of chamber pot, with a flat-topped rim (Type 2), dated to the late 17th century, and this is confirmed by the London evidence. Candlesticks may be green- or yellow-glazed, but a higher proportion are green than in the above mentioned forms. Brown glaze is generally restricted to forms used at the table: mugs, flanged dishes, wide bowls and porringers. With the exception of mugs, for which brown is undoubtedly the preferred colour, all these forms are more commonly green- or yellow-glazed. Bichrome glazing is unusual, but again follows the tradition of medieval Surrey whitewares, for example Kingston-type ware metal-copy baluster jugs and Coarse Border ware lobed cups (Pearce and Vince 1988, 20, 66–7). The only forms from London to carry more than one glaze colour are a small number of mugs and two jars. Glaze colours used on Red Border wares seem to have the same significance as they do for whitewares. The majority of vessels have clear or green glaze, appearing khaki or olive, with little discernible relation to date or form. The exception is again provided by mugs which typically have a brown-stained glaze in common with their whiteware counterparts.

Firing

Collections of liquid glaze and runs and dribbles of glaze can indicate the way in which pots were stacked in the kiln for firing. Certain forms appear generally to have been placed in an upright position. Settling of glaze inside the base and glaze-runs from the rim downwards are common on drinking jugs and mugs. Such forms were probably safer standing on their bases, but not all were fired in such a position. Forms which were commonly stacked in an inverted position include tripod pipkins and chamber pots, as shown by glaze running from base to rim and drips of glaze around the rim. However, it would be dangerous to make too firm a generalisation, since there is evidence that all these forms were fired in a variety of positions, as most conveniently accommodated in the kiln. Glaze-runs and settling of glaze also shows that many flatwares such as dishes and bowls, as well as many saucer candlesticks and porringers, were laid in a slightly tilted position, resting on the rim or side (Fig 47).

Kiln scars, common on all forms, are frequently found around the rim or under the base, appearing as circular scars, or impressions from the rim of an

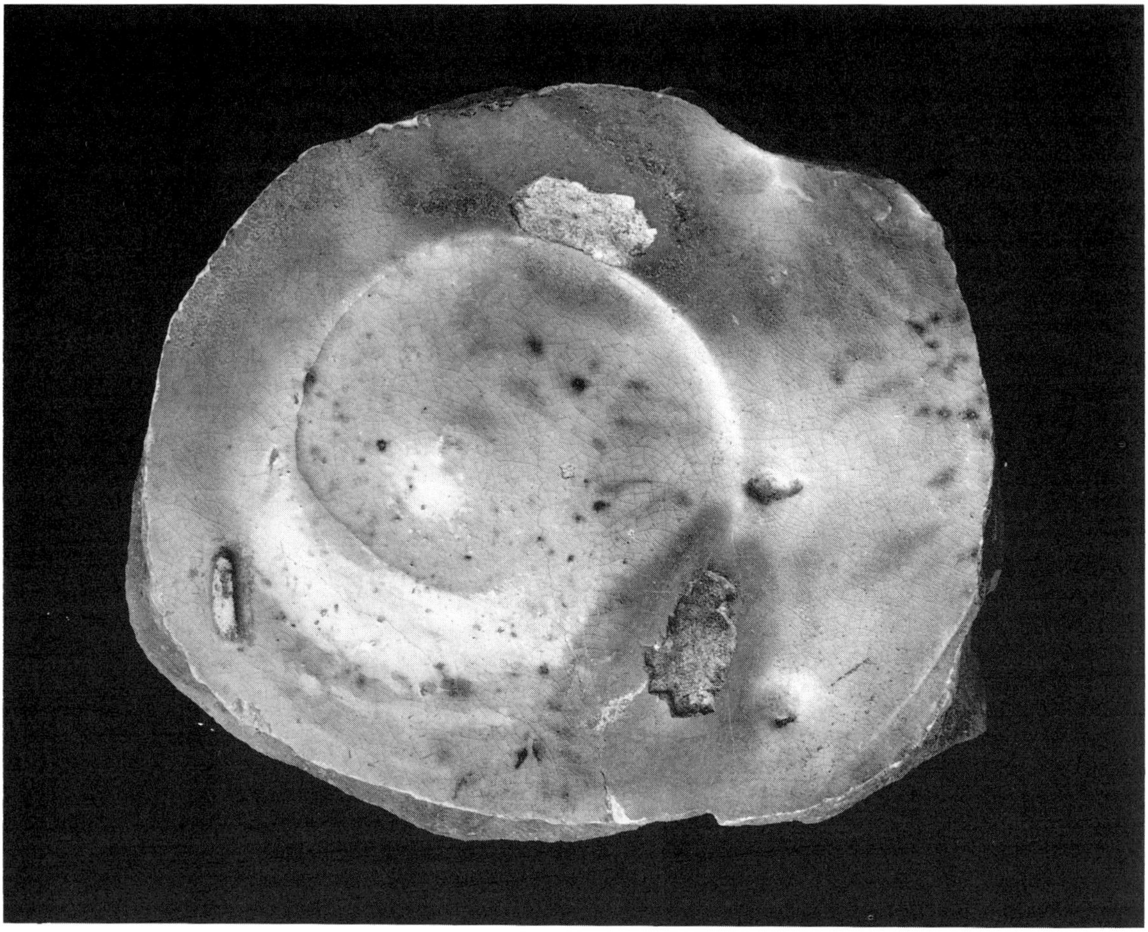

Fig 55 *Detail inside base of tripod pipkin showing marks left by ring-prop*

underlying pot. However, scars are also found in other positions. Together with accidental glaze-runs of a different colour from that intended, they show clearly that pots with all the main glaze colours were fired at the same time as a standard practice. Patches of an alien glaze often spread from a kiln scar. Although manganese-stained glaze was limited principally to mugs and certain tablewares (see above), brown spots, patches and spreads are found on most other forms, from chamber pots to cooking vessels. This suggests that vessels belonging to the finer end of the range were made and fired together with more utilitarian household products, and illustrates something of the diversity of the individual potting centres. A potter or a production centre might specialise in one form in particular, as in the case of mugs at Cove, but this by no means limited the scope of their total output. Moreover, both redwares and whitewares were stacked together in the same firing, as shown by scars of red-firing clay on whiteware vessels and vice versa. On this evidence, it might be suggested that the co-operative use of kilns by a number of potters was practised in the Border ware industry, as discussed by Peacock (1982, 126–7) in relation to samian production at La Graufesenque. More work is required on the known kiln sites, and the considerable quantities of pottery produced by some of them, in order to clarify the picture.

There is no evidence for the use of saggars at any of the kiln sites. Ring-props made in both red- and white-firing clay were found at Ash (Holling 1969, 28, fig 7, K1, K2) and in large numbers at Hawley (Castle Arch Museum, Guildford). A number of vessels found in London have three or four light scars left in a circular pattern by the use of such props (Fig 55). These are found either inside the base of large vessels, such as tripod pipkins or chamber pots, or underneath the base of smaller forms, such as mugs, which were either stacked upright on the base of a larger, inverted pot, or inside it. Additional evidence for this comes from a yellow-glazed tripod pipkin with brown glaze spread around each of the internal scars. There are also examples from London of white clay ring-prop scars underneath a Red Border ware saucer candlestick, and of red clay scars inside a green-glazed whiteware chamber pot.

Holling has shown that the late medieval finewares or 'Tudor Green' from Farnborough Hill were biscuit-fired (Holling 1977, 63). There is no evidence that this practice was still in use by the time the Border ware industry was fully established in the late 16th century, or later, nor would it have been necessary for the more robust wares made in that industry. Holling has also suggested, on the basis of experimental firings, that the whitewares had a very narrow tolerance of kiln temperatures, between 900°C and 1000°C (Holling 1971, 64). Harder, higher-fired whitewares tend to have a greyish surface and margins, and clear glaze accordingly appears olive. Grey patches on the surface are quite common, probably resulting from smoke inside the kiln during firing, rather than from any subsequent usage. Both whitewares and, to a greater extent, redwares may have lighter or darker patches in the fabric, demonstrating an uneven firing.

· 7 ·
Chronological Perspective

Examining the Data

The dating of each assemblage included in this book is considered in the site summaries (Appendix 1) and is based largely on a combination of documentary and stratigraphic evidence, ceramic spot dates and, more closely datable finds such as tokens and clay tobacco pipes. The dating adopted, such as 'early 16th century' or 'mid-17th century', represents convenient groupings of excavated contexts for the purposes of discussion and is explained more fully in Appendix 1. It is unfortunate that there is an imbalance in the number and size of assemblages available for comparison during the 16th and 17th centuries. Those selected as the basis for this series of volumes are stratigraphically sound and undisturbed. However, more large assemblages, many of which come from brick-lined cesspits sealed by the Great Fire, are available for the mid-to late 17th century than for earlier periods. This renders quantitative comparison difficult and must be borne in mind when considering the conclusions drawn from the quantified data. Moreover, it was not possible in the time available to quantify fully the pottery from all the assemblages included here. With the exception of a number of mid-17th-century and Great Fire groups, only the major wares – Border wares, Post-medieval redwares and Tin-glazed wares – have been quantified as yet. The Border ware data are presented as a series of histograms in the following discussion. These must be viewed in conjunction with the text as certain less common forms are apparently over-represented in the figures. For example, there is an unusually high proportion of candlesticks and money-boxes in the late 16th-century group (see p 94). It must be stressed that the relative proportions of forms given in this chapter are based on excavated material and are not the same as those based on the corpus given in the Description and Type-Series (Chapters 2–5). Form codes in Figs 57, 59, 61, 63 and 65 are given in Appendix 3.

It is difficult to determine the average survival rate of any particular form. Cooking vessels are more substantial than drinking vessels and therefore more durable, but were subjected to heavier, more vigorous use, rendering them more vulnerable to damage. Tablewares and finer quality wares may be more susceptible to the dictates of fashion, but are also liable to have been treated more carefully and kept longer because of their intrinsic appeal. The composition of any one assemblage does not necessarily, therefore, accurately reflect the state of the market. With these caveats in mind, it is still possible to build a general picture, to detect trends within the ceramic market, to make comparisons with kiln groups and to note the presence of new forms and features.

Origins and Affinities of the Border Ware Industry

The medieval industry

The Border ware industry forms part of a long continuum of potting in the region of the Surrey–Hampshire borders, and can, in a wider context, be seen as the post-medieval development of the flourishing Surrey whiteware tradition. Kingston-type ware started production in the first half of the 13th century (Pearce and Vince 1988, 82–9) and gained a large market in the capital which came to an end by the beginning of the 15th century. By this time, the only Surrey whitewares in circulation were Cheam whiteware and Coarse Border ware, which is the commonest type of pottery found in 14th- to 15th-century excavated assemblages from the city of London. The two industries produced complementary ranges of pottery, Cheam concentrating on tablewares, such as jugs and drinking vessels, and the Border potters on larger forms for cooking and storage. High quality, fine, untempered tablewares were made in all three Surrey whiteware industries, particularly from the late 14th century onwards. Grouped together under the misleading term 'Tudor Green', these finewares continued in production at least until the late 15th and probably into the early 16th century, by which time Coarse Border ware is rare in London, and probably residual.

The early 16th century

The history of the post-medieval Border ware industry in the first half of the 16th century remains obscure. No kiln groups dating to this period have yet been recognised, and inferences about developments in this crucial, transitional stage must be drawn from a few scattered sites in London and elsewhere. Large, coarse cooking forms in the medieval tradition were still made at Farnborough Hill in the late 15th century (Holling 1977), but were phased out of production during the first half of the 16th century, and were no longer being made by the time the known Border ware kilns were operating during the second half of the century. The decline in coarseware production must have been influenced, at least in part, by a fall in demand for the range of cooking pots, cauldrons and pitchers, which formed the main output of the late medieval industry.

London was always the major outlet for Surrey whitewares, but during the 15th and 16th centuries the cooking and storage requirements of Londoners were largely met by the various redware industries situated closer to the capital. Between them, they produced a wide range of household pottery and were quick to respond to changes in ceramic fashions prompted by new methods of cooking and food preparation. During this period the increased importation of pottery from the Continent, particularly from the Low Countries and the Rhineland, also provided a great stimulus to the potters of the London area, and indeed elsewhere in the country. This was a time of great change in the English pottery industries which flourished during the more settled period of economic growth following the accession of the Tudors.

Of all the early 16th-century contexts excavated by the DUA (from seven selected sites, listed in Appendix 1), only five contained fine, green-glazed whitewares or 'Tudor Green'. These come from Baynard's Castle (BC72); Gateway House (ER161B), Rangoon Street (RAG82) and Bridewell Place (BRI78) which is dated to the 1520s by documentary and cartographic evidence. The value of these contexts is somewhat limited by their small size. The large and important early 16th-century assemblage from Mansell Street (MAN82) contained Post-medieval redwares and imports, but very little 'Tudor Green' or pottery from the Surrey-Hampshire borders. A further problem is that fine whitewares, particularly drinking vessels, are very light and fragile, and break easily into very small sherds. This can distort the statistical picture when comparison is made with more substantial vessels such as costrels, and this is reflected in Fig 57 and Appendix 3. Nevertheless, it appears that small quantities of finewares made in the same fabric and forms as found at the late 15th-century kiln at Farnborough Hill were still being sent to London in the early 16th century. There is virtually no Coarse Border ware in London at this date, and very little Cheam whiteware.

The evidence from the City, supported by limited information from the production area, suggests that the Border industry of the late 15th to early 16th centuries was characterised by specialisation and change. The introduction into the flourishing late medieval Surrey whiteware industries of high quality, thin-walled, untempered drinking vessels of various forms was very likely the result of influences from the Continent. The initial impetus may well have been provided by the migration of potters from areas which produced comparable green-glazed, fine whitewares (Moorhouse 1971a, 185; Moorhouse 1979, 57). This is supported by the close similarity in fabric and form between late 15th- and early 16th-century green- and yellow-glazed Beauvais earthenware jugs, including those with medallions (Hurst 1970–71, figs 1–23; Hurst *et al.* 1986, 106, fig 50, nos 156–7), and fine, 'Tudor Green' globular drinking jugs, as found in the late 15th-century kiln material at Farnborough Hill (Holling 1977, fig 1, nos 1–2). This form is also comparable with Cologne and Frechen stoneware drinking jugs common in the second half of the 16th century, and with the early 16th-century Cologne form (Hurst *et al.* 1986, figs 101, 106). However, the suggested connection with Beauvais provides a more likely inspiration for the Border vessels, if external influence was involved. Drinking jugs were already established as part of the medieval Surrey whiteware repertoire, and Orton

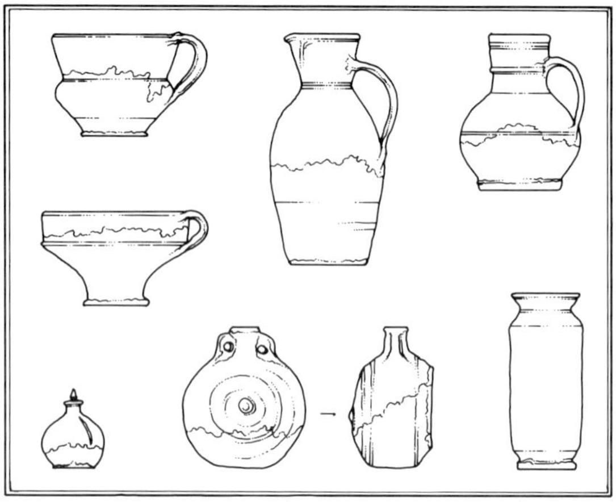

Fig 56 *The range of 'Tudor Green' and Border ware forms found in early 16th-century excavated contexts from London. (Scale 1/8)*

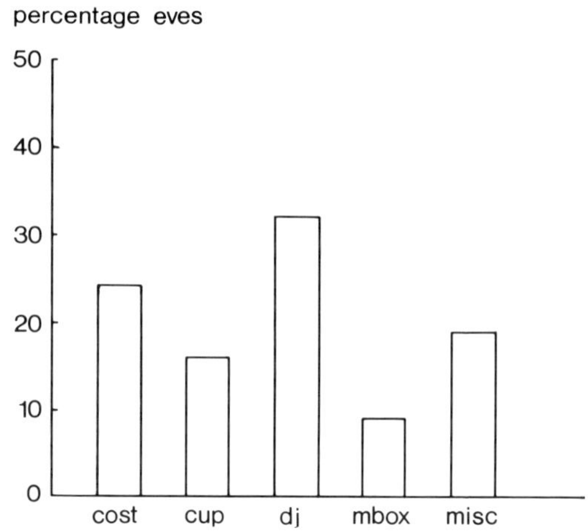

Fig 57 *Relative proportions of the main 'Tudor Green' and Border ware forms found in early 16th-century contexts from London*

has suggested that the development of the Cheam whiteware industry was partly a response to the growing demand for drinking jugs during the 14th and 15th centuries, in line with contemporaneous continental fashions (Orton 1982, 79–82). Both forms of late 15th-century 'Tudor Green' drinking jug were found in the early 16th-century assemblages from London mentioned above, although the type is not always easy to recognise from small sherds. They continued in production with little alteration in form throughout the late 16th and 17th centuries in the fully developed Border ware fabric.

Two different forms of 'Tudor Green' cups without lobes were found at Bridewell Place (Plate 8; Nos 194–7) and can be paralleled in the late 15th-century group from Farnborough Hill (Holling 1977, fig 1, nos 3–4, 7). The influence of Siegburg stoneware cups or drinking bowls, which were common in the second half of the 15th and early 16th centuries, may be seen in the form of the wide, handled cup (Hurst *et al.* 1986, 178, fig 88, no 257). Interestingly, a similar form was also made at this period in Beauvais stoneware, perhaps reinforcing the connection with this area suggested above (ibid., 105, fig 48, no 145; Morisson 1970–71, pls 6–7, 13). These 'Tudor Green' cup forms are found very rarely, as small sherds, in late 16th-century contexts in London, where they are probably residual. There is no evidence that they were made at any of the kiln sites at this date or later. It could be argued that finds of 'Tudor Green' drinking jugs and cups in early 16th-century contexts in London were also residual. However, the survival of similar forms in various contemporaneous assemblages elsewhere in the country suggests that they were still made at this time (see Chapter 1).

The only other 'Tudor Green' forms found in early 16th-century contexts from London are money-boxes, mammiform costrels, and possibly goblets. Money-boxes follow a long-established tradition in medieval Surrey whitewares and continue with little change in form throughout the 16th and 17th centuries. Mammiform costrels were made in 'Tudor Green' from the 15th century, but were later replaced in Border ware by the bottle-shaped form. The full range of forms found in early 16th-century contexts is illustrated in Fig 56 and Plate 8 (see also Appendix 3).

Holling has suggested that unlocated early 16th-century kilns in the Border area continued to produce finewares as part of a wider output including coarser cooking vessels and other forms, much as they had done in the late 15th century (Holling 1977, 64). This is supported by the early 16th-century finds from Guildford High Street, including vessels in 'Surrey ware' (termed fabric F in this report) which is described as finer than the medieval whiteware and which bears a close resemblance to Border ware (Holling 1984, 295, fig 1, no 2; fig 2, nos 11, 15–19, 25, 27). A small number of drinking jug sherds in a similar fabric, indistinguishable from Border ware proper, were found in early 16th-century contexts in London, both at Bridewell Place and Baynard's Castle. Part of a tall, straight-sided jar again in a similar fabric and with a thin, clear glaze comes from Gateway House, and is an unexpected find at this date, unparalleled in the late 15th- or 16th-century kiln material, or at Guildford. None of the other forms found in Guildford were recognised. These appear largely to have been made for local consumption, rather than for trade with the capital. During the first half of the 16th century, the Border industry obviously underwent great changes, its potters experimenting with fabrics, developing new forms and adapting others which had been part of their earlier repertoire. The coarsely tempered fabric (Coarse Border ware) used in the 14th and 15th centuries for green-glazed whiteware cooking and storage vessels, which had gained such a profitable outlet in the London market, was discontinued as new local industries began to take over the production of everyday domestic pottery. The fine, fragile tablewares, which may well have begun under continental influence, probably continued in production until they were replaced, by the second half of the 16th century, by the more robust pottery known as Border ware. 'Tudor Green' had a wide distribution throughout the country, but only took a small part of the lucrative London market. It was undoubtedly attractive and of high quality, but the skill, time and attention required to make and fire it would have restricted its commercial viability, especially as part of a broader domestic pottery industry. Centres producing a single whiteware fabric which could be used for a wide range of forms were better able to serve the needs of the pottery-buying public, and to gain a much larger market in the major towns and cities of the south and south-east.

The late 16th century

During the second half of the 16th century, the industry of the Surrey–Hampshire borders began to consolidate its hold on the London market. The known kilns at Farnborough Hill were producing green- and yellow-glazed whitewares in a distinctive fabric, different from the typical products of the late medieval kilns of the area. This fabric (Border ware proper) is coarser than the earlier finewares or 'Tudor Green' and forms a significant proportion of pottery from most late 16th-century assemblages excavated in London. However, none of the contexts included can be more closely dated than to the second half of the century, and some probably extend in date of deposition beyond the turn of the century. The largest single assemblage, from the Abacus House site (ABC87), contained a considerable quantity of Border ware, as well as yellow- and green-glazed whitewares with visually similar fabric from sources in the Low Countries and Rhineland. Other large assemblages come from Holy Trinity Priory (HTP79) and Leadenhall Street (LEA84).

By the second half of the 16th century, a much wider range of forms than was available in 'Tudor Green' was being made in the Border potteries and sent to London (see Fig 58 and Appendix 3). The commonest form in the assemblages from Abacus House and Holy Trinity Priory is the flanged dish, with green or yellow glaze, although the quantified data are somewhat unbalanced by the unusual number of candlesticks and money-boxes found in the former (Fig 59). Curvilinear, combed or incised decoration appears to be more prevalent at this date than later. The form of the flanged dish is a newcomer to the Surrey white-ware tradition and emerges as a ceramic equivalent to the platters and trenchers of wood and pewter commonly used at table. There is a close similarity in form between Border ware flanged dishes and plates or saucers made in pewter at least as early as the 14th century (Hornsby *et al.* 1989, figs 13–14, 36–8), and these could well have provided the stimulus for the 16th-century potters. Shallow flanged dishes, often highly decorative, were also being made in a number of other ceramic industries both in this country and on the Continent at about the same time, for example, in Werra ware (Jennings 1981, 78–9, fig 31), in Beauvais sgraffito (Hurst *et al.* 1986, fig 52, no 161), and in plain earthenwares from Duisburg (Gaimster 1988b, fig 5, no 1). The advantages of having cheap, easily cleaned pottery dishes or plates are obvious and were being widely exploited. This ceramic takeover of forms made in other materials is also reflected in the production of Border ware drinking jugs, which began to replace wooden and pewter cups at the Inns of Court during the 16th century (Matthews and Green 1969, 6). The vitality of the industry is demonstrated by its ability to respond effectively to the demand of its customers and perhaps to create or influence requirements in the develop-

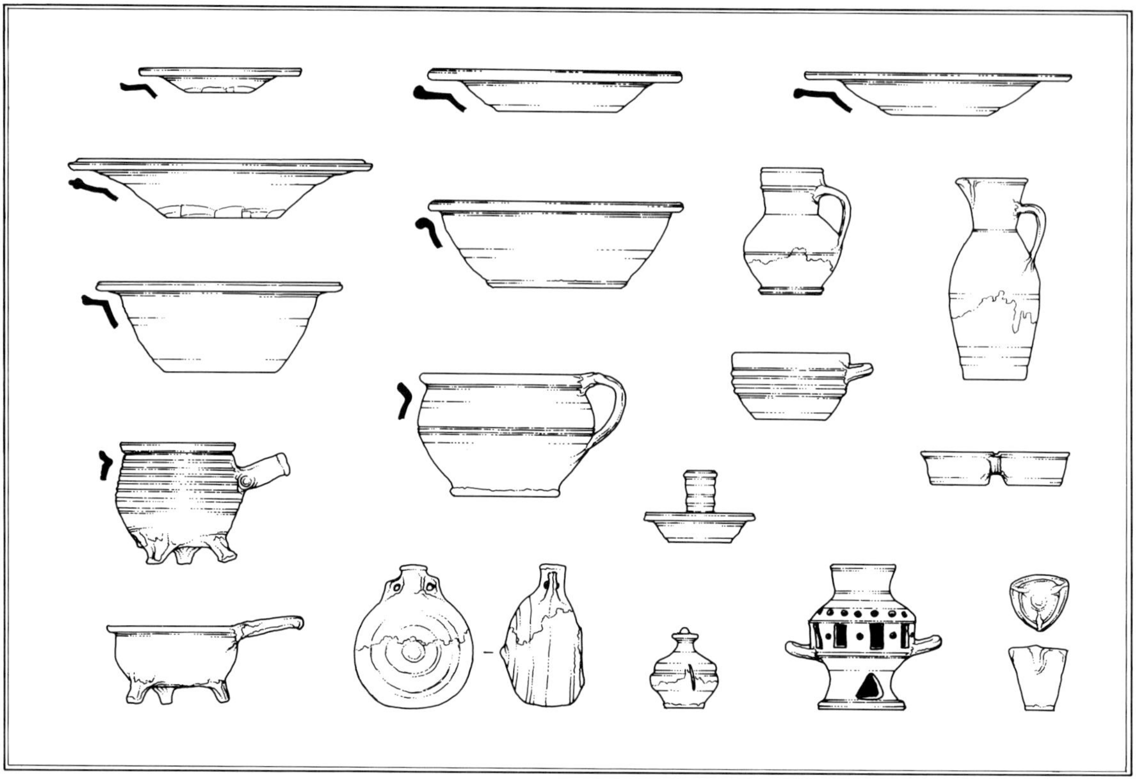

Fig 58 *The range of Border ware forms found in late 16th-century excavated contexts from London. (Scale 1/8)*

ment of a number of new forms. Its success in competition with other industries is shown by its growing hold on the London market by the end of the 16th century.

Another form which is relatively common in late 16th-century assemblages from London is the tripod pipkin (see Fig 59). During the 14th and 15th centuries, the various Surrey whiteware industries largely produced jar-shaped cooking pots without feet or handles, and cauldrons with long legs and two loop handles (Pearce and Vince 1988, fig 94; figs 114–16; fig 124, nos 564–70). Small tripod pipkins with a single solid handle were made only in Kingston-type ware (ibid., fig 95, nos 318–19). Nevertheless, it was the tripod pipkin, with short feet and a single tubular handle, which became the standard cooking pot form of the Border ware industry from the late 16th century onwards. The adoption of the tubular handle is a significant feature, since the majority of contemporaneous industries, in south-east England at least, were making tripod pipkins with a single, solid handle or one or two loop handles (e.g. Orton 1988, fig 127, nos 1203, 1214). This was also fashionable in those continental industries which were exporting pottery to Britain, such as Dutch red earthenware and Low Countries whiteware (Jennings 1981, fig 56; fig 55, nos 923–7). However, ribbed whiteware tripod pipkins with tubular handles were being made in the second half of the 16th century at Duisburg in the west German Rhineland (Gaimster 1988b, 157, fig 5, nos 2, 8). The close similarity in form to Border ware vessels makes a connection between the two industries a tempting proposition, strengthened by the presence of German and Low Countries white earthenwares, including tripod pipkins, at Abacus House in London. This raises the possibility of direct imitation or cross-fertilisation between pottery industries.

The pottery of the Low Countries and the Rhineland had a widespread effect on traditional forms of English cooking pot during the early 16th century. This was the result both of healthy trading connections and the emigration of potters from the Continent. The adaptability of the

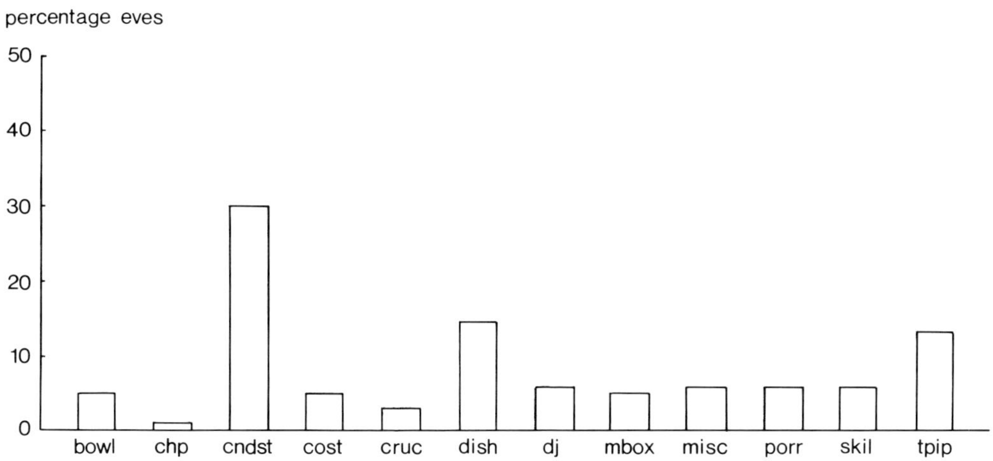

Fig 59 *Relative proportions of the main Border ware forms found in late 16th-century contexts from London*

Border industry to new fashions and trends shows that the climate was right for such influences to be absorbed. Similar forms of tripod pipkin, including those with tubular handle, were also made at this time at Fulmodeston in Norfolk (Wade-Martins 1983, fig 20, nos 136–43), a part of the country that was very open to influences from the Low Countries and the Rhineland. Against this, it must be said that tubular handles were made in late medieval Coarse Border ware on certain forms of cooking vessel, such as frying pans and dripping dishes (Pearce and Vince 1988, fig 117, nos 492–8) and were consequently part of the potting tradition in this area. Moreover, Holling notes the presence of two-handled, whiteware cooking pots apparently predating the late 16th century kilns at Farnborough Hill (Holling 1977, 66). However, this form never became popular in Border ware and it is the tubular-handled tripod pipkin which became the standard form.

Skillets are another new form to the Border industry. Their function, to heat small quantities of food or liquids, with a provision for pouring, was probably served by pipkins without feet before the 16th century. These are well represented in medieval Surrey whitewares (Pearce and Vince 1988, fig 95, nos 311–17; fig 124, nos 571–3). The adaptation of the form by the addition of feet may therefore have been a purely local innovation, although skillets with feet were also made in Dutch red earthenware in the 16th century and were imported into London and Norwich (Jennings 1981, fig 58, nos 990, 993–5). Their form, however, does not compare very closely with that of the Border ware skillets from London. The straight-sided form found in the late 16th-century kiln groups at Farnborough Hill, but not in London, is much closer in shape to the imported material (Holling 1971, fig 4, F1), but the extent of the influence of continental forms, if any, is by no means clear. It is tempting to trace influences from large and flourishing continental industries on English potteries, rather than in the other direction. Such arguments must always be treated with caution as the picture is seldom clear cut. Similarities are noted here and tentative parallels are made. In some instances similarity of forms across industries is so striking, as with tripod pipkins, that imitation or influence by one of the other seems likely. However, independent local development within existing potting traditions must also be considered.

Border ware porringers are found for the first time in London in late 16th-century contexts (Fig 59; Appendix 3). They are not present in large numbers, but examples from Leadenhall Street, Holy Trinity Priory and the site of the Horntavern Public House, Knightrider Street (TAV82), show that the form was current at this period. Early porringers with a distinctly carinated profile were made at Farnborough Hill (Holling 1971, fig 2, B1b), but not at later sites, and this form is found occasionally in London. Porringers of the fully developed and more common Border ware form made at Hawley and Cove in the early 17th century are also found in London in late 16th-century contexts. Moorhouse (1970, 53) has suggested that porringers or 'side-handled cups' were not made in this country until the early 17th century and that the English potters were inspired by contemporaneous Tin-glazed forms. Evidence from Farnborough Hill and London shows that they were introduced into Border ware during the late 16th century. Small handled bowls were made at various centres on the Continent from at least the 16th century, with notable examples in plain earthenware from Duisburg (Gaimster 1988b, fig 5, no 7) and in North Holland slipware (Hurst *et al.* 1986, 154–68, figs 77–80) which was common in the 17th century and was certainly imported into this country in the late 16th century. Examples are known in both London and Norwich, where Dutch influence was strong (Jennings 1981, 85–8, fig 34). Similar Dutch red earthenware bowls were also imported to London and East Anglia, and elsewhere, during the 16th century. They were copied in the Norwich area at the same period, in a visually similar red fabric, difficult to distinguish from the prototypes, and in other early post-medieval local wares (ibid., 157–8, fig 68, nos 1196–1201; 134–6, fig 57, nos 961–2, 965–9). The carinated shape of the early Border ware porringers bears a close resemblance to the Dutch vessels, although the English examples have a flat base and a single handle. Just as the indigenous East Anglian potters were influenced by continental fashions, the thriving import trade of London acted as a stimulus to the local pottery industries of the south-east. A further influence on the development of the porringer in Border ware and other ceramic industries may have come from pewter forms. Shallow bowls with one or two lobed handles have been dated to the middle of the 16th century and were probably current earlier (Hornsby *et al.* 1989, 40, figs 30–2). Whatever the origins of the porringer, it was quickly absorbed into the standard range of Border ware forms, assuming, at least by the early 17th century and probably earlier, the characteristic shape that remained little altered until the end of the whiteware industry.

The full range of Border ware forms found in late 16th-century contexts in London is illustrated in Plate 9 and Fig 58. Apart from those discussed above, they include wide bowls, money-boxes, saucer candlesticks, drinking jugs, crucibles; and single examples of a fuming pot, a condiment dish, a mammiform costrel and a chamber pot. With the exception of the drinking jugs, costrel and money-boxes, all these forms are new to the industry. There are at least 10 money-boxes and 14 candlesticks, including two in Red Border ware, in the late 16th-century material from Abacus House, an unusually large number for either form at any period in a single assemblage. Within each form, all the vessels bear a close resemblance to each other and they may well have been bought as a single batch; the reasons for their being discarded together remain a puzzle. There seems little doubt that they were all made at the same kiln. Finds at the various kiln sites, admittedly fragmentary, suggest that manufacture of the saucer type of candlestick was restricted to the second quarter of the 17th century, at Hawley and Cove (see p 37). Similar examples in Midlands Yellow ware have been found in Civil War debris of the 1640s in the Midlands (Brears 1971, 31, 36, type 7). It is therefore interesting to note the presence in London of this type at an earlier date, especially in Red Border ware, suggestive of undiscovered phases of production or dumps at the known kiln sites, or unknown production centres. No upright candlesticks of the type made at Farnborough Hill in the late 16th century have been found in London at this period.

Green and yellow are the only glaze colours found on any of the late 16th-century Border wares in London. The introduction of a clear lead glaze, which appears yellow over a buff body, was a feature of the development of the early post-medieval industry. Formerly, green had been the characteristic glaze colour of the medieval Surrey whiteware tradition and of the late 15th- and early 16th-century finewares. Green remained the preferred colour for certain forms, notably those most closely related to or derived from the medieval repertoire. Yellow glaze was used, although not exclusively, for the new forms. A common feature of the 16th-century Border ware glazes is their mottled appearance, suggestive of poor mixing of the raw glaze, and providing a further link with the medieval glazes. Clear or yellow glazes are often speckled with dark brown to black spots of iron-rich compound, sometimes quite large and sometimes covering the glazed surface profusely. During the course of the 17th century, there is a tendency for the glazes to be more even and better mixed. Many Border ware forms of the late 16th century also have thin walls by comparison with later 17th-century vessels, even of the same form. This again suggests a continuation of earlier 15th- and 16th-century traditions and methods of throwing into the second half of the century, although none of the pottery made at this time matches 'Tudor Green' for fineness.

Red Border ware was made at Farnborough Hill alongside whitewares, but the only examples yet found in London in late 16th-century contexts are the two candlesticks from Abacus House. The forms made at the kiln site are heavier and less attractive than the whitewares and include large storage jars and chafing dishes. They were probably made for a more local market, while industries situated nearer London provided the capital with its redwares.

The second half of the 16th century saw the Border ware industry entering the London market with a new range of forms, a relatively robust, attractive and obviously desirable fabric, stronger than the fineware which had been a speciality of the 15th- to early 16th-century Border potters. It was easier and cheaper to make and was not restricted to fragile, quality tablewares with their more limited use and appeal. The Border ware potters were, therefore, in a strong position to compete in the London market, as well as in other more local markets, where there was probably less competition. This they achieved with great success during the next century, as the industry grew, flourished and diversified.

The early 17th century (1600–c. 1640)

Just as some of the assemblages dated broadly to the late 16th century may extend in date into the opening years of the next century, so those contexts which have been given an early 17th-century date may have been deposited over a number of years and cannot be more closely dated. Large and medium-sized assemblages dated before c. 1640 were found in the New Fresh Wharf watching brief (FRE78) and at River Plate House, Finsbury Circus (RIV87) (see Appendix 1).

Although it was not possible to quantify all the pottery from most of the sites considered here, the impression gained from examination of Border ware and other major wares is that it was becoming increasingly important as a source of London's pottery during the first half of the 17th century. There are however few significant changes or innovations in the major forms found in early 17th-century assemblages. The range of forms current in London at this time is shown in Plate 10 and Figure 60.

Flanged dishes are still the commonest form (see Fig 61 and Appendix 3), continuing virtually unchanged in shape from the late 16th-century vessels found in London and in the kilns at Farnborough Hill. Rims are still relatively simple, bevelled externally. Decoration is rare, limited to curvilinear combed patterns on the flange, as seen on the late 16th-century pottery from Abacus House, and paralleled at Farnborough Hill. Bowls, however, are more frequent and varied in form than in earlier assemblages (see Figs 60–1). They include wide flanged bowls, deep bowls (Types 1 and 2), comparable with porringers in shape, and a handled bowl of the type described by Holling as a 'stool pan' (Fig 25, No 100). Tripod pipkins are all ribbed at least over the upper half of the body and have an everted rim or internal lid-seating, although no lids of this date have yet been found in London. In form, they are comparable with vessels of Holling's phase 2a, from Hawley.

There is a noticeable increase in the number of porringers found in early 17th-century contexts (see Fig 61 and Appendix 3). By this date, they have the standard carinated profile with ribbed upper half, typical of the main output from Hawley and Cove, both of which are dated to the second quarter of the 17th century. Although the form of the porringer may have been developed under continental influence (see above), by the time it had been fully integrated into the Border ware potters' repertoire they had adapted it to their own taste, so that it is clearly distinguishable from the prototypes.

There is a higher proportion of drinking jugs, of both main forms, in early 17th-century assemblages than in later material. The form is never common in excavated pottery from the city of London, although there is a considerable number in the Reserve Collection. The survival of numerous complete vessels at the various Inns of Court contrasts strikingly with the paucity of finds from excavations. It is possible that institutions such as the Inns monopolised the market for this particular form of drinking vessel and continued to maintain contracts with individual kilns, which tended not to supply the general public. The existence of agreements between the Inns of Court and the Border potteries is well attested by documentary sources (see p 3), as is the propensity of the

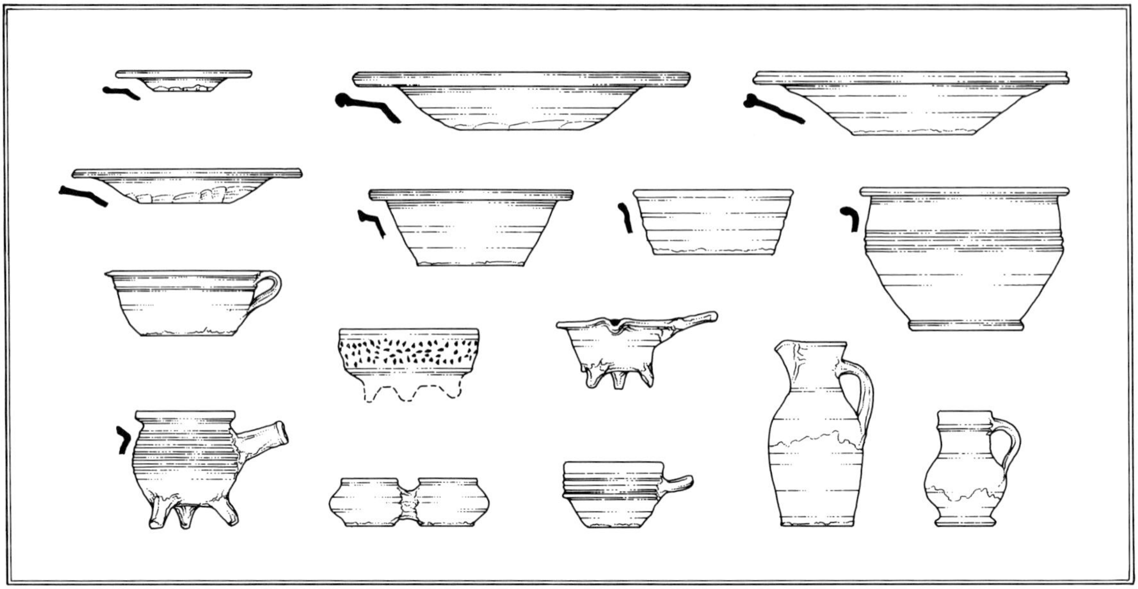

Fig 60 *The range of Border ware forms found in early 17th-century excavated contexts from London. (Scale 1/8)*

Inns to store and preserve such utensils, which has ensured their survival.

The proportion of Red Border ware in early 17th-century assemblages is minimal compared with the amount of whiteware being imported into London in this period, and in comparison with other, more local, redwares (Bown and Nenk forthcoming). The only form represented – a skillet – mirrors the whiteware forms current at this date. The predominance of whitewares is also reflected in the output of the two centres known to be producing Border ware in the early 17th century – Hawley and Cove. At Cove (Minley Road), the ratio of white to red fabrics was about 6:1 (Haslam 1975, 167). The redwares continued to be marketed over a more limited area, but as far as the London market was concerned, it was the whitewares which were considered more desirable. It was during the 17th century that the sale of Border wares in London reached its peak, only to decline in the early 18th century as redware production began to predominate.

Early 17th-century whitewares were still glazed principally green and yellow, with similar relationships between glaze colour and form as in the late 16th century. However, a small number of vessels – tripod pipkins and dishes – have the indeterminate pale yellow-green glaze described as olive, a colour not found in earlier material. Brown glaze also occurs for the first time in London, on a single porringer, becoming more common later in the century.

The early years of the 17th century, after the latest phase at Farnborough Hill and before the start of the known kilns at Hawley and Cove, are rather nebulous in terms of recognised production centres. No kilns dated firmly to the first quarter of the 17th century have yet been located. However, the picture drawn from London shows that the industry was being consolidated and was growing without any great innovations in form or technology. Rather, potters were continuing to make forms introduced in the late 16th century and were developing them as recognisable products of their own particular industry. Questions as to whether production continued at Farnborough Hill, or what other centres were in operation at this date, must await further discoveries.

The mid- to late-17th century (c. 1640–1700)

One of the largest and most important mid-17th-century assemblages comes from Capel House, New Broad Street (CAP86). Other assemblages dated to the period between c. 1640 and the Great

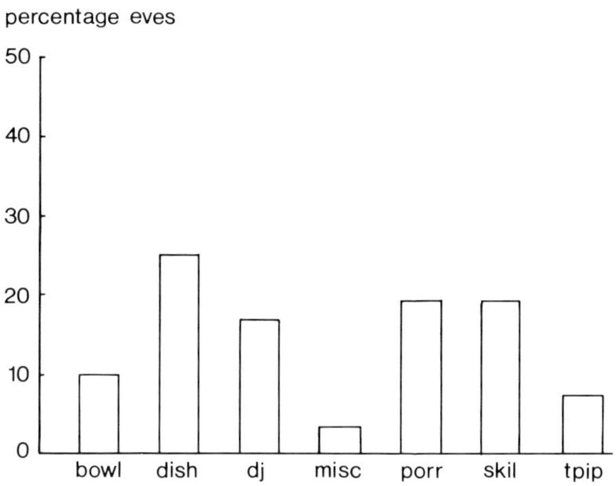

Fig 61 *Relative proportions of the main Border ware forms in early 17th-century contexts from London*

Fire come from Swan Lane (SWA81); Bishopsgate (BOP82); Lime Street (LIM83); St Peter's Hill (PET81); St Swithin's Lane (SL75); Peninsular House (PEN79); Billingsgate Lorry Park (BIG82); and Minories (MIO86) where the stratigraphic sequence extended into the late 17th century. Assemblages deposited after the Great Fire came from Ludgate Broadway (LBY85); Carter Lane (CAT86); Ludgate Hill (LGA87); Cutler Street Warehouse, Harrow Place (CUT78), and Watling Court (WAT78). A full list of sites is given in Appendix 1.

The greater number and size of assemblages belonging to the second half of the 17th century makes quantitative and qualititive comparison with earlier material rather difficult. Nevertheless, general trends can be detected, and full quantification of certain mid-17th-century contexts shows that white Border wares were the commonest type of pottery in the large assemblages from Capel House and Swan Lane (26% and 29% respectively of all pottery by 'eves' – estimated vessel equivalents). Border ware was the second most common fabric at St Swithin's Lane (29% by eves) and at Lime Street (13%). A similar trend may be seen at Aldgate (Orton and Pearce 1984, fig 30). At most of these sites Red Border ware formed a relatively small proportion of all pottery (no more than 7%), but at Swan Lane it was the second most common fabric (16%). (The full quantified record is stored in the DUA archive.)

By the middle of the 17th century, the Border industry had become one of the major suppliers of everyday, domestic pottery to London and remained so at least until the end of the century. A broadening of the range of vessels available is apparent (see Plate 11; Figs 62, 64; Appendix 3). New forms were introduced, and established forms, such as tripod pipkins, show signs of development in shape and rim form. Such changes may be the result of natural evolution at a particular production centre or may indicate an unknown source. Evidence for the late 17th-century industry in the area of production is somewhat scant. The only site where pottery dating from this period has been found is Ash (Holling 1969). However, it was not possible to conduct a controlled excavation here, and apart from a quantity of kiln furniture, no evidence for a kiln was found. The kiln sites at Cove (Minley Road) and Hawley were both probably in operation during the second quarter of the 17th century, but no good evidence for continued production in the second half of the century has been found at either site. However, although the picture from its source area is unclear, the evidence from London shows that Border ware was thriving.

The commonest Border ware forms found in London from *c.* 1640 to *c.* 1700 are tripod pipkins, flanged dishes, porringers, bowls and chamber pots (Figs 63, 65; Appendix 3; see also Orton and Pearce 1984, figs 32–3). Certain of these forms can be seen to change or develop during this period. Ribbed tripod pipkins with everted rim or internal lid-seating are still found in contexts dating to the last quarter of the 17th century. However, from *c.* 1650 onwards, vessels with plain or only slightly ribbed bodies are also found, and by the end of the century they are at least as numerous as the ribbed version (Figs 62, 64). This pattern conforms with Holling's findings in the later phases at Hawley and at Ash where the ribbed tripod pipkin was no longer being made (see p 18). The earliest occurrence of an external lid-seating on tripod pipkins from London is in the 1640s at Capel House, which is again roughly contemporary with their introduction at Cove and Hawley. This innovation probably came about as a means of providing a better seal around the rim of the cooking vessel, keeping in the heat and preventing spillage more effectively. It was used especially on larger vessels, but does not appear to have replaced the more common internal lid-seating. The earliest known lids from London also

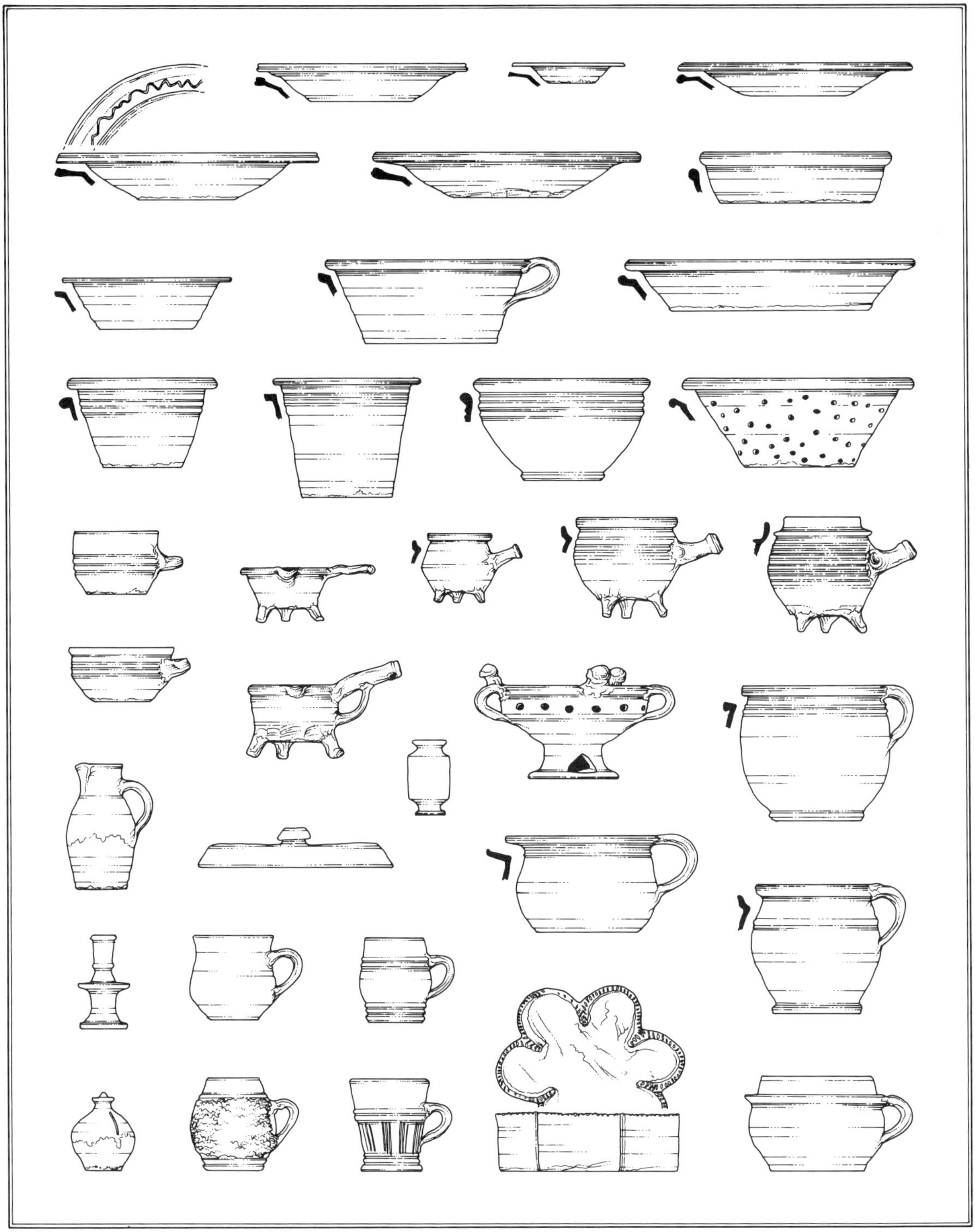

Fig 62 *The range of Border ware forms found in mid-17th-century excavated contexts from London. (Scale 1/8)*

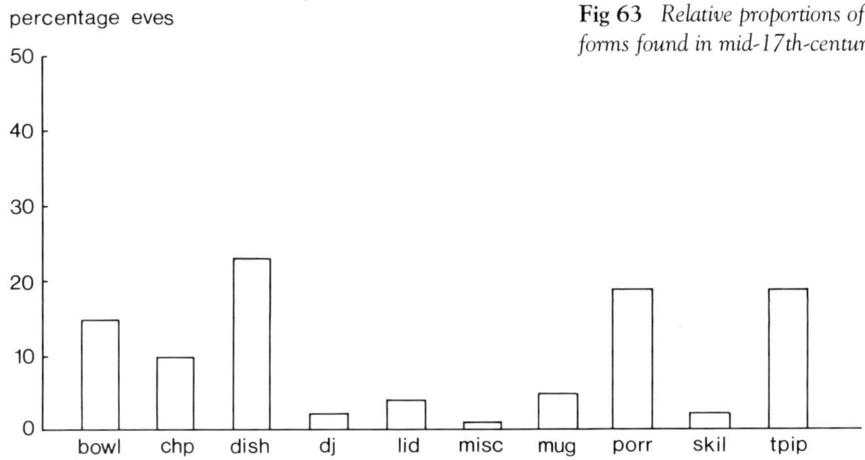

Fig 63 *Relative proportions of the main Border ware forms found in mid-17th-century contexts from London*

date to the 1640s and are of a shape and size ideally suited to tripod pipkins. With their flat or slightly domed top and straight sides, they are clearly adapted to fit over the rim of the cooking pot and to rest on its external flange, rather than inside the rim.

Flanged dishes continue throughout the second half of the 17th century with many of the same rim forms as in the late 16th century. However, a number of new forms were also introduced, including hammerhead rims, which were typical of Werra and Weser ware dishes during the 17th century (Hurst *et al.* 1986, 242–4, figs 115–17; fig 119, no 375). Combed decoration is rare after the 1640s, but pinched rims, or piecrust decoration, occur in contexts dated from *c.* 1650 onwards. This again conforms with the evidence from Hawley and Ash. Piecrust decoration is not common in the other contemporaneous pottery industries supplying London, but was known during the late 16th and early 17th centuries in north-west Europe, for example on vessels very similar in form to Border ware flanged dishes made in Weser ware and in north German slipware (ibid., 260–2, plate XVI, fig 123).

The only recognisable development in the form of the porringer is a tendency towards a plain, unribbed body, or at least less pronounced ribbing, by the end of the 17th and start of the 18th centuries. Plain porringers are found in the latest context at Minories and at Ludgate Broadway. Although chamber pots are one of the commonest forms during the second half of the 17th century, they are found only in certain contexts. This may suggest a selective pattern of disposal, since a number of cesspits contain many broken chamber pots at the expense of other forms. For example, at Aldgate, a cesspit dated *c.* 1650–75, contained a markedly higher proportion of 'sanitary wares', than any other group from this site (Orton and Pearce 1984, fig 31). Their absence from the early 17th-century contexts considered here does not necessarily mean they were not supplied to London at this date. It may simply be that the pits in which they were discarded have not been found. Type 1 chamber pots with a comparatively tall body and thickened, folded rim, as made at Hawley, are found in London throughout the second half of the 17th century. The most developed form in Border ware is seen in squatter vessels with a pear-shaped profile and broad, everted or flat-topped rim (Type 2; Figs 62, 64). Their earliest occurrence in London is in pottery from Swan Lane dated *c.* 1640–60, and they become more common towards the end of the century and into the early years of the 18th century.

The earliest known Border ware mugs from London come from Capel House in contexts dated to the 1640s. During the second quarter of the 17th century, the Cove potteries were producing a wide range of high quality mugs in large numbers. Mugs of Haslam's Types 1–3 are found in London in mid- to late 17th-century assemblages, although very few of the more elaborately decorated types are represented. Haslam has drawn attention to the close parallels between Type 1–3 mugs from Cove and vessels of the same types made in Tin-glazed ware at Southwark and Lambeth and dated between 1628 and 1642 (Haslam 1975, 184–5,

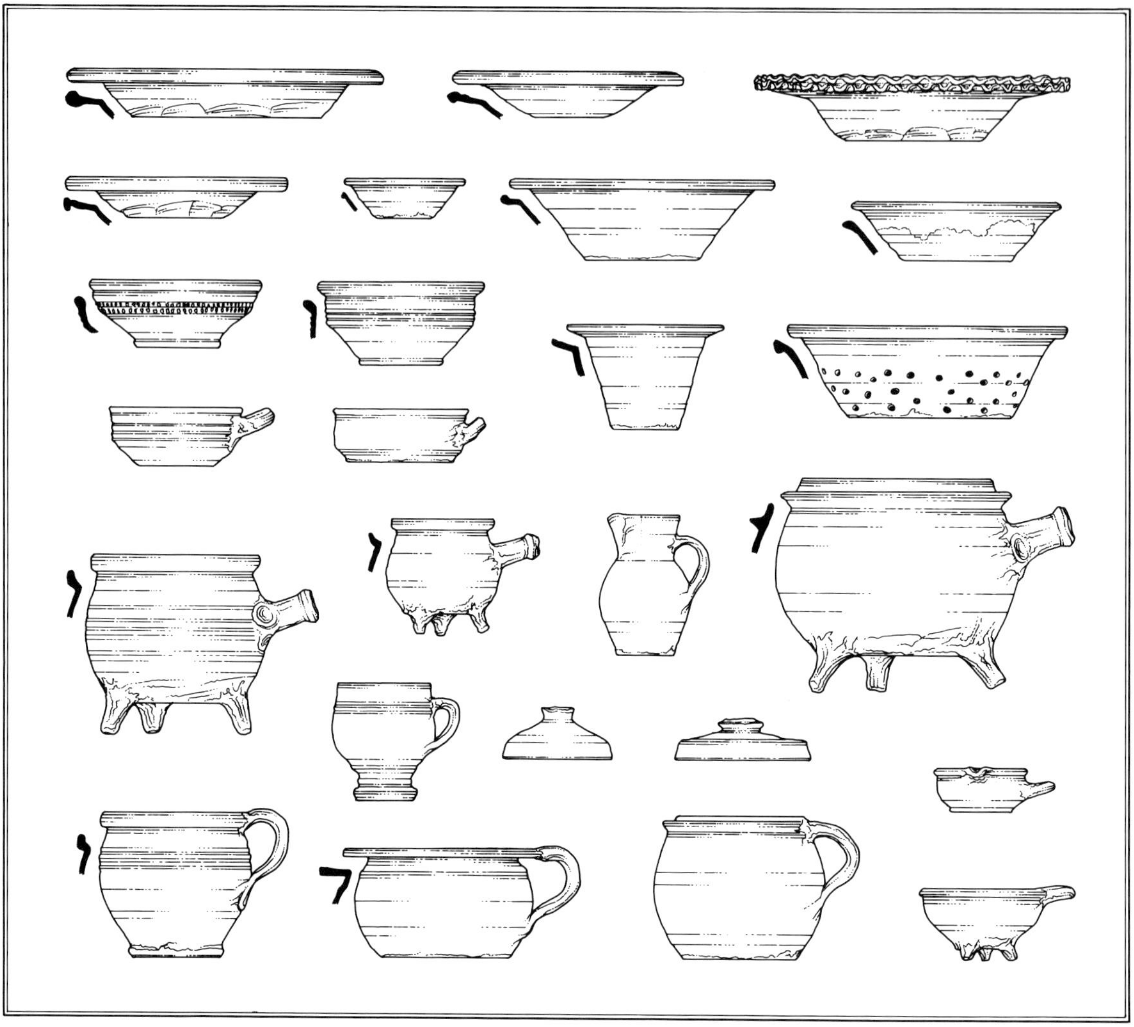

Fig 64 *The range of Border ware forms found in late 17th-century excavated contexts from London. (Scale 1/8)*

fig 11). In fact, these parallels play an important role in the dating of the pottery from Minley Road. Mugs of Type 1 were also made at Hawley, probably at the same time. Haslam suggests that the Cove potters, and by inference those at other production sites, were influenced by the London Tin-glazed wares in the introduction of these drinking vessel forms. This could well be true, for the similarities are very striking. Moreover, there are close parallels between the form of the London S-shaped mugs related to Type 1 and Tin-glazed vessels of the mid-17th century (e.g. Orton 1988, 309–11, fig 131, nos 1272–4).

Drinking vessels comparable with Border ware mugs and variously known as mugs, cups and tankards were made in a large number of pottery industries with a wide distribution in southern England in the late 16th and early 17th centuries, including Midlands Yellow ware (Brears 1971, 31, no 2) and Post-medieval black-glazed ware (Bown and Nenk forthcoming). It is also possible to find parallels with forms made in various continental industries, such as Weser ware (Hurst *et al.* 1986, fig 121, no 380) and Raeren stoneware (ibid., fig 94). The use of encrusted decoration on Border ware was also known on the Continent. The technique was widespread throughout Germany in the late 16th and early 17th centuries and may well have been copied by the Border potters from this source (ibid., 237–40, fig 113). On the other

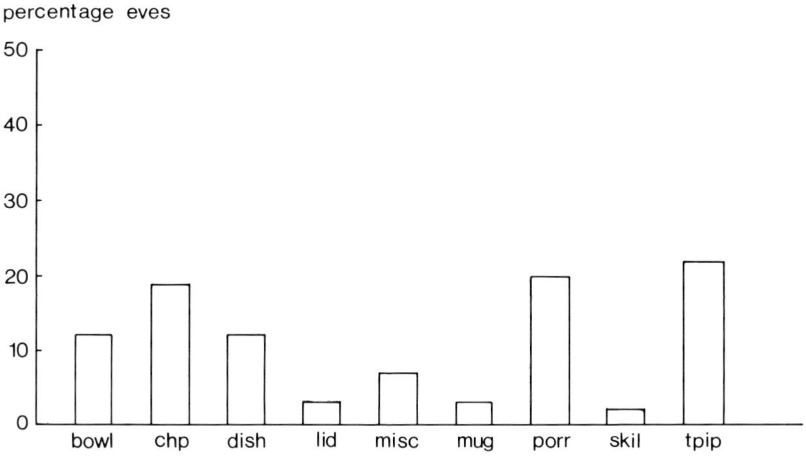

Fig 65 *Relative proportions of the main Border ware forms found in late 17th-century contexts from London*

hand, drinking vessels and measures made in other materials such as wood, leather or pewter may have provided some inspiration for the ceramic forms. The bands of raised cordons on mugs, for example, could have been transposed into pottery from the binding on wooden mugs. However, whatever influences may have been involved, Border ware was only one of a number of industries which responded to a growing demand for strong, serviceable and attractive earthenware drinking vessels during the late 16th and 17th centuries. It may be that the mug form was evolved by these various industries more or less simultaneously to meet the new fashion, drawing indirectly on a number of varied sources and existing traditions.

Border ware forms which continue with little change into the second half of the 17th century are money-boxes, rounded drinking jugs, and various types of bowls and skillets. Bowls are both more varied in form and more common in the mid- to late 17th century than earlier (see Figs 62–5). Colanders are first found in Great Fire deposits. Certain forms are rare among excavated pottery from London, although better represented in the undated Reserve Collection. Chafing dishes are found occasionally in mid-17th-century contexts. The form was made in Border ware at Farnborough Hill in whiteware and redware (unpublished material in Castle Arch Museum, Guildford), but none from this date has yet been found in London. Upright candlesticks and bottle-shaped costrels are also very rare, and the only datable examples belong to the mid- to late 17th century, although they may be difficult to identify when broken and incomplete. There are no Border ware dripping dishes or large storage jars in any of the excavated material from London. Heavy-duty forms such as these were instead supplied by the more local redware industries.

It has already been noted that there is a higher proportion of Red Border ware in mid- to late 17th-century assemblages from London than in earlier material, although in relation to the quantity of whiteware found it remains low throughout the century. This does not reflect the quantity produced at source, and it seems that while the whiteware continued to flourish, redwares had a more limited local distribution. Forms found in London at this period include flanged dishes, bowls, tripod pipkins, porringers, skillets, chamber pots, colanders and lids. By the mid-17th century whiteware glazes are generally more evenly mixed than in the late 16th and early 17th centuries. Yellow and green glazes still predominate (see Appendix 3), but brown glaze is also found increasingly from the middle of the 17th century, particularly on mugs, but also on flanged dishes, bowls, colanders, porringers and chafing dishes.

It is possible to detect a wide range of parallels, particularly with pottery from Germany and the Low Countries, in the Border ware products of the late 16th and early 17th centuries. By the late 17th century, these influences, certainly in inspiring new forms, appear to have been thoroughly absorbed into the local idiom. There is no evidence that continental potters were directly involved in the border ware industry, at least from the late 16th century onwards. Rather, the industry expanded by being adaptable and receptive to popular fashions from other sources. Once a form was introduced, its evolution was primarily due to local inspiration.

The end of the whiteware Industry

During most of the 17th century, the Border ware industry was of major importance in supplying the London market. From about the middle of the century until the early years of the 18th century, Border ware was one of the principal sources of good quality household pottery used in the capital. With its buff fabric and different coloured glazes, it was aesthetically pleasing, well-made and available in a comprehensive range of forms that catered for the kitchen, the table, sanitary needs and various other domestic uses. This volume has concentrated on the evidence from London, but Border ware was clearly not dependent on the London market alone for its continued existence, however lucrative that market was. As Haslam notes, it was 'of considerable importance in the economy of the south of England as a whole' (Haslam 1975, 187), and it is widely distributed throughout the major centres of this part of the country. However, during the early decades of the 18th century, the whiteware industry went into decline. By the second quarter of the century, very little Border ware is found in excavated assemblages from London (Orton and Pearce 1984, 65–7). The reasons for this are complex, but it appears that the rise of the various Staffordshire potteries was largely responsible for the falling market for white earthenware. With the wide availability of Staffordshire salt-glazed stoneware from the 1720s onwards, the Border ware industry was no longer able to compete in the London market. This agrees with Holling's suggestion that whitewares went out of production in the early 18th century, in the face of growing competition from the Midlands and from the various centres producing Tin-glazed wares (Holling 1971, 64). The redware industry continued well into the 19th century, but never seems to have been as influential as the whiteware.

Summary

The pottery industry centred on the borders between Surrey and Hampshire in the early post-medieval period grew out of a long ceramic tradition in the area. The late-medieval Surrey whitewares known as Coarse Border ware were made in the late 15th-century kilns at Farnborough Hill, together with finewares, also known in Kingston-type ware and Cheam whiteware and referred to collectively, if erroneously, as 'Tudor Green'. These finewares, which appear to have been introduced into the medieval industry under French influence, were still in circulation, and probably in production, in the early 16th century after the coarsewares had been abandoned.

By the late 16th century, 'Tudor Green' was no longer made, but the kilns at Farnborough Hill used the local white-firing clays of the Reading Beds to make a fine, white earthenware, glazed green or yellow. The term 'Border ware' describes the products of this and other centres in the Farnham area. Kiln waste was found at Hawley and Cove, dating to the second quarter of the 17th century, and at Ash, from the second half of the century. Redwares, or Red Border ware, were made at Farnborough Hill, Hawley and Cove in the same range of forms as whitewares. By the second half of the 16th century, Border ware proper was being exported to London, and was gaining an influential hold on the market by the middle of the 17th century. From this time until the end of the century, it was one of the main sources of domestic pottery used in the capital. The full extent of the industry is not yet known, and there remain certain chronological gaps in our knowledge of its development. The material from the known kiln groups has not yet been fully published, and it is difficult to attribute finds of Border ware to individual production centres. These questions must await further research and discoveries in the source area.

In its heyday, the Border ware industry was a major force in the supply of good quality, attractive domestic pottery to London and the south of England as a whole. Its potters were able to respond quickly and effectively to new fashions and influences from contemporaneous industries, both in the London area and on the Continent. Although Red Border ware was traded to London and other centres, it remained more important locally, and it was the whitewares which brought about the long-standing success of the industry outside its area of production. When the major markets of the south began to be flooded with the wares of the flourishing Midlands potteries in the early 18th century, the whitewares were finally abandoned, although the redwares continued to be made in the area well into the next century.

Appendix · 1 ·

The Excavations

David Lakin

The quantified pottery used in the post-medieval series as a whole comes from 37 DUA sites, and one earlier Guildhall Museum site (Excavation Register). In the following site summaries, bold face is used to indicate those sites and contexts which contained Border wares. Many of the deposits selected are individual features from particular excavations; however, study of the stratified sequence from Area A at Cutler Street provided a comparison for evaluating isolated deposits from other sites. A brief site summary, together with more detailed description of the quantified deposits, is given for each of the sites selected. Following the summaries and list of additional sites, is a chronological listing of the sites and contexts, together with their summarised

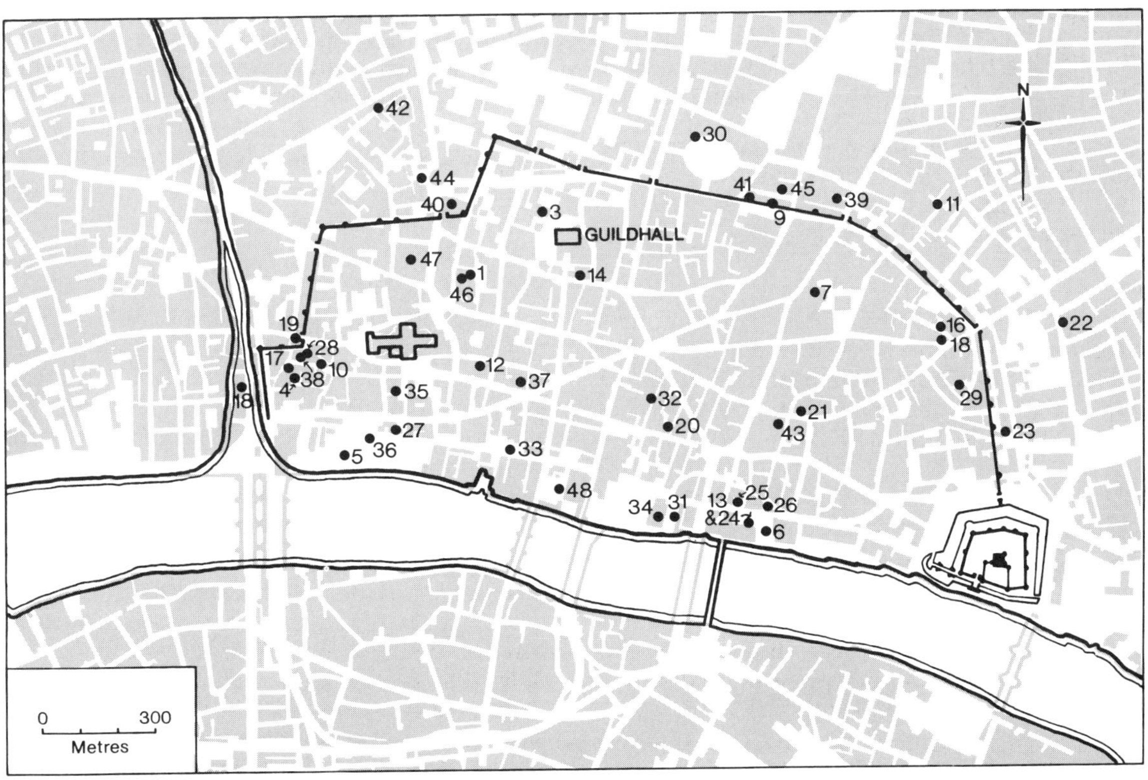

Fig 66 *The City of London, showing the location of DUA excavations which produced Border wares. The numbers refer to the numbered site summaries in Appendix 1*

dating evidence. Contexts dated to 1660–80 may be placed in either the mid- or late 17th century groups. They have been assigned to the mid-17th century when associated with Great Fire debris.

1. ABC87 Abacus House, 33–39 Gutter Lane, EC2

Supervisor I Blair

An extensive plan excavation recovered a sequence of Roman buildings sealed by a deposit of dark earth which was extensively pitted in the medieval period. From 1520 the site was occupied by Embroiderers' Hall to whom probably belonged a brick and ragstone lined cesspit located on the Gutter Lane frontage. Context **[793]** filled this feature while context **[1061]** filled an earlier rubbish pit identified in the bottom of the cesspit and truncated by it. Both features were dated to the late 16th/early 17th century.

2. ACE83 77–79 Gracechurch Street, EC3

Supervisor A Upson

A controlled excavation revealed a sequence of early Roman structures sealed by the courtyard of the 2nd-century Forum. Modern basements had destroyed all other horizontal deposits to this level leaving only unrelated intrusions. One of these was a stone lined cellar which was later extended and partly lined with brick. Context [10] represented the backfilling of this feature in the 17th century.

3. AMB87 58–63 Aldermanbury, EC2

Supervisor G Brown

An extensive post-demolition plan excavation took place. However, modern basementing had removed archaeological deposits and only deeply cut features survived, the earliest of which were Roman. Many of the medieval features were cesspits which, together with the foundations of two 14th-century buildings, show that the area was occupied by domestic buildings. Context **[104]** was one of the fills of a brick-lined well dating to the late 17th century, indicating that the site remained in domestic use in the post-medieval period.

4. APO81 20–26 Blackfriars Lane, EC4

Supervisor R Bluer

Recording, largely by means of drawn sections, recovered traces of early medieval defensive ditches. These were backfilled and consolidated with gravel dumps prior to the establishment of the Dominican friary of Blackfriars in the late 13th century and the consequent westward extension of the City walls. Remains of the friary church, guest house, and porter's lodge were identified. After the Dissolution, the church, at least, may have remained relatively intact until the late 17th century. However at some point its west wall was cut by the insertion of a brick and chalk lined well, whose fill constitutes context **[153]**. In the area of the body of the church a deep pit was dug to dispose of rubble debris **[8]**. Both features seem to mark the eventual demise of the church, possibly as a result of the Great Fire of 1666.

5. BC72 Baynard House, Queen Victoria Street, EC4

Supervisor P Marsden

Excavation located the later medieval Baynard's Castle and a dock and wharf to the west. The dock was initially constructed in timber but was rebuilt in stone in the 14th century. Contexts **[1]**, **[10]**, **[23]** and **[23B]** were from a group of pits robbing the stone-lined dock (P Marsden, pers comm), and have been dated to the first half of the 16th century.

6. BIG82 Billingsgate Lorry Park, Lower Thames Street, EC3

Supervisor S Roskams

A large plan excavation uncovered an extensive Roman and medieval sequence of waterfronts and associated buildings including the church of St Botolph. In the late medieval period an area adjacent to the church was enclosed to create a small private chapel within which a series of burials was made. Later, in the south-east of the area, an industrial building was constructed. This had a main north–south culvert, which was also fed by a smaller one running east–west. Context **[1389]** was the latest fill of the subsidiary culvert and **[1627]** one of the fills of the main culvert.

7. BOP82 28–34 Bishopsgate, EC4

Supervisor C Evans

A large plan excavation uncovered an extensive sequence of Roman deposits cut by post-medieval features which included a substantial brick-lined and vaulted cesspit. Context [241] appeared to be the remains of the cess fill of the feature whilst contexts [199], [224], and [233] (all of which contained a high proportion of rubble and discarded non-organic rubbish) seem to represent the deliberate infilling of the feature at some point in the mid-17th century.

8. BRI78 9–12 Bridewell Place, EC4

Supervisor D Gadd

A plan excavation uncovered parallel brick foundations (including brick arches on pile-supported chalk piers). Documentary and cartographic evidence identifies these as the southern half of the east range of the principal courtyard of Bridewell Palace (1515–23). The beginning of the south range, the base of a corner stair, and traces of the brick courtyard surface were also recorded; as were, in the east of the site, later brick foundations perhaps associated with the chapel of Bridewell Hospital. Context [129] was a reclamation dump associated with the construction of the Palace.

9. CAP86 54–62 New Broad Street, EC2

Supervisor I Blair

An extensive pre-demolition excavation comprised seven trenches grouped at the east and west ends of the site. The Roman sequence, which showed silting and the establishment of the City defences, was followed in the medieval period by further silting and ground-raising dumps. In the 16th century a wide defensive ditch was aligned on the wall to the south. Its primary fills were contexts [29], [48], [520], [591], [603], and [605]. In the western group of trenches the backfill and disuse of the ditch was represented by [4], [5], [8], [12], [16], [20], [22], [23], [24], [25], [27], [42], [43], [44], [47], [49], [61], [64], [66], [74], [75], and [83]; in the eastern group the equivalent deposits were [510], [511], [515], [516], [517], [522], [525], [556], [559], [560], [562], [563], [565], [568], [576-9], [586], [587] [588], [589], [590], [594], [595], [600], [601], [602], [604] and [609]. Drains and wells were subsequently laid out over the backfilled ditch as gardens were established over its line. Faithorne's map of 1643–7 (Fisher 1981) shows that this part of the ditch had been backfilled by the mid-17th century. The finds from the fills show that this probably took place after 1600.

10. CAT86 52 Carter Lane, EC4

Supervisor B Watson

The principal early feature on the site discovered by a controlled excavation, was a large defensive ditch aligned NW–SE cut in the 11th/12th century and backfilled in the 13th century, possibly as a preliminary to the building of the Dominican friary of Blackfriars. Nineteenth-century basements removed horizontal deposits later than the backfilling of the ditch, leaving only later cut features. These appear to show that a house was built on the site in the 16th century and that its subsequent replacement in the later 17th century featured a cellar with an icehouse beneath it. The cellar had a pier base at its centre which was eventually robbed out and backfilled with [102] and [108] in the late 17th century. The icehouse was a large, sunken, brick-lined feature with wooden shelves and a flagstone floor, the bedding for which – [74] – survived. It was covered by a vaulted brick roof and access was by a hatchway in the vault. The vaulting, or possibly the drainage, of this feature seems to have been unsatisfactory and it was partly demolished and backfilled, [63], [65], [66] and [124]. It was subsequently converted into a somewhat smaller cesspit – of which [58] and [121] were construction debris. Possibly contemporary with the conversion of the icehouse was the cutting of a pit outside the building which was filled with humic material [56].

11. CUT78 Cutler Street Warehouse, Harrow Place, E1

Supervisor S O'Connor Thompson; report by J Drummond Murray

A pre-demolition excavation was coupled with an extensive watching brief during the demolition of the old East India Company warehouses. The Roman sequence consisted of graves belonging to the extra-mural cemetery outside Bishopsgate. In the medieval period the site was part of the garden of Holy Trinity Priory and a few features from this phase and the immediate post-Reformation period were recorded before more extensive occupation in the 17th century which culminated in extensive building of brick terraces and associated gardens as shown in the Ogilby and Morgan map of 1677. Most of the contexts used in this study were connected with these buildings.

Preceding the building phase, context [1594]

filled a pit of late 16th century date. Contexts **[713]**, **[851]** and **[857]** were make-up dumps dating from the early 17th century; [682] was an external occupation layer of similar date and [854], [880] and **[925]** were posthole fills. Context **[814]** was an external dump, [815] the primary fill of a pit and **[882]** an occupation layer, all dating from the early to mid-17th century. Contexts [772] and [778] were the primary fills of a wooden barrel dating to the early 17th century and [740] a later fill. [763] was backfill around the barrel and [774] a contemporary external occupation layer. [676] was the fill of a posthole and [678] an external accumulation, both provisionally dated to the mid-17th century. Contexts [881], **[905]** and **[917]** of later 17th century date were make-up for a surface and **[852]** an external dump.

Contexts **[322]**, [323], **[690]**, **[695]** and **[696]** were construction trench backfills and [728] and **[580]** an associated dump connected with the construction of Building 5. **[572]** was a foundation cut for this building. **[312]** and **[595]** were dumps of construction debris and [320] a construction surface. Contexts [330] and [315] were bedding layers for floors and [306] was the backfill around a wooden barrel found within the building. [420] and [679] were brick floors and [738] another floor surface; **[729]** was the make-up for a floor, [737] the mortar bedding for a brick wall and [509] a posthole. Contexts [347] [421] and **[433]** were accumulations of construction debris for structures associated with this building. Associated dumps, **[201]**, **[337]** and **[344]**, produced tobacco pipe kiln waste; dumps **[305]**, [422], [507] and **[508]** were of the same phase. [377] was the fill of a beam slot for an associated structure within which [386] was an occupation surface. Context **[395]** was an external surface associated with the buildings. Context [357] was the levelling for a brick floor within Building 6. **[360]** filled a construction cut and **[835]** was an internal brick floor. Contexts [601] and [633] filled a construction trench for Building 7, also built in the late 17th century.

Contexts **[504]** and **[789]** were fills of a large pit dating from the mid-17th century. **[310]**, **[503]**, **[758]** and [833] filled a large pit of similar date and **[348]** was the backfill of a smaller 17th century pit. Context **[809]** was a layer of robbing debris dating from the late 17th/early 18th century. Context **[1119]** filled a wood-lined pit. **[1120]**, **[1383]**, **[1389]** and **[1394]** filled a brick-lined cesspit. Both features were recorded in the watching brief and are of 17th century date.

12. ER161B Gateway House, 1 Watling Street, EC4
Supervisor P Marsden

Overlying various Roman structures the post-Roman sequence consisted of medieval rubbish pits and post-medieval pits, wells and cellars. Context **[161B]** is the lower fill of a chalk-lined cesspit or garderobe.

13. FRE78 Fresh Wharf, New Fresh Wharf, Lower Thames Street, EC3
Supervisor L Miller

A watching brief, in an area adjoining the controlled excavations at New Fresh Wharf (NFW74) and St Magnus (SM75), (Miller *et al.* 1986), revealed a waterfront sequence from the early 2nd century, followed by medieval rebuilding which continued until destruction by the Great Fire. Context **[511]** is the fill of a drain predating the Great Fire.

14. GDH85 Guildhall House, 81–87 Gresham Street, EC1
Supervisor K Steedman

Extensive excavations revealed Roman features (including part of the amphitheatre) overlain by dark earth. As a consequence of disturbance by modern basements evidence for later activity was confined to features which cut these deposits, such as early medieval pits and a 13th-century cellar. Despite generally poor stratigraphic survival, context **[841]**, destruction debris from the demolition of a post-medieval building, remained intact as it had slumped into a large underlying pit. This was in turn cut by a stone-lined cesspit (fill context **[740]**) which probably served the late 16th-century successor to the building.

15. HOU78 Chatsworth House, 47–56 Houndsditch, EC3
Supervisor C Harding

Features on this site were recorded in section only, the main section running north–south across the supposed line of the City ditch. The excavation uncovered a series of ditches and metalled surfaces. The ditches were thought to be defensive features associated with the city walls, the earliest being of 12th century date and the latest being backfilled in the 16th century or later. The metalled surfaces were interpreted as tenter-grounds known to exist in this area from the late medieval period. Contexts [3], [7], [9], [12] and [19] formed part of the infilling of the latest ditch.

16. HTP79 Mitre Square, 11–12 Mitre Street, EC3

Supervisor J Schofield

Excavation and a watching brief revealed foundations of the range on the west side of the cloister of Holy Trinity Priory, Aldgate, founded in 1108. The cloister range was adapted after the Dissolution. Context **[220]** is the fill of a pit containing domestic and industrial debris deposited in the late 16th or early 17th century.

17. LBY85 7 Ludgate Broadway, EC4

Supervisor J Hill

Plan excavation recovered the foundations of the medieval Dominican friary church of the Blackfriars which overlay the Roman city ditch. After the Dissolution most of the friary was leased out for housing development. The church itself may not have been immediately affected by this but was certainly no longer in existence by the time of the post-Great Fire reconstruction when domestic plots with cellars and cesspits were laid out over it. Several early cellars belonging to this post-fire phase were later consolidated into one larger cellar with a higher floor. Likewise the associated cesspits of the post-Fire phase were backfilled as a result of this remodelling. Context [20] was a levelling deposit for the larger cellar built after 1695, and contexts **[66]** and **[67]** were backfill deposits in a cesspit (deposited after 1680).

18. LEA84 71–77 Leadenhall Street, EC3

Supervisor S Rivière

Controlled excavation uncovered an extensive sequence of Roman buildings and a late Saxon graveyard. Over this lay part of Holy Trinity Priory, founded in 1108. The remains of the south transept, an apsidal chapel, and a second chapel attached to the choir were discovered. At some point, probably after the Dissolution, considerable modifications were made although some of the monastic structures remained in use, albeit in a modified form. Material was dumped to the south of the transept, the south-east corner of the apsidal chapel was demolished and a structure founded on massive timber posts was built in the space between the two chapels. This wooden structure was subsequently demolished and the emptied postholes allowed to silt up [226]. Further dumping and pitting occurred to the south, where [283] was the backfill behind the lining of a brick-lined cesspit, as well as in the area of the demolished wooden structure where [212] and [308] were the fills of rubbish pits and **[181]**, **[200]**, and [268] were successive dumped deposits sealing the pits. The apsidal chapel was considerably modified and in its final form functioned as a cellar with a considerably lowered floor. Pitting continued in the south of the site – **[127]** was the fill of a rubbish pit and [246] and [247] were successive dumped layers. All activity described above took place before 1600. The chapel/cellar had its last reflooring and was backfilled by 1760.

19. LGA87 41–43 Ludgate Hill, EC4

Supervisor W McCann

Evidence was recovered for the position of the early medieval city ditch and its subsequent infilling resulting from the westward extension of the City defences after the establishment of the Dominican friary of Blackfriars in the late 13th century. Several medieval buildings fronting on to Ludgate Hill were demolished in the post-medieval period and the site became waste ground. Context **[125]** was the fill of a rubbish pit dug on the waste ground in the last half of the 17th century.

20. LIB82 119-121 Cannon Street, EC4

Supervisor P Rowsome

A detailed watching brief revealed an extensive Roman sequence cut by several discrete features of much later date. Cutting one of these brick features was a circular chalk-lined pit filled with organic rubbish deposits, one of which **[157]**, dated to the mid-17th century.

21. LIM82 25–6 Lime Street, EC3

Supervisor T Williams

A short plan excavation and watching brief recovered a series of Roman buildings, the latest of which was a masonry structure with a deeply sunken cellar. Although modern basements had destroyed any horizontal stratigraphy later than the construction of the cellar, it was apparent that it was rediscovered and reused in the 11th century, continuing in use until backfilled after the Great Fire. In the eastern part of the site were pits contemporary with the occupation of the building which had reused the cellar. Context [50] was the rubble fill of a brick-lined cesspit or sub-cellar within the building and was part of a general horizon of demolition debris marking the demise of the pre-Great Fire building.

22. MAN82 21–29 Mansell Street, E1

Supervisor A Upson

The entire area was sealed by a series of dumps that had accumulated between c. 1350–1800. The surfaces of individual dump layers were occasionally cut by small pits, apparently for the disposal of rubbish, suggesting that the area lay open for a while. A major property boundary (dated to the 17th century) was established by means of an east–west brick–built wall across the full extent of the site. This formed the north wall of a brick–lined cesspit and another cesspit lay immediately to the south. A number of small pits to the south of the main property boundary cut into the sequence of dumped material and contained industrial type debris. Documentary sources suggest that the area to the north of the boundary was a Nonconformist burial ground in the 18th century. Context [213] was the backfill of one of a series of gravel extraction pits, and [107] and [205] were two of the dumps which subsequently sealed those pits; context [204] filled a feature cut into these dumps, while [206] was the fill of a small pit.

23. MI086 118 Minories, EC3

Supervisor P McCullough

Controlled excavation revealed two successive large ditches, both aligned north–south, the later of which was backfilled after 1650. An horizon of dumped building material overlay the backfill, and over this was a humic deposit. A series of pits cutting the humic material were in turn sealed by further dumped deposits [1007] and [1065]. Cut into these deposits were more features including a ditch-like feature running east–west along the southern limit of excavation which was filled with industrial debris [1010]. Later a clay and brick furnace was built in the centre of the western part of the site. This was eventually demolished and its insertion cut backfilled with [1016], [1020], [1025] and [1029]. The backfill was disturbed by a later cut of uncertain purpose filled with [1002]. All activity later than the infilling of the large ditches seems to have taken place in the late 17th century.

24. NFW74 New Fresh Wharf, Lower Thames Street, EC3

Supervisor L Miller

An extensive plan excavation yielded much evidence for the development of the waterfront area from the Roman to the post-medieval periods. A series of early medieval tenements were continuously modified into the 17th century. On one of these plots a house (Building H) was erected in the late 14th or early 15th century – context [40] was one of the dumps sealing the earlier building on the plot. The new building was continuously altered until well into the 17th century. For example, in one basement room a cesspit was inserted in which humic deposit [2] accumulated and which was eventually backfilled with rubble deposit [1]. Another house (Building J) was erected on an adjacent tenement in the 16th century and in the 17th century, possibly following the Great Fire, it was demolished and its basement backfilled with rubble dumps which included deposits [39] and [41].

25. PDN81 118–127 Lower Thames Street, EC3

Supervisor G Milne

An extensive excavation uncovered a sequence of Roman and later waterfront structures. Two brick-lined cellars with associated drains and cesspits were constructed in the post-medieval period and were backfilled following the Great Fire. Context [42] was part of a thick deposit of fire debris filling both cellars and marking their disuse in the late 17th century.

26. PEN79 Peninsular House, 112–116 Lower Thames Street, EC3

Supervisor G Milne

Extensive excavations produced a sequence of Roman and later waterfront structures. In the post-medieval period, a building with a brick-lined cellar was constructed and the cellar used to store what appeared to be barrels of tar. The cellar was modified at least once during its lifetime. Context **[361]** was part of the initial construction of the cellar; context **[359]** was part of its subsequent modification; contexts [322], [337], [338] and [342] were deposits of burnt material and rubble indicating the destruction and disuse of the building following the Great Fire; and context **[319]** was the fill of a pit which was dug into the rubble backfill, possibly indicative of a short term reuse of the site after the demolition of the cellared building.

27. PET81 St Peter's Hill, EC4

Supervisor T Williams

Large scale excavations revealed an extensive Roman sequence with subsequent Saxon occupation. Buildings established in the latter period were demolished in the 12th century and replaced by new properties aligned on Upper Thames Street and St Peter's Hill, which were laid out at this time. The church of St Peter was also built. The roads, houses and church continued to be modified until the Great Fire.

Contexts **[1659]**, **[1667]** and [1772] were separate dumps of make-up material indicating the continued use of Upper Thames Street in the post-medieval period. To the north the medieval properties continued to be occupied. Context **[76]** was the fill of a shallow pit cut into cobbled yard surface [184]; **[622]** was the fill of a robber trench cutting into the earlier Roman masonry structure (probably used as a source of building material); and [214] was the fill of a pit. These features seem on the whole to precede the brick refurbishment of the Thames Street properties. Contexts [108], [471], **[636]**, [661], **[1763]** [1789], [1791], and **[1831]** represented the continued build up of floor layers within the cellar of one of these properties. In another property **[307]** was the fill of a pit sealed by the bedding material **[238]** for a cellar floor of which **[194]** was a repair, **[160]** and **[199]** were the fills of pits cut into the floor, and **[22]** was a new floor layer sealing all the foregoing features. Contexts **[104]** and **[486]** were the fills of rubbish pits associated with these properties (**[104]** was the upper fill of a large feature which also contained much redeposited Roman and medieval material). All these features were dated to the first half of the 17th century and were overlain by an extensive dump of fire and demolition debris including contexts **[101]**, [344], [352], [353], **[357]**, **[362]**, [373], [374], **[488]**, [2198] and [2203] probably resulting from the Great Fire of 1666.

28. PIL75 5 Pilgrim Street, EC4

Supervisor J Schofield

A visit to this site during construction work resulted in the recording of a brick-lined two-chambered cesspit, filled by context **[1]**. No other features were observed.

29. RAG82 1–12 Rangoon Street/61–65 Crutched Friars, EC3

Supervisor D Bowler

A plan excavation uncovered several Roman features sealed by a deposit of dark earth into which were cut a number of medieval features, including numerous levels from the construction and use of a timber-lined well [101, **112**, 114, 153–4, 175 179–80, **81**, 184, 190, **191**, 198] rebuilt and in use before 1550.

30. RIV87 River Plate House, Finsbury Circus, EC2

Supervisors P Askew, D Lees

Plan excavations recovered evidence of Roman activity sealed by the accumulation across the entire site of marsh deposits. Beginning in the medieval period, these deposits were sealed by dumps of material intended to stabilise the marshy ground. Contexts [3], **[4]**, **[114]** and **[115]** were amongst the uppermost of these dumps and lay directly below the modern basement slab.

31. SH74 Seal House, 106–108 Upper Thames Street, EC4

Supervisor J Schofield

A plan excavation uncovered a series of medieval buildings, which continued in use until their destruction by the Great Fire of 1666. Context **[47]** is part of a foundation deposit established on top of the rubble of the buildings destroyed in the fire.

32. SL75 10 St Swithin's Lane, EC4

Supervisor J Schofield

Three cellars, possibly constructed in the early 17th century, were recorded during a watching brief. Two of these, were divided by an arched chalk wall, beneath which lay a chalk-lined well. The northern cellar was fire-blackened and its contents [21] included fire debris, whilst the other cellar contained dumped material [10] and [17].

33. SLO82 Beaver House, Sugar Loaf Court, EC4

Supervisor M Barker

Five trenches were excavated on the site of the Hudson's Bay Company fur warehouse in an area which was believed to have been open ground from the 18th- until the 20th century. Roman and medieval sequences were recorded and at the eastern end of the site were the remains of an undercroft. This was built principally of chalk blocks and was at least 56 m^2 in area (the north and east sides lying beyond the limits of excavation). It appears to have been covered by a vaulting of Reigate stone and may have been entered by a stairway located at the eastern end of the southern wall. A series of subsequent modifications included the construction of a cesspit within the undercroft which was filled with deposits [15] and [16].

34. SWA81 Swan Lane NCP site, 95–103 Upper Thames Street, EC4

Supervisor G Egan

A small excavation and an extensive watching brief disclosed post-medieval features which were represented by a brick-lined cesspit, [980], [981], [986], a pit fill [952], and a barrel lined pit [2172]. The cesspit was apparently abandoned at the time of the Great Fire but showed no signs of burning and included material dated to at least the preceding 20 years.

35. TAV82 29–33 Knightrider Street, EC4

Supervisor J Burke-Easton

A short plan excavation on the site of the Horntavern Public House revealed deep post-medieval pits cutting all earlier levels. Contexts [12], [14], [16], [17], [146], [147], and [149] were fills of an unlined pit with an initial rubbish fill covered with a soil capping. The lower fill of this feature consisted mainly of large fragments of late 16th to early 17th century pottery and other finds, mostly copper and iron, including a portable sundial inscribed 'Anno 1561'. The clay pipes found indicate a deposition date of *c.* 1580 or later.

36. UT74 Upper Thames Street, EC4

Supervisor D Jones

A plan excavation of a 24m^2 section of the western part of Upper Thames St was undertaken to resolve questions raised by earlier work on the nearby site of the later medieval Baynard's Castle. Evidence was obtained for the construction and modification of the curtain wall of the castle. In the mid-15th century the original stone wall was demolished and after a general levelling of the site, a brick faced wall with a rubble core was constructed. Context [34] was the rubble base of a buttress for the rebuilt wall. In the 17th century (possibly as a result of the Great Fire), the curtain wall and buttress were demolished and rubble layers, including [14], were dumped over the site. Subsequent to this dumping a brick-lined cellar, [32], with a mortar floor, [29], was constructed. The cellar was then remodelled and another rubble layer, [24], was deposited to provide a base for a new brick floor and drain. Later the cellar was refloored, with context [25] being a make-up layer of mortar on which a greensand and mortar floor, [26], was constructed.

37. WAT78 41–53 Watling Court, EC4

Supervisor D Perring

A plan excavation uncovered an extensive Roman sequence. The latest periods of occupation were, however, represented by a series of pits and wells. Context [2501] was the backfill of a cesspit with a collapsed timber superstructure. Context [2528] was the backfill of a brick-lined cesspit.

38. WAY83 12–13 Ludgate Broadway, EC4

Supervisor P Rowsome

A short controlled excavation provided evidence for the establishment of the Roman defensive ditch and its subsequent modifications in the medieval period, until the establishment of the Dominican friary of Blackfriars in the late 13th century. The site fell within the northern part of the friary precinct and may have formed part of the monastic cemetery. After the Dissolution the area was redeveloped for secular purposes and after some initial industrial use a building was established fronting on to Pilgrim St, to the north. Contexts [56] and [57] were the fills of a brick-lined cesspit located in the garden at the rear of the property.

Additional Sites

The following sites, although not included in the summaries, produced Border ware vessels that have been illustrated because of their intrinsic interest.

39. ADM81 Alderman's House, 34–37 Liverpool Street, EC2

40. ALG84 7–12 Aldersgate Street, EC1

41. BLM87 Blomfield House, 85–86 London Wall, EC2

42. CLO83 62–67 Long Lane/Cloth Fair, EC1

43. FEN83 5–12 Fenchurch Street, EC3

44. LBT86 Little Britain, EC1

45 NEB87 35–45 New Broad Street, EC2

46. OST82 7–11 Foster Lane, EC2

47. POM79 Newgate Street, EC1

48. TEX88 Thames Exchange Buildings, EC4

Summarised Dating Evidence

Julie Edwards

The non-ceramic dating evidence for each site and context is summarised here. Ceramic spot dates for each context fall within the broad chronological groupings under which these are listed. Tobacco pipe dates are based on the type-series drawn up by Atkinson and Oswald (1969), with revisions for some sites by Davey and Higgins (forthcoming). Glass wine bottles, coins and dated artefacts are also included. The coins, jettons and tokens were identified by members of staff of the DUA, and the Early Department of the Museum of London.

Context	**Tobacco pipes**	**Wine bottles**	**Dated finds and coins**
First Half of the 16th Century (Early 16th Century)			
BC 72			
1	–	–	jetton 1475–early 16th century
10	–	–	–
23	–	–	–
23B	–	–	jetton 1475–early 16th century
BRI 78			
129	–	–	–
ER 161B	–	–	–
HOU 78			
3	–	–	–
7	–	–	–
9	–	–	–
12	–	–	–
19	–	–	–
MAN 82			
107	–	–	–
204	–	–	–
205	–	–	–
206	–	–	–
213	–	–	–
RAG 82			
101	–	–	–
112	–	–	–
114	–	–	–
153	–	–	–
154	–	–	–
175	–	–	–
179	–	–	–
180	–	–	–
181	–	–	–
184	–	–	–
190	–	–	–
191	–	–	–
198	–	–	–

Context	Tobacco pipes	Wine bottles	Dated finds and coins
WAT 78			
2501	–	–	–
Second Half of the 16th Century (Late 16th Century)			
ABC 87			
793	1610–40	–	–
1061	–	–	–
CUT 78			
1594	–	–	–
GDH 85			
740	–	–	–
841	–	–	–
HTP 79			
220	stem	–	–
LEA 84			
127	–	–	Nuremberg jetton early 16th century
181	–	–	–
200	–	–	–
212	–	19th century intrusive	–
226	–	–	–
246	–	–	–
247	–	–	–
268	–	–	–
283	–	–	–
308	–	–	–
TAV 82			
12	–	–	–
14	–	–	–
16	stems	–	Nuremberg jetton of Hans Krauwinckel c. 1580–1610 sundial inscribed '1561'
17	–	–	–
146	–	–	–
147	–	–	–
149	–	–	–
First Half of the 17th Century (Early 17th Century)			
CUT 78			
682	–	–	–
713	–	–	–
740	–	–	–
763	–	–	–
772	–	–	–

Context	Tobacco pipes	Wine bottles	Dated finds and coins
774	1680–1710 intrusive	–	–
778	–	–	–
814	–	–	–
815	–	1650+ intrusive	–
851	1600–1700	1650+ intrusive	–
854	–	–	–
857	–	–	–
880	–	–	–
882	–	–	–
925	–	–	–
FRE 78			
511	1610–40		
RIV 87			
3/4	1700–70 intrusive	–	–
114/115	–	–	–
Mid-17th Century (Includes Great Fire Deposits)			
ACE 83			
10	1660–80	1650–80 (stamp c. 1660)	–
APO 81			
8	1640–70	1650–60	–
153	–	1680–1730	–
BIG 82			
1389	1660–80	1650+	rose farthing of Charles I 1635–44 Nuremberg jetton of Hans Krauwinckel c. 1586–1635
1627	1660–80	–	–
BOP 82			
199/224/ 233/241	1640–60	–	17th-century trade token or royal farthing token of James I or Charles I
CAP 86			
4	1610–40	–	–
5	–	–	–
8	–	–	–
12	1610–40	1760–1900 intrusive	–
16	–	–	–
20	–	–	–
22	–	–	–

Context	Tobacco pipes	Wine bottles	Dated finds and coins
23	–	–	–
24	–	–	–
25	–	–	–
27	1610–40	–	–
29	1610–40	–	–
42	–	–	–
43	–	–	–
44	–	–	–
47	–	–	–
48	1610–40	–	Nuremberg jetton of Matheus Lauber 1619
49	1610–50	–	Nuremberg jetton of Hans? Krauwinckel c. 1580–1610
61	–	–	–
64	–	–	–
66	–	–	–
74	–	–	–
75	–	–	–
83	–	–	–
510	1610–50	–	–
511	1610–50	–	–
515	1610–50	–	–
516	1610–40	–	–
517	–	–	–
520	–	–	–
522	–	–	–
525	–	–	Nuremberg jetton of Hans Schultes late 16th century
556	–	–	–
559	–	–	–
560	–	–	–
562	1610–50	–	–
563	1610–50	–	–
565	–	–	–
568	–	–	–
576	–	–	–
577	1610–40	–	–
578	1610–50	–	–
579	–	–	–
586	–	–	–
587	–	–	–
588	–	–	–
589	–	–	–
590	–	–	–
591	–	–	–
594	–	–	–
595	–	–	–
600	–	–	–
601	–	–	–
602	–	–	–
603	–	–	–

Context	Tobacco pipes	Wine bottles	Dated finds and coins
604	–	–	–
605	–	–	–
609	–	–	–
LIB 82			
157	1660–80	1650+	–
LIM 83			
50	1640–60	–	–
MIO 86			
1007	–	–	–
1010	1640–60	1650+	farthing of James I 1613–25
1016	1610–40	–	–
1020	stem	–	Irish penny 1602
1025	1580–1610	–	–
1029	1640–60	–	–
1065	–	–	–
NFW 74			
1	1660–80	?1680+	–
2	1650–80	–	–
39	1600–1700	–	–
40	1650–80	–	–
41	1660–80	–	leather bucket inscribed 'SB 166?'
PDN 81			
42	1660–80	1650–80 and intrusive 1760+	–
PEN 79			
319	stem	1650+	–
322	–	–	–
337	*c.* 1666	1650+	sixpence of Elizabeth I 1561–99
338	–	–	–
342	1660–80	–	–
359	–	–	–
361	–	–	–
PET 81			
22	stems	–	–
76	1680–1710	–	–
101	–	–	–
104	–	–	–
108	–	–	–
160	1640–60	–	–
184	–	–	–
194	1660–80	–	–
199	1610–40	–	–
214	–	–	–
238	1640–60	–	–

Context	Tobacco pipes	Wine bottles	Dated finds and coins
307	1640–70	–	–
344	stem	–	–
352	stem	–	–
353	stem	–	–
357	–	–	–
362	1600–80	–	–
373	stem	–	–
374	stem	–	–
471	1660–80	–	–
486	1660–80	–	–
488	–	–	–
622	–	–	–
636	–	–	–
661	–	–	–
1659	stem	–	–
1667	1640–60	–	–
1763	1640–60	–	–
1772	stem	–	–
1789	–	–	–
1791	–	–	–
1831	–	–	–
2198	stem	–	–
2203	–	–	–
PIL 75			
1	1640–60 and intrusive 1740+	–	–
SH 74			
47	1640–80	–	–
SL75			
10	1660–80	1650+ and intrusive 1720–60	–
17	stem	–	–
21	–	–	–
SLO 82			
15	1660–80	–	–
16	1660–80	1660–80	–
SWA 81			
952/980/	1610–80	–	–
981/986	1640–80	–	trade token of William Swift Worcester 1648–72 corroded Nuremberg jetton
2172	1640–70	–	–

Context	Tobacco pipes	Wine bottles	Dated finds and coins
UT 74			
14	stem	–	–
24	1660–80	–	–
25	1660–80	–	–
26	1660–80	–	–
29	–	–	–
32	–	–	–
34	1640–60	–	–
Second Half of the 17th Century (Late 17th Century)			
AMB 87			
104	*c.* 1680	1650–1700	–
CAT 86			
56	–	–	–
58	1660–80	–	–
63	1660–80	–	–
65	1660–80	–	–
66	1660–80 and intrusive 1700–70	–	–
74	–	–	–
102	–	–	–
108	–	–	–
121	1660–80	–	–
124	1660–80	–	–
CUT 78			
201	1650–80	1650+	–
305	1600–1700	–	–
306	1600–1780	1650+	–
310	–	–	–
312	1660–80	–	–
315	1750–80 intrusive	–	–
320	1660–80	–	–
322	–	–	–
323	1660–80	–	–
330	1600–1700	–	–
337	1660–80	1650+	–
344	1660–80	–	–
347	1660–80	–	–
348	1660–80	–	–
357	1750–80 intrusive	–	–
360	1640–60	–	–
377	1600–1800	–	–
386	1660–80	–	–
395	1610–40	–	–
420	–	–	–
421	1600–1700	–	–
422	1660–80	1650+	–
433	1660–80	–	–
503	1600–1700	–	–

Context	Tobacco pipes	Wine bottles	Dated finds and coins
504	1610–40	–	–
507	1660–80	–	–
508	1660–80	–	–
509	1660–80	–	–
572	–	–	–
580	1640–70	1650+	–
585	1600–1700	–	–
601	1600–1700	–	–
633	1770–1800	–	–
676	–	–	–
678	1600–1700	–	–
679	1640–60	–	–
690	1660–80	1650+	–
695	–	–	–
696	1600–1700	–	–
728	–	–	–
729	1600–1700	1650+	–
737	1660–80	–	–
738	1600–1700	–	–
758	1660–80	1650+	–
789	1600–1700	–	–
809	1600–1700	–	–
833	1660–80	–	–
835	1600–1700	–	–
852	1640–1700	–	–
881	1600–1700	–	–
905	–	–	–
917	–	–	–
1119	1640–60	–	–
1120	1660–80	–	–
1383	1600–1700	–	–
1389	–	–	–
1394	1650–70	–	–
LBY 85			
20	c. 1700	1730–60 intrusive	farthing of William III 1695
66	1660–80	–	–
67	1660–80	1700–1800 intrusive	–
LGA 87			
125	–	–	–
MIO 86			
1002	1640–60	–	–
WAT 78			
2528	1640–70	1650–80	–
WAY 83			
56	1680–1710	–	–
57	1680–1710	1690–1720	–

Appendix · 2 ·

Concordance of Illustrated Vessels

Pottery from DUA excavations is referred to by site code and context number. Full expansions of these codes and additional codes are listed in Appendix 1. All other illustrated vessels are in the collection of the Museum of London, and museum accession numbers are given here.

Figure Number	Provenance
Fig 2	CAP86 42
Fig 3	RIV87 3
Fig 4	MIO86 1002
Fig 5	BIG82 1389
Fig 6	From left to right: 6093 A25377 24576
Fig 7	SWA81 980
Fig 8	From left to right: 88.94/11 26735 A4570
Fig 9	CAP86 29
Fig 10	13590
Fig 11	26212
Fig 12	From left to right: A20785 5801 33.104/21 A4571
Fig 13	From left to right: 23877 34.285/9
Fig 14	From left to right, back row: A9429 A28571 5950 A9430 Front row: A26006 5956

Figure Number	Provenance
Fig 15	5975
Fig 16	A4539
Fig 17	A4542
Fig 18	A19341
Fig 19	1 OST82 251 2 FRE78 511 3 OST82 251 4 A27467 5 A5165 6 SL75 21 7 ABC87 793 8 18840 9 CAP86 53 10 TAV82 16 11 CAP86 42 12 FRE78 511 13 OST82 251 14 22796 15 17989 16 26728 17 ABC87 793 18 CAP86 42
Fig 20	19 CUT78 690 20 6004 21 SWA81 981/980 22 OST82 55 23 BLM87 200 24 ABC87 793 25 BLM87 200 26 6083 27 CUT78 961 28 1949.50 29 ABC87 793 30 OST82 251

Figure Number	Provenance	
	31	MIO86 1002
	32	A27929
Fig 21	33	23845
	34	BLM87 200
	35	MIO86 1010
	36	ABC87 793
	37	21264
	38	CAP86 520
	39	FRE78 511
	40	LGA87 125
	41	BIG82 1389
	42	FRE78 511
	43	CUT78 1119
	44	23921
	45	85.3/53 (11)
	46	18458
	47	22731
	48	BLM87 200
	49	SL75 10
Fig 22	50	APO81 153
	51	ER269
	52	LBY85 67
	53	25930
	54	17888
	55	22795
	56	21134
	57	17996
	58	M1086 1025
	59	FRE78 511
	60	21151
	61	21448
	62	ABC87 793
	63	BLM87 200
	64	Z3448
Fig 23	65	23881
	66	21152
	67	CUT78 895
	68	22797
	69	18390
	70	5947
	71	A22549
	72	CLO83 30
	73	GDH85 740
	74	APO81 8
	75	CUT78 905
	76	63.10
	77	FRE78 511
	78	23878
	79	21135
	80	FRE78 511
	81	24579
Fig 24	82	LBY85 67
	83	18716
	84	FRE78 511
	85	CUT78 690A
	86	BIG82 1389
	87	21357
	88	21423
	89	OST82 9
	90	CAT86 5
	91	ADM81 58
	92	MIO86 1010
	93	5998
	94	6114
Fig 25	95	5995
	96	5913
	97	21425
	98	11214
	99	RIV87 3
	100	MIO86 1010
	101	LBT86 1205
	102	BLM87 200
	103	PET81 199
	104	MIO86 1002
	105	MIO86 1016
	106	MIO86 1010
Fig 26	107	5924
	108	80.93/16
	109	37.222/53
	110	15958
	111	6009
	112	CAP86 42
	113	A25377
	114	6093
	115	MA1903
	116	24575
	117	CAT86 58
	118	CAT86 124
	119	LBY85 65
	120	BIG82 1389
	121	L220/2
	122	21214
	123	6010
	124	BIG82 1389
	125	FRE78 511
	126	CAT86 63
	127	CUT78 201
	128	A25738
	129	6095
	130	B46
Fig 27	131	LBY85 65
	132	37.222/56
	133	MA2228
	134	21341
	135	P311
	136	LBY85 63

Figure Number	Provenance
	137 MIO86 1010
	138 37.222/60
	139 88.94/11
	140 A1409
	141 ALG84 604
	142 ALG84 603
	143 MIO86 1037
	144 1939–95
	145 GDH85 740
	146 24863
Fig 28	147 24590
	148 AMB87 104
	149 27.30/18
	150 18394
	151 5930
	152 25382
	153 22788
	154 ER191B
Fig 29	155 18707
	156 81.566/2
	157 BOP82 224
	158 A24031
	159 10639
	160 68.11/10
	161 B44
	162 A4570
	163 SWA81 980
	164 18921
	165 29.163/12
	166 AMB87 104
	167 21333
	168 26735
Fig 30	169 5931
	170 A23377
	171 LBY85 65
	172 CUT78 675B
	173 5825
	174 BLM87 200
	175 CAP86 595
	176 ABC87 793
	177 A13139
	178 CUT78 337
	179 FRE78 511
	180 A4916
	181 5923
	182 CAP86 562
	183 SWA81 952
	184 CAP86 29
	185 CUT78 1041
	186 23958
	187 MIX410
Fig 31	188 SWA81 980
	189 MI086 unstratified

Figure Number	Provenance
	190 MIO86 1010
	191 16751
	192 5076
	193 SL75 10
	194 5812
	195 13359
	196 ER161B
	197 A22776
	198 5905
	199 A5603
	200 A28242
	201 A6651
	202 A4557
	203 POM79 2002
Fig 32	204 A15325
	205 5898
	206 5813
	207 80.93/11
	208 70.62/2
	209 5731
	210 5730
	211 A22530
	212 5781
	213 A1403
	214 A4561
	215 80.93/12
	216 5778
	217 A16119
Fig 33	218 5792
	219 37.194/6
	220 A11469
	221 5854
	222 A8390
	223 BLM87 9
	224 A9284
	225 80.93/22
	226 81.42/1
	227 25615
	228 A4546
	229 A4566
	230 A733
	231 A4576
	232 80.93/13
	233 A22767
Fig 34	234 A24921
	235 472 56-72-1
	236 22748
	237 A4924
	238 70.62/1
	239 A23697
	240 A22626
	241 A25741
	242 A4564

Figure Number	Provenance	
	243	24949
	244	A9428
	245	80.93/2
	246	A4547
	247	A1509
	248	A737
	249	13590
	250	5873
	251	24710
Fig 35	252	5991
	253	A4536
	254	A4543
	255	A7457
	256	A9427
	257	A9426
	258	A13138
	259	A10673
	260	A23538
	261	21187
	262	NEB87 456
	263	26212
	264	FEN83 1746
	265	6348
	266	SWA81 980
	267	A1528
	268	CAT86 65
	269	6034
	270	MIO86 1010
Fig 36	271	A4504
	272	6063
	273	Z1342
	274	10538
	275	Z1343
	276	TEX88 1150
	277	TEX88 1150
	278	TEX88 1150
	279	A24351
	280	A20317
	281	MIO86 1010
	282	A4492
	283	MIO86 1002
	284	5749
Fig 37	285	80.93/18
	286	No accession number
	287	A3906
	288	A5166
	289	5894
	290	A4580
	291	5887
	292	A4571
	293	A4551
	294	A11303
	295	A723

Figure Number	Provenance	
	296	6065
	297	37.194/7
	298	A11533
	299	33.104/21
	300	24948
Fig 38	301	24948
	302	A1512
	303	A1513
	304	A4544
	305	21684
	306	80.93/15
	307	80.93/4
	308	5801
	309	5803
	310	A11285
	311	ABC87 793
	312	18577
	313	ER166 3
Fig 39	314	26730
	315	ER166 A
	316	23877
	317	SWA81 952
	318	25383
	319	CAT86 65
	320	CAT86 66/124
	321	15247
	322	26732
Fig 40	323	ABS86 208
	324	80.93/8
	325	5973
	326	SWA81 952
	327	ER289 B
	328	23279
	329	24583
	330	24245
	331	22738
Fig 41	332	ER332 B
	333	A1980
	334	559
	335	17669
	336	34.285/9
	337	WAY83 49
	338	11647
	339	LBY85 67
	340	A916
	341	A1502
	342	A14559
	343	No accession number
	344	61.9/5
	345	80.93/17
Fig 42	346	15244
	347	A9429

Figure Number	Provenance	
	348	A4550
	349	80.364/3
	350	A4573
	351	5950
	352	5950
	353	L199-88?
	354	A28571
	355	MIX449
	356	86.66/29
	357	A4569
	358	ABC87 793
	359	ABC87 793
	360	16187
	361	13469
	362	15519
	363	A26006
	364	A25257
	365	A16778
Fig 43	366	A14561
	367	A27806
	368	52.85/3
	369	A4548
	370	5967
	371	A7354
	372	A4664
	373	A4663
	374	25641
	375	947
	376	23721
	377	37.194/8
	378	10286
	379	12401
	380	73.138/2
	381	18749
	382	23722
	383	5830
	384	86.66/35
	385	21313
	386	26227
	387	A1171
	388	SWA81 980
	389	A27528
	390	A11528
	391	HTP79 220
	392	77.182/11
	393	RIV87 73
Fig 44	394	A4565
	395	A26493
	396	83.463/25
	397	FRE78 511
	398	23723
	399	Z3372
	400	A4568
	401	77.182/3

Figure Number	Provenance	
	402	77.182/12
	403	A20230
	404	77.182/23
	405	5960
	406	13370
	407	A24905
	408	16203
	409	5275
	410	MA2760
	411	A4562
	412	80.93/10
	413	A17184
	414	5946
	415	A23206
	416	5946
	417	No accession number
	418	A19197
	419	23077
	420	5809
	421	ER161B
	422	A5061
	423	12400
	424	A3913
	425	A16812
Fig 45	426	5870
	427	A5246
	428	No accession number
	429	A5205
	430	ABC87 793
	431	5979
	432	A778
	433	A4545
	434	A24788
	435	23726
	436	BLM87 200
	437	MIO86 1010
	438	SWA81 2172
	439	APO81 8
	440	CAT86 66
	441	23049
	442	A27632
	443	CUT78 1016
	444	No accession number
	445	A27624
Fig 46	446	5975
	447	A27902
	448	A4539
	449	A19575
	450	22794
	451	FRE78 511
	452	MIO86 1030
	453	17990
	454	A19341
	455	ABC87 793

Figure Number	Provenance
	456 ABC87 793 457 5764 458 5815 459 5902 460 5763
Fig 47	CAP86 16
Fig 48	MIO86 1002
Fig 49	CAP86 16
Fig 50	SWA81 980
Fig 51	POM79 2002
Fig 52	ABC87 793
Fig 53	AMB87 104
Fig 54	No accession number
Fig 55	CUT78 344
Plate 1	MIX410
Plate 2	From left to right: A23538 21187
Plate 3	Top row, left to right: MIX467 A24351 Bottom row, left to right: 6063 A20317
Plate 4	MIX449
Plate 5	A778
Plate 6	A27632
Plate 7	From left to right: 5763 5764
Plate 8	From left to right: A6651 13359 A4541 5812
Plate 9	From left to right: A1409 6004 ABC87 793 A9426 A4556
Plate 10	From left to right: 5930 5971 25930 Front: 52/85/1
Plate 11	Top row, from left to right: 68.11/10 21423 L220/2 Bottom row, from left to right: WAT78 2528 A19324 A10439

Appendix · 3 ·

Quantified Data

The data given here are based on the total quantities of Border wares, by weight and rim percentage or 'eves', estimated vessel equivalents (Orton 1975) from all contexts within any one chronological period. All sites and contexts which produced Border wares are highlighted in the site summaries in Appendix 1.

Two quantified data tables are given below for each period. One (A) gives the relative proportion of forms by glaze colour and fabric. 'Tudor Green' is included only in the early 16th century since in later periods it is residual and present only in minute quantities, if at all. Classes of vessels are not subdivided into forms or types in the data, since the fragmentary nature of some of the excavated pottery rendered such identification difficult. In the case of dishes, however, the great majority are of the flanged form. A second table (B), from which the histograms of Figs 57, 59, 61, 63 and 65 are derived, summarises the evidence by combining all Border wares irrespective of glaze colour or fabric and amalgamates minor forms under MISC. Form types respresented by less than 1% are indicated by an asterisk. There is no table (B) for the early 16th century as there were too few identifiable forms for presentation in this way.

The following fabric and form codes have been used in these tables:

Computer Code	Expansion
BORD	Unglazed Border ware (mostly unglazed sherds from glazed vessels – colour unidentified)
BORDB	Brown-glazed Border ware
BORDG	Green-glazed Border ware
BORDO	Olive-glazed Border ware
BORDY	Yellow-glazed Border ware
RBOR	Red Border ware
TUDG	Tudor Green
Form	
BEDP	Bed pan
BOT	Bottle
BOWL	Bowl
CHAFD	Chafing dish
CHP	Chamber pot
CNDST	Candlestick
COL	Colander
COND	Condiment dish
COST	Costrel
CRUC	Crucible
CUP	Cup
DISH	Dish
DJ	Drinking jug
FUM	Fuming pot
JAR	Jar
LID	Lid
LOBED DISH	Lobed dish
MBOX	Money-box
MISC	Miscellaneous forms
MUG	Mug
PORR	Porringer
SKIL	Skillet
STRAINER	Strainer
TPIP	Tripod pipkin
WARMING PAN	Warming pan

Early 16th Century

Fabric/Form	Weight	% Weight	Eves	% Eves
TUDG/COST	216	11	100	24
TUDG/CUP	135	7	64	16
TUDG/BORDG/ DJ	1256	64	129	32
BORDY/JAR	173	9	–	–
TUDG/MBOX	23	1	35	9
TUDG/BORDG/ MISC	164	8	43	19
Total	1967	100	409	100

Late 16th Century (A)

Fabric/ Form	Weight	% Weight	Eves	% Eves
BORD/CRUC	184	2	57	3
BORD/DJ	24	*	–	–
BORD/MBOX	16	*	–	–
BORD/MISC	14	*	–	–
BORDG/BOWL	189	2	26	1
BORDG/CNDST	310	4	134	7
BORDG/COND	34	*	35	2
BORDG/COST	488	6	100	5
BORDG/DISH	1062	13	169	9
BORDG/DJ	476	6	116	6
BORDG/MBOX	405	5	100	5
BORDG/MISC	33	*	–	–
BORDG/PORR	153	2	72	4
BORDG/SKIL	379	5	118	6
BORDG/TPIP	312	4	106	6
BORDY/BOWL	718	9	60	3
BORDY/CHP	453	5	25	1
BORDY/CNDST	539	7	291	15
BORDY/DISH	723	9	95	5
BORDY/FUM	150	2	75	4
BORDY/MISC	129	1	–	–
BORDY/PORR	22	*	32	2
BORDY/TPIP	1222	15	149	8
RBOR/CNDST	226	3	144	8
Total	8261	100	1904	100

Late 16th Century (B)

Form	Weight	% Weight	Eves	% Eves
BOWL	907	11	86	5
CHP	453	5	25	1
CNDST	1075	13	569	30
COST	488	6	100	5
CRUC	184	2	57	3
DISH	1785	22	264	14
DJ	500	6	116	6
MBOX	421	5	100	5
MISC	360	4	110	6
PORR	175	2	104	6
SKIL	379	5	118	6
TPIP	1534	19	255	13
Total	8261	100	1904	100

Early 17th Century (A)

Fabric/ Form	Weight	% Weight	Eves	% Eves
BORD/MISC	4	*	–	–
BORDB/PORR	72	2	–	–
BORDG/BOWL	475	16	51	7
BORDG/DISH	25	18	133	18
BORDG/DJ	94	3	126	17
BORDG/MOX	10	*	–	–
BORDG/PORR	66	2	29	4
BORDG/SKIL	195	7	100	13
BORDG/TPIP	32	1	–	–
BORDG/STRAINER	58	2	23	3
BORDO/TPIP	34	1	25	3
BORDY/BOWL	225	8	25	3
BORDY/COND	48	2	–	–
BORDY/COST	6	*	–	–
BORDY/DISH	609	20	57	7
BORDY/MISC	12	*	–	–
BORDY/PORR	444	15	112	15
BORDY/SKIL	32	1	32	4
BORDY/TPIP	26	1	30	4
RBOR/SKIL	35	1	13	2
Total	2998	100	756	100

Early 17th Century (B)

Form	Weight	% Weight	Eves	% Eves
BOWL	700	23	76	10
DISH	1134	38	190	25
DJ	94	3	126	17
MISC	134	5	23	3
PORR	582	19	141	19
SKIL	262	9	145	9
TPIP	92	3	55	7
Total	2998	100	756	100

Mid-17th Century (A)

Fabric/ Form	Weight	% Weight	Eves	% Eves
BORD/BOWL	1564	3	227	2
BORD/CHP	4158	7	402	4
BORD/CNDST	22	*	16	*
BORD/COL	91	*	15	*
BORD/COST	377	1	–	–
BORD/DISH	243	*	28	*
BORD/DJ	798	1	77	1
BORD/FUM	28	*	–	–
BORD/JAR	9	*	–	–
BORD/LID	1389	2	262	3
BORD/MBOX	605	1	–	–
BORD/MISC	210	*	–	–
BORD/MUG	439	1	68	1
BORD/PORR	1677	3	491	5
BORD/SKIL	135	*	47	1
BORD/TPIP	1509	3	348	3
BORDB/BOWL	85	*	8	*
BORDB/CHAFD	8	*	–	–
BORDB/CHP	165	*	–	–
BORDB/COL	19	*	–	–
BORDB/DISH	521	1	75	1
BORDB/MUG	998	2	171	2
BORDB/PORR	495	1	204	2
BORDB/TPIP	17	*	–	–
BORDG/BOWL	1108	2	142	1
BORDG/CHAFD	228	*	15	*
BORDG/CHP	317	1	49	1
BORDG/CNDST	24	*	–	–
BORDG/COL	32	*	6	*
BORDG/COST	56	*	–	–
BORDG/DISH	3813	6	569	6
BORDG/DJ	589	1	149	1
BORDG/FUM	28	*	–	–
BORDG/MBOX	114	*	–	–
BORDG/MISC	223	*	37	*
BORDG/MUG	96	*	–	–
BORDG/PORR	1496	3	471	5
BORDG/SKIL	19	*	25	*
BORDG/TPIP	1219	2	283	3
BORDO/CHP	191	*	47	1
BORDO/DISH	244	1	28	*
BORDO/MISC	6	*	–	–
BORDO/PORR	4	*	–	–
BORDO/SKIL	68	*	14	*
BORDO/TPIP	637	1	92	1
BORDY/BEDP	36	*	8	*
BORDY/BOWL	3550	6	502	5
BORDY/CHAFD	204	*	7	*
BORDY/CHP	2825	5	238	2
BORDY/CNDST	34	*	40	*
BORDY/COL	831	1	83	1
BORDY/COST	18	*	–	–
BORDY/DISH	5808	10	1184	12
BORDY/DJ	451	1	–	–
BORDY/FUM	14	*	–	–
BORDY/JAR	111	*	–	–
BORDY/LID	56	*	16	*
BORDY/LOBED DISH	219	*	10	*
BORDY/MBOX	48	*	–	–
BORDY/MISC	174	*	15	*
BORDY/PORR	1303	2	443	4
BORDY/SKIL	380	1	156	2
BORDY/TPIP	4747	8	788	8
BORDY/ WARMING PAN	99	*	–	–
RBOR/BOWL	2856	5	416	4
RBOR/CHP	3925	7	296	3
RBOR/COL	1069	2	75	1
RBOR/DISH	1901	3	391	4
RBOR/LID	292	1	97	1
RBOR/MUG	632	1	236	2
RBOR/PORR	1240	2	262	3
RBOR/SKIL	36	*	13	*
RBOR/TPIP	1288	2	362	4
Total	60225	100	10004	100

Mid-17th Century (B)

Form	Weight	% Weight	Eves	% Eves
BOWL	11206	19	1474	15
CHP	11582	19	1032	10
DISH	12530	21	2275	23
DJ	1838	3	226	2
LID	1737	3	375	4
MISC	2896	5	148	1
MUG	2165	3	475	5
PORR	6215	10	1871	19
SKIL	638	1	255	2
TPIP	9417	16	1873	19
Total	60225	100	10004	100

Late 17th Century (A)

Fabric Form	Weight	% Weight	Eves	% Eves
BORD/BOWL	613	3	69	2
BORD/CHP	24	*	–	–
BORD/DISH	158	1	154	4
BORD/DJ	6	*	–	–
BORD/JAR	24	*	27	1
BORD/LID	135	1	100	3
BORD/MISC	98	1	6	*
BORD/MUG	34	*	33	1
BORD/PORR	86	*	24	1
BORD/TPIP	367	2	51	1
BORDB/BOWL	14	*	7	*
BORDB/DISH	92	*	10	*
BORDB/MISC	2	*	–	–
BORDB/MUG	318	2	60	1
BORDB/PORR	38	*	–	–
BORDB/TPIP	12	*	10	*
BORDG/BOWL	323	2	61	2
BORDG/CHP	1952	9	189	5
BORDG/COND	2	*	10	*
BORDG/DISH	439	2	63	2
BORDG/DJ	144	1	–	–
BORDG/JAR	6	*	5	*
BORDG/MISC	228	1	–	–
BORDG/PORR	373	2	217	5
BORDG/TPIP	108	1	67	2
BORDO/CHP	12	*	–	–
BORDO/TPIP	16	*	5	*
BORDY/BOT	62	*	100	3
BORDY/BOWL	2000	10	229	6
BORDY/CHP	2303	11	334	8
BORDY/CNDST	70	*	75	2
BORDY/COST	114	1	–	–
BORDY/DISH	1173	6	216	5
BORDY/LOBED DISH	310	2	32	1
BORDY/MISC	182	1	–	–
BORDY/PORR	1309	6	494	12
BORDY/SKIL	206	1	96	2
BORDY/TPIP	3489	17	659	17
RBOR/BOWL	583	3	119	3
RBOR/CHP	2293	11	212	6
RBOR/COL	108	1	19	*
RBOR/DISH	204	1	42	1
RBOR/LID	40	*	20	1
RBOR/MISC	506	2	–	–
RBOR/MUG	155	1	23	1
RBOR/PORR	86	*	49	1
RBOR/TPIP	338	2	80	2
Total	21155	100	3967	100

Late 17th Century (B)

Form	Weight	% Weight	Eves	% Eves
BOWL	3533	17	485	12
CHP	6584	31	735	19
DISH	2066	10	485	12
LID	175	1	120	3
MISC	1862	9	274	7
MUG	507	2	116	3
PORR	1892	9	784	20
SKIL	206	1	96	2
TPIP	4330	30	872	22
Total	21155	100	3967	100

Appendix
· 4 ·

Thin-Section Analysis

Thin-section slides were made of 23 different samples of Border wares, both whiteware and redware, although the size of the sample was necessarily limited.

Sherds from the kiln waste at Yeoman's Potteries, Cove and from Farnborough Hill were included, as well as pottery from various excavated contexts in London spanning the 16th and 17th centuries. The kiln material was kindly loaned by the Hampshire County Museums Service. Three sherds of whiteware, visually similar to Border ware but with a suspected Low Countries or Rhenish origin, were also included for comparison. The characteristics of these sherds were distinctive enough to enable them to be distinguished from the range recognised as typical of Border ware. However, too few examples could be sectioned to allow detailed analysis and a much larger sample needs to be examined before the results of such analysis are put into print.

The results of the thin-section analysis are given in the faric descriptions (Chapter 1). The sectioned sherds are housed in the DUA Fabric Reference Collection. The following list gives fabric and form codes (see Appendix 3), identification and provenance by site code and context (see Appendix 1). Fabric codes not included earlier are FRECWW (Frechen whitewares) and LCWW (Low Countries whitewares). Sherds from the kiln sites are marked with an asterisk and additional site codes are: FH69 Farnborough Hill, Surrey, and COVEYP Yeoman's Potteries, Cove, Hampshire.

Number	Fabric	Form	Site	Context
1494	RBOR	DISH	SWA81	980/1
1495	RBOR	PORR	BIG82	1389
1496	RBOR	CHP	SWA81	952
1497	RBOR	TPIP	SL75	10
*1498	BORDY	TPIP	FH69	C1 3
*1499	RBOR	DISH	COVEYP	
*1550	RBOR	JAR	COVEYP	
1501	BORDO	TPIP	LBY85	20
1502	BORD	TPIP	COVEYP	
1503	BORDB	MUG	SWA81	980
1504	BORDG	BOWL	GDH85	740
1505	BORDY	BOWL	CLO83	30
1506	BORDG	CHP	AMB87	104
1507	BORDG	MUG	MIO86	1010
1508	BORDG	CUP	BRI78	129
1509	RBOR	DISH	SWA81	980
1510	LCWW?	TPIP	ABC87	793
1511	BORDG	DJ	GDH85	841
1512	BORDG	DJ	ER161B	
*1513	BORDY	TPIP	COVEYP	
1514	BORDG	DJ	BRI78	129
1515	FRECWW?	CUP	CAP86	42
1516	BORDY	TPIP	LBY85	67
1517	BORDY?	MUG	CLO83	30
1518	LCWW?	TPIP	ABC87	793
1519	BORDY	PORR	LEA84	127

Bibliography

AMIS, P, 1968 'Some domestic vessels of southern Britain: a social and technical analysis', *J Ceramic Hist*, **2**

ATKINSON, D and OSWALD, A, 1969 'London clay tobacco pipes', reprinted from *J Brit Archaeol Ass*, **32**

BLOICE, B J and DAWSON, G J, 1971 'Classification of shapes' in Bloice, B J, 'Norfolk House, Lambeth: excavations at a delftware kiln site, 1968', *Post-Medieval Archaeol*, **5**, 99–159

BOWN, L and NENK, B, forthcoming *Post-Medieval Pottery in London, 1500–1700: Vol 3, Redwares*

BREARS, P C D, 1971 *The English Country Pottery, its History and Techniques*, Newton Abbot

—, 1974 *The Collector's Book of English Country Pottery*, Newton Abbot

BRITTON, F, 1987 *London Delftware*, Milton Keynes

CASPALL, J, 1987 *Making Fire and Light in the House pre-1820*, Woodbridge

COLEMAN-SMITH, R and PEARSON, T, 1988 *Excavations in the Donyatt Potteries, Somerset*, Chichester

DAVEY, P and HIGGINS, P, forthcoming *Clay Tobacco Pipes from the City of London*, HMSO

EDWARDS, J, forthcoming *Post-Medieval Pottery in London, 1500–1700: Vol 2, Tin-glazed Wares*

EDWARDS, R, 1974 'London Potters *c.* 1570–1710', *J Ceramic Hist*, **6**

FARLEY, M, 1979 'Pottery and pottery kilns of the post-medieval period at Brill, Buckinghamshire', *Post-Medieval Archaeol*, **13**, 127–52

FISHER, J, 1981 *A collection of Early Maps of London 1553–1667*, London

GAIMSTER, D R M, 1987 'The supply of Rhenish stoneware to London, 1350–1600', *London Archaeol*, **5**, 339–47

—, 1988a 'Post-medieval ceramic stove-tiles bearing the Royal arms: evidence for their manufacture and use in southern Britain', *Archaeol J*, **145**, 314–43

—, 1988b 'Pottery production in the Lower Rhineland: the Duisburg sequence *c.* 1400–1860', *Zur keramik des Mittelalters und der beginnenden Neuzeit in Rheinland*, BAR, **440**, 151–71

HASLAM, J, 1975 'The Excavation of a 17th-century pottery site at Cove, east Hampshire', *Post-Medieval Archaeol*, **9**, 164–87

HOBSON, R L, 1903 *Catalogue of the Collection of Pottery in the British Museum*, British Museum

HOLLING, F W, 1969 'Seventeenth-century pottery from Ash, Surrey', *Post-Medieval Archaeol*, **3**, 18–30

—, 1971 'A preliminary note on the pottery industry of the Hampshire–Surrey borders', *Surrey Archaeol Collect*, **68**, 57–88

—, 1977 'Reflections on Tudor Green', *Post-Medieval Archaeol*, **11**, 61–6

—, 1984 'Early post-medieval pottery from no 137 High Street, Guildford', *Surrey Archaeol Collect*, **75**, 295–301

HORNSBY, P R G, WEINSTEIN, R and HOMER, R F, 1989 *Pewter: A Celebration of the Craft 1200–1700*, Museum of London

HURST, J G, 1964 'Tudor-Green Ware', in Cunliffe, B W, *Winchester Excavations 1949–1960*, **1**, 140–43

—, 1970–71 'Sixteenth century Beauvais drinking-jugs', *Groupe de Recherches et d'Études de la Ceramique de Beauvaisis*, **3**, 6–15

—, NEAL, D S and VAN BEUNINGEN, H J E, 1986 *Pottery produced and traded in north-west Europe 1350–1650*, Rotterdam Papers, **6**

JENNINGS, S, 1981 'Eighteen centuries of pottery from Norwich', *East Anglian Archaeol*, **13**

LONDON TYPOGRAPHICAL SOCIETY, 1905 *An exact delineation of the Cities of London and Westminster and the Suburbs, by Wm. Faithorne*, sheet 2

MCCARTHY, M R and BROOKS, C M, 1988 *Medieval Pottery in Britain AD 900–1600*, Leicester
MATTHEWS, L G and GREEN, H J M, 1969 'Post-medieval pottery of the Inns of Court', *Post-Medieval Archaeol*, **3,** 1–17
MILLER, L, SCHOFIELD, J and RHODES, M, 1986 *The Roman Quay at St. Magnus House, London. Excavations at New Fresh Wharf, Lower Thames Street, London 1974–78*, London Middlesex Archaeol Soc Special Paper, **8**
MILLETT, M, 1979 'An approach to the functional interpretation of pottery', in Millett, M (ed) *Pottery and the Archaeologist*, Inst Archaeol Occ Publ, **4,** 35–47
—, 1981 'Yeomans Potteries, Cove Road, Cove', *Archaeol in Hampshire*, 24
MOORHOUSE, S, 1970 'Finds from Basing House, Hampshire c. 1540–1645', *Post-Medieval Archaeol*, **4,** 31–91
—, 1971a 'A sixteenth-century Tudor Green group from Overton, Hampshire', *Post-Medieval Archaeol*, **5,** 182–5
—, 1971b 'Two late medieval and post-medieval pottery groups from Farnham Castle, Surrey', *Surrey Archaeol Collect*, **58,** 39–55
—, 1979 'Tudor Green: some further thoughts', *Medieval Ceram*, **3,** 53–61
MORISSON, H, 1970–71 'Pots et godets du Beauvaisis', *Groupe de Recherches et d'Etudes de la Ceramique du Beauvaisis*, **3,** 43–75
MUNSELL, 1969 *Book of Color*, Baltimore

NELSON, S, 1981 'A group of pottery waster material from Kingston', *London Archaeol*, **4,** 96–102

OGILBY, J and MORGAN, W, 1677 *A Large and Accurate Map of the City of London*, reprinted by Harry Margary, Lympne Castle, Kent
ORTON, C R, 1975 'Quantitative pottery studies: some progress, problems and prospects', *Science and Archaeology*, **16,** 30–5
—, 1980 *Mathematics in Archaeology*, London
—, 1982 'The excavation of a late medieval/transitional pottery kiln at Cheam, Surrey', *Surrey Archaeol Collect*, **73,** 49–92
—, 1988 'Post-Roman pottery', in Hinton, P (ed), *Excavations in Southwark 1973–76, Lambeth 1973–79*, London Middlesex Archaeol Soc/Surrey Archaeol Soc Joint Publ, **3,** 295–364
— and PEARCE, J E, 1984 'The Pottery', in Thompson, A, Grew, F and Schofield, J, 'Excavations at Aldgate, 1974', *Post-Medieval Archaeol*, **18,** 34–68

PEACOCK, D P S, 1982 *Pottery in the Roman World: An Ethnoarchaeological Approach*, London
PEARCE, J E, 1984 'Getting a handle on medieval pottery', *London Archaeol*, **5,** 17–23
— and VINCE, A, 1988 *A Dated Type-Series of London Medieval Pottery, Part 4: Surrey Whitewares*, London Middlesex Archaeol Soc Special Paper, **10**
—, — and JENNER, M A, 1985 *A Dated Type-Series of London Medieval Pottery Part 2: London-Type Ware*, London Middlesex Archaeol Soc Special Paper, **6**
—, — and WHITE, R, with Cunningham, C M, 1982 'A Dated Type-Series of London Medieval Pottery Part 1: Mill Green Ware', *Trans London Middlesex Archaeol Soc*, **33,** 266–98
PLATT, C and COLEMAN-SMITH, R, 1975 *Excavations in Medieval Southampton 1953–1969: Vol 2 The Finds*, Leicester

RACKHAM, B, 1952 'Farnham pottery of the 16th century', *Surrey Archaeol Collect*, **52,** 50–5

TYERS, P, 1984 *Pottery Archive Users' Handbook*, London

VAN DER LEEUW, S, 1975 'Medieval pottery from Haarlem: a model', in Renaud, J G N (ed), *Rotterdam Papers*, **2,** 67–87
VINCE, A G, 1981 'Coarse Pottery', in Vince, A G and Egan, G, 'The contents of a late 18th century pit at Crosswall, City of London', *Trans London Middlesex Archaeol Soc*, **32,** 162–4
—, 1985 'Saxon and medieval pottery in London: a review', *Medieval Archaeol*, **29,** 25–93

WADE-MARTINS, P, 1983 'Two post-medieval earthenware pottery groups from Fulmodeston, Norfolk', *East Anglian Archaeol*, **19**
WEBSTER, G (ed), 1976 *Romano–British Coarse Pottery: A Student's Guide*, CBA Res Rep, **6** (3rd ed)

Index